Diagnosis and Management of Learning Disabilities

An Interdisciplinary/Lifespan Approach

Third Edition

Diagnosis and Management of Learning Disabilities

An Interdisciplinary/Lifespan Approach

Third Edition

Diagnosis and Management of Learning Disabilities

An Interdisciplinary/Lifespan Approach

Third Edition

By

Frank R. Brown, III, Ph.D., M.D.
Professor of Pediatrics
Baylor College of Medicine, and
Director, Meyer Center
   for Developmental Pediatrics
Texas Children's Hospital
Houston, Texas

Elizabeth H. Aylward, Ph.D.
Associate Professor
Department of Psychiatry and Behavioral Sciences
The Johns Hopkins University School of Medicine
Baltimore, Maryland

Barbara K. Keogh, Ph.D.
Professor
Department of Education
The University of California, Los Angeles
Los Angeles, California

SINGULAR PUBLISHING GROUP, INC.
SAN DIEGO · LONDON

Singular Publishing Group, Inc.
4284 41st Street
San Diego, California 92105-1197

19 Compton Terrace
London, N1 2UN, UK

© 1996 by Singular Publishing Group, Inc.

Typeset in 10/12 English Times by So Cal Graphics
Printed in the United States of America by BookCrafters, Inc.

Library of Congress Cataloging-in-Publication Data

Brown, Frank R., III 1943–
   Diagnosis and management of learning disabilities: an
interdisciplinary/lifespan approach / Frank R. Brown III, Elizabeth
H. Aylward, Barbara K. Keogh. —3rd ed.
    p.   cm.
   Includes bibliographical references and index.
   ISBN 1-56593-420-2
   1. Learning disabilities.   2. Learning disabled children—
Rehabilitation.   3. Learning disabled children—Education.
I. Aylward, Elizabeth H., 1954–   .   II. Keogh, Barbara K.
III. Title.
   [DNLM: 1. Learning Disorders—diagnosis.   2. Learning Disorders—
therapy.   3. Remedial Teaching. LC 4704 B877d 1995]
RJ506.L4B76   1995
618.62'85889—dc20
DNLM/DLC
for Library of Congress   95-34199
                                                      CIP

Contents

Planning for Follow-up
Conclusion

Frank R. Brown, III and Elizabeth H. Aylward

GLOSSARY, APPENDICES, AND REFERENCES

Preface

Of all childhood disorders, learning disabilities and its concomitant condition, attention-deficit/hyperactivity disorder, are by far the most prevalent, occurring in approximately 10 to 15% of school-aged children. It is important, therefore, that all professionals who work with children understand basic concepts in the identification and treatment of these disorders. The third edition of this book, like its predecessor, is designed primarily for practitioners who are involved to some degree with diagnosis and treatment of children with learning disabilities. At the same time, it is written at a level that can be understood by parents or professionals who have little familiarity with learning disorders.

Children with learning disabilities often have a multitude of problems that span many facets of their lives, including academic, social, emotional, behavioral, and familial. It is imperative, therefore, to consider the total child from several points of view. Practitioners must consider the difficulties encountered in each sphere, as well as the interactions among the various problem areas. In the case of the child with learning disabilities, the whole is greater than the sum of the parts. We believe that an interdisciplinary approach allows for the most thorough understanding of the child's problems and needs. When an interdisciplinary approach is used, professionals from many disciplines come together to plan the evaluation, to share results of the assessments they have conducted individually, to discuss how results from evaluation in one discipline relate to results from another discipline, to formulate diagnoses, and to plan for treatment and follow-up.

In this third edition we additionally expand our earlier presentations of psychological and educational assessment to include the most current instruments, we introduce a chapter on neuropsychological assessment approaches to the identification of learning disabilities, and we critically discuss the role of sensory motor integration in diagnosis and treatment. Finally, considering the current trend toward increased identification and treatment of children with attention-deficit/hyperactivity disorder (AD/HD), we include an in-depth review of the differential diagnosis of deficits of attention span, impulse control, and excessive motor activity, and of the role of medication in multimodal treatment of AD/HD.

As in the prior editions, we continue to be brief and direct. Our plan in writing remains to answer the question "What do you, as a practitioner, do from the moment you first suspect that a child might have a learning disability?" We intend for this third edition to continue to be a part of the practitioner's working library, as a guide to be used on a day-to-day basis.

Contributors

Robert D. Annett, Ph.D.
Department of Pediatrics
University of New Mexico
  School of Medicine
Albuquerque, New Mexico

Lucinda P. Bernheimer, Ph.D.
Key Investigator—Sociobehavioral Group
The University of California, Los Angeles
Los Angeles, California

Douglas R. Bloom, Ph.D.
Assistant Professor
Department of Pediatrics
University of Texas-Houston Medical School
Houston, Texas

Margaret H. Briggs, Ph.D.
Private Practice in Pediatric
  Speech/Language Pathology
Pasadena, California

Winnie Dunn, Ph.D., OTR, FAOTA
Professor and Chair
Occupational Therapy Education
University of Kansas Medical Center
Kansas City, Kansas

Linda K. Elksnin, Ph.D.
Professor
Coordinator of Graduate Special Education Programs
The Citadel
Charleston, South Carolina

Nick Elksnin, Ph.D., NCSP
Adjunct Professor of Education
The Citadel
Charleston, South Carolina

Jack M. Fletcher, Ph.D.
Professor of Pediatrics
University of Texas-Houston Medical School
Houston, Texas

Judith Margolis, Ph.D.
Professor of Education
Department of Special Education
California State University, Los Angeles
Los Angeles, California

Robert G. Voigt, M.D.
Assistant Professor of Pediatrics
  Baylor College of Medicine, and
Meyer Center for Developmental Pediatrics
  Texas Children's Hospital
Houston, Texas

Dedication

To our spouses, Mitten, Bob, and Jack; and to Reggie and Riggs Brown, Laura and Caitlin Aylward.

CHAPTER 1

Introduction

Frank R. Brown, III
Elizabeth H. Aylward

LEARNING DISABILITIES: WHAT ARE THEY?

Since the term *learning disabilities* was first used by Samuel Kirk in 1962, there has been a great deal of confusion and controversy regarding the nature of this disorder. Special educators, other school personnel, psychologists, physicians, and researchers have proposed many definitions and descriptions of the disorder, a myriad of terms used interchangeably with *learning disabilities*, many theories regarding the etiology of the disorder, and many programs for its remediation.

In 1975 the United States Congress recognized learning disabilities as a handicapping condition and assured free and appropriate education for all children with learning disabilities. At this time, it became imperative that schools devise a system for making decisions about the eligibility of individual students for participation in the required special education programs. The federal government's definition of *specific learning disabilities* was included in the Education for All Handicapped Children Act as part of Public Law 94-142 (1975). The definition cited in the act is as follows:

> Specific learning disability means a disorder in one or more of the basic psychological processes involved in the understanding or in using language, spoken or written, which may manifest itself in an imperfect ability to listen, think, speak, read, write, spell, or to do

1

mathematical calculations. The term includes such conditions as perceptual handicaps, brain injury, minimal brain dysfunction, dyslexia, and developmental aphasia. The term does not apply to children who have learning problems which are primarily the result of visual, hearing, or motor handicaps, of mental retardation, or emotional disturbance, or of environmental, cultural or economic disadvantages. (Public Law 94-142, 34 C.F.R. 300.5 [b] [9])

To further clarify the term *learning disabilities*, the government provided educators with a separate set of federal regulations for the implementation of Public Law 94-142. These regulations are the "Procedures for Evaluation of Specific Learning Disabilities" (U.S. Office of Education, 1977). According to these regulations, a child has a specific learning disability if:

1. The child does not achieve commensurate with his or her age and ability levels in one or more of seven specific areas when provided with learning experiences appropriate for the child's age and ability level.
2. The team finds that a child has a severe discrepancy between achievement and intellectual ability in one or more of the following areas:
   a. oral expression
   b. listening comprehension
   c. written expression
   d. basic reading skills
   e. reading comprehension
   f. mathematics calculation
   g. mathematics reasoning. (p. 65083)

Despite federal efforts to clarify the definition of learning disabilities, many professionals launched criticisms based on the definition's ambiguity, redundancy, and unnecessary restrictions (see Berk, 1984, for further discussion). In order to address these criticisms, the National Joint Committee for Learning Disabilities (NJCLD) (1981), composed of representatives from six professional organizations, proposed a new definition, which was presented as follows:

Learning disabilities is a generic term that refers to a heterogeneous group of disorders manifested by significant difficulties in the acquisition and use of listening, speaking, reading, writing, reasoning, or mathematical abilities. These disorders are intrinsic to the individual and presumed to be due to central nervous system dysfunction.

Even though learning disabilities may occur concomitantly with other handicapping conditions (e.g., sensory impairment, mental retardation, social and emotional disturbance) or environmental influences (e.g., cultural differences, insufficient/inappropriate instruction, psychogenic factors), it is not the direct result of those conditions or influences. (p. 5).

Most school systems have used a combination of these definitions and regulations as the basis for establishing procedures to identify children with learning disabilities. In doing so, they have made an attempt to determine the existence of "severe discrepancy" between achievement and intellectual ability in the individual. Because no federal guidelines have been established for defining "severe discrepancy," state and local education agencies have been forced to establish their own procedures for measuring achievement and intellectual ability, and for identifying severe discrepancy. Even within states or regions where procedures have been established, many different approaches are used by various professionals to identify students with learning disabilities. Especially for parents and professionals not specializing in the identification of learning disabilities on a day-to-day basis, there continues to be a great deal of confusion in determining whether or not any particular child is or is not learning disabled.

When eligibility definitions for learning disabilities were developed in response to Public Law 94-142, there was little initial focus on infants and toddlers at risk for subsequent learning disabilities, and eligibility definitions for learning disabilities were developed solely with school-age children in mind. In 1986, Public Law 99-457 was introduced, focusing on development of comprehensive, coordinated, multidisciplinary, and interagency programs of early intervention services for infants and toddlers at risk for learning disabilities and their families. As a result of this legislation, there has evolved a thrust to identify preschool-age children "at risk" for subsequent developmental disabilities, including learning disabilities. Professionals involved with preschoolers at risk for learning disabilities have been forced to develop alternatives to discrepancy definitions of this disorder. Some of these alternative approaches will be discussed in subsequent chapters.

Focus has expanded to include not only preschoolers at risk for learning disabilities, but also young adults with ongoing learning disabilities. In 1984, the Carl D. Perkins Vocational Act (P.L. 98-524) mandated services to aid in the transition from high school for individuals with learning disabilities. As a result, professionals are now accountable to individuals with learning disabilities across the life span of their disability.

DEFINITION OF TERMS

It is our opinion that much of the confusion regarding learning disabilities reflects a lack of understanding of the underlying basis and natural history of this disorder. This lack of understanding is reflected in the large number of terms that are often used imprecisely and inappropriately to suggest more understanding of the disorder than is justified. These include terms such as *specific learning disability, minimal brain dysfunction, attention-deficit/hyperactivity disorder,* and *dyslexia.* In this book the use of terms reflects our philosophy regarding the neurological basis of learning disabilities. These definitions are presented in a format that, it is hoped, will clarify a distinction that the authors wish to make between primary (neurologically based) and secondary (derivative of primary) disorders.

Primary (Neurologically Based) Disabling Conditions

The primary disabling conditions for children with learning disabilities are assumed to reflect brain "damage," albeit often of subtle degree and undetectable, given current medical technologies. Like all disorders, mild degrees of brain damage are far more common than more serious degrees. This is reflected in the high incidence of learning disabilities and associated primary disabling conditions, in comparison to more serious neurological dysfunctions, such as mental retardation and cerebral palsy.

The brain damage assumed in children with learning disabilities is typically diffuse, meaning that multiple brain functions are affected. Two important areas of neurological functioning for the child with learning disabilities are cognitive and motor skills. Diffuse cognitive dysfunction might involve expressive or receptive language, visual-spatial perceptual abilities, or the ability to focus and maintain attention. Diffuse motor dysfunction might include weaknesses in gross motor, fine motor, or oral motor skills.

The typical child with learning disabilities will show some mixture of difficulties in cognitive and motor function. Because the motor and cognitive difficulties frequently are subtle, parents and professionals sometimes may not appreciate their impact on the child. It is especially important to look not just at the "tip of the iceberg" (i.e., see the obvious and most major disabling condition), but also to be alert to less obvious associated difficulties.

The primary disabling conditions most often seen in children with learning disabilities (and requiring careful definition) are defined as follows.

Learning Disabilities

In the case of the school-age child, the definition of learning disabilities that we use is based on the 1975 federal definition included as part of Public Law 94-142, the 1977 U.S. Office of Education (U.S.O.E.) regulations, and the 1981 NJCLD definitions. We limit the use of the term *learning disability* in the school-age child to a condition whereby an individual's academic achievement level is significantly below the level that would be predicted from the level of intellectual ability. The cause for the discrepancy between academic achievement and intellectual ability is presumed to be neurologically based. Although learning disabilities can occur concomitantly with other disabling conditions or environmental influences, they are not the direct result of these conditions or influences. Learning disabilities can occur in the areas of listening, speaking, reading, writing, reasoning, or mathematical abilities. Primary focus, however, is placed on learning disabilities in three areas:

READING. A specific learning disability in reading (also termed *dyslexia*) occurs when individual reading skills (e.g., word attack, reading comprehension) or general reading ability are significantly below the level that would be predicted from the individual's level of intellectual ability, assuming other disabling conditions or environmental influences have been ruled out. If the reading disability is thought to be caused by an overall weakness in language skills, it may be referred to as a "language-based" learning disability.

MATHEMATICS. A specific learning disability in mathematics (also termed *dyscalculia*) occurs when individual math skills (e.g., acquisition of number facts, written calculations, mathematical reasoning) or general mathematical ability are significantly below the level that would be predicted from the individual's level of intellectual ability, assuming other disabling conditions or environmental influences have been ruled out.

WRITTEN LANGUAGE. A specific learning disability in written language (also termed *dysgraphia*) occurs when individual written language skills (e.g., spelling, application of grammar, punctuation, usage skills, organization of thoughts in writing) or general written language ability are significantly below the level that would be predicted from the individual's level of intellectual ability, assuming other disabling conditions or environmental influences have been ruled out. Although it may be considered a specific learning disability in itself, poor handwriting is not included in the term *dysgraphia*, as we use it.

In response to P.L. 99-457 and the desire to identify children with learning disabilities as early as possible, many professionals have attempted to identify preschoolers "at risk" for subsequent learning disabilities. We believe, as discussed in Chapter 9, that currently no diagnostic procedure(s) reliably identifies the preschool child who subsequently will demonstrate significant discrepancies between cognitive functioning and academic achievement (i.e., will evidence learning disabilities). However, many identifiable factors can predict subsequent *slow academic achievement*, if not necessarily academic achievement that is deviant from cognitive expectation. Children who are at risk for subsequent *slow academic achievement* (not necessarily learning disabilities) may be identified by delays in language, visual-perception, attention span and/or impulse control, and problems with behavior. For the remainder of the book, we will use the term at risk for learning difficulties to refer to those children who can be expected to encounter difficulties in academic achievement, whether or not these difficulties represent true learning disabilities.

Attention-Deficit/Hyperactivity Disorder

The definition used by the authors is based on the criteria set in the *Diagnostic and Statistical Manual of Mental Disorders* (Fourth Edition, DSM-IV) of the American Psychiatric Association (1994). DSM-IV criteria for diagnosis of attention-deficit/hyperactivity disorder (AD/HD) require the establishment of a persistent pattern of inattention and/or hyperactivity-impulsivity at a level more frequent and severe than is "typically observed in individuals at a comparable level of development" (p. 78). DSM-IV criteria for AD/HD additionally require that there exists clear evidence of interference with developmentally appropriate social, academic, or occupational functioning in at least two settings (e.g., at home and at school or work).

DSM-IV criteria for diagnosis of AD/HD make allowance for the fact that symptoms of attention-deficit, impulsivity, and hyperactivity may occur together (attention-deficit/hyperactivity disorder, combined type) or separately (attention-deficit/hyperactivity disorder, predominantly inattentive type versus attention-deficit disorder, predominantly hyperactive-impulsive type). This allowance for the occurrence of symptoms of attention deficit, impulsivity, and hyperactivity either together or separately is consistent with the neurodevelopmental principle of associated deficits. This term implies that although delays in one area of development appear most prominent (e.g., attention-deficit), professionals examining children should be on the lookout for associated domains of intercurrent developmental delay (e.g., impulse or motor control). The subtle presence of the "/" in AD/HD implies that symptoms of attention-deficit, impulsivity, and hyperactivity may occur together ("combined type") or separately.

The authors of this text endorse the current definition of AD/HD. We believe it is consistent with a neurodevelopmental model in which the attention deficit is viewed as a primary, neurologically based disabling condition. As such, AD/HD would be expected to manifest at an early age (below age 7 as per DSM-IV criteria) and symptoms would be expected to generalize across all functional settings (e.g., at school [or work] and at home as per DSM-IV criteria). Additionally, as a neurologically based disabling condition, it might reasonably be assumed that AD/HD would manifest across time; that is, symptoms of AD/HD might extend into adulthood. This would relate to the residual type AD/HD.

Minimal Brain Dysfunction

We use the term *minimal brain dysfunction* (MBD) to refer to the child who has a mixture of some or all of the subtle cognitive and motor dysfunctions described previously. Components of MBD may include learning disabilities, language disabilities, other inconsistencies among various cognitive functions, AD/HD, and gross-, fine-, and oral-motor dyscoordinations. What is clear from this listing is that AD/HD is part of a larger syndrome that was originally termed MBD. Developmentalists and educators have, with the term AD/HD, focused on that part of this larger MBD syndrome that they felt was most significant in terms of school dysfunction, that is, deficits of attention span and impulse control. Clearly, a number of children exhibit a much wider spectrum of symptoms than are accounted for by the term AD/HD, and for these children the term MBD may still be an appropriate description.

Secondary (Derivative of Primary) Disabling Conditions

Unlike the primary disabling conditions described previously, secondary disabling conditions do not have a direct neurological basis. They are instead the *result* of the primary disabling conditions, especially when the primary disabling conditions have not been properly managed. The most common secondary disabling conditions are poor self-concept and inappropriate attention-seeking behaviors. Poor self-concept is often the result of academic failure, especially when the child is blamed or told that the failure is due to lack of motivation. When children with learning disabilities are unable to receive recognition for positive achievements (e.g., academic success) they sometimes resort to inappropriate behaviors in order to obtain recognition, despite the fact that the recognition is often negative. In addition to these two common secondary disabling conditions, children with learning disabilities may also exhibit such secondary characteristics as poor peer relationships, compliance problems, oppositional behaviors, depression, school phobia, and other problems of adjustment.

Slow Learner

Although children with learning disabilities demonstrate slow achievement in some or all academic areas, their cognitive functioning is usually average or better. The authors wish to distinguish between children with learning disabilities and children labeled "slow learners." *Slow learner* is a term used to describe the child whose learning ability in all areas is delayed in comparison to children of the same chronological age. These children are characterized by low-normal to borderline intelligence, with corresponding slow academic progress. These children are not considered learning disabled because there is no discrepancy between cognitive expectations and academic achievement. Although generally not eligible for special education services, these children are often in need of a modified curriculum and more individual attention than their nonaffected peers. We will not address this population except to point out that the number of slow learners is at least as great as the number of students with learning disabilities, and to express an opinion that these students need and deserve special education services as much as do students with learning disabilities. A resource for children and families experiencing a slow learning course is the Center for Success in Learning (17000 Preston Road, Suite 400, Dallas, Texas 75248).

PREVALENCE OF LEARNING DISABILITIES

Failure to define terms precisely has led to confusion over prevalence rates. Prevalence rates for learning disabilities range between 3 and 15% of the school-age population and vary according to geographic area (Sixth Annual Report to Congress, 1984). Boys are diagnosed as being learning disabled four to eight times as often as girls (Marsh, Gearhart, & Gearhart, 1978). Although there are no definite figures regarding the prevalence of AD/HD within the population with learning disabilities, estimates vary from 33 to 80% (Interagency Committee on Learning Disabilities, 1987). Safer and Allen (1976) estimated that approximately 30% of hyperactive children are learning disabled, although Halpern, Gittleman, and Klein (1984) put the figure at 10%.

ETIOLOGY OF LEARNING DISABILITIES

In discussing learning disabilities, many parents ask, "Why is my child learning disabled?" In most cases, professionals must answer "I don't know," as the etiology of learning disabilities can rarely be determined for certain. However, it is known that the incidence of learning disabilities increases among family members of children with the disorder, suggesting a genetic link. Parents (especially fathers) will sometimes remark that their child's difficulties are similar to problems they experienced themselves as children. Children who have experienced certain types of birth trauma (e.g., lack of sufficient oxygen at or around the time of birth, difficult delivery, prematurity) also have a higher incidence of learning disabilities as well as other developmental delays. However, it must be kept in mind that causality cannot be presumed from the fact that two conditions frequently occur together. It is, therefore, rarely possible to pinpoint for certain the exact "cause" of the problem in an individual child.

As the term *learning disabilities* is usually defined, the assumption is made that the disorder is due, at least in part, to some type of neurological irregularity. The nature of the irregularity has, however, been much debated. One general view presumes that the neurological abnormalities are a consequence of aberrant organization or dysfunction of the central nervous system (Critchley, 1970; Hinshelwood, 1917; and others). The neurological "deficits" referred to in this "deficit" model are very subtle and cannot be recognized or localized using present technologies. An alternative view is the "no defect" or maturational lag hypothesis (Bender, 1957; Kinsbourne, 1975; and others). This hypothesis suggests that children with learning disabilities merely have a slower rate of normal development of neural processes relevant to the acquisition of academic skills. It implies that children with learning disabilities will eventually develop the requisite neural processes and will then learn with normal or near-normal facility (McKeever & VanDeventer, 1975).

Witelson (1977) points out that there is no empirical support for the hypothesis implied by the "developmental lag" model that children with learning disabilities eventually "catch up" and become normal. We agree that most children with learning disabilities, especially those with a concomitant AD/HD, continue to demonstrate weaknesses in academic achievement, despite all remedial efforts, well into adolescence and beyond. As Witelson notes, a "deficit model" does not preclude the manifestation of a lag in development of cognitive skills. Most disorders, she states, result in test performance that is at least superficially comparable to that of normal children at some earlier chronological age.

Parents will occasionally ask if their child is learning disabled or merely suffering from some type of developmental lag or delay. We generally would answer these parents by agreeing that the child does, indeed, have a delay that makes him or her appear "immature" or poorly developed in certain areas. Parents would, however, be discouraged from believing that the child will "catch up" (with or without intervention) and eventually appear normal. Of course, children with mild delays, especially if they are bright, may learn ways to circumvent their weaknesses. However, it would be a mistake to say that the neurological abnormalities underlying these weaknesses do not continue to exist. It should also be noted that individuals with learning disabilities often experience few difficulties once they have finished school because they can avoid situations that demand those skills that caused problems for them in the school setting.

It may be inappropriate to assume that all symptomatology related to learning disabilities and especially to AD/HD will prove ultimately to be so maladaptive. Levine, Brooks, and Shonkoff (1980) have suggested that many of the symptoms of AD/HD may have some positive facets and potential for good prognosis. The child with disabling distractibility in school may prove to make interesting observations with less confined associations as an adult. The child with AD/HD and fast-paced cognitive tempo may prove to be an extremely productive adult. In essence, when the child with AD/HD is permitted as an adult to develop strengths (and the opportunity to bypass areas of weakness), the "disorder" of attention-deficit/hyperactivity disorder may evolve into some areas of strength.

Finally, in discussing the etiology of learning disabilities, we must mention that investigators over the years have proposed many theories to explain what is "wrong" in the brains of children with learning disabilities. For example, investigators have proposed that these children suffer from inadequate lateralization of the brain hemispheres, from language processing deficits, from deficits in visual discrimination, from poor auditory-visual integration, from poor visual closure, or from poor auditory sequential memory. (See Johnson, 1981, for a thorough history of these theories.) We will not add to this list of theories by attempting to identify *the* underlying problem that leads to learning disabilities. We assume, however, that children with learning disabilities are not a homogeneous group. Learning disabilities are not the result of one etiology (e.g., genetics or birth trauma) and are not caused by one type of deficit (e.g., language-processing or lack of cerebral lateralization). The diagnostic process is designed primarily to identify which children are actually experiencing learning disabilities, not to theorize about possible underlying causes.

INTERDISCIPLINARY PROCESS IN DIAGNOSIS AND TREATMENT

What Is the Interdisciplinary Process?

We wish to distinguish between a *multidisciplinary* and an *interdisciplinary* process. The former involves a series of individual evaluations and treatment plans by several disciplines (e.g., special education, medicine, psychology). The latter involves a comprehensive integrated and systematic approach, whereby professionals from several disciplines come together to plan the diagnostic procedures to be used, carry out a variety of evaluative procedures, meet again to share the results of the evaluations, formulate diagnoses based on these evaluations, work together to devise appropriate treatment procedures, and assign responsibility to individual team members for carrying out various parts of the plan.

Who Is Involved?

The interdisciplinary process can be carried out in a variety of settings. One common setting would be a diagnostic and evaluation clinic, whose staff would probably include physicians, psychologists, and special educators, as well as professionals in allied fields such as speech-language therapy and occupational and physical therapy. In this case, outside professionals who are familiar with the child, especially school personnel, would be asked to participate. Alternatively, the interdisciplinary process could be initiated by the school, with participation solicited from the child's physician and any other outside professionals familiar with the child. An individual professional working privately with the child, such as a physician, private language therapist, tutor, or psychologist, might initiate and coordinate the process. On rare occasions, the procedure might even be initiated by parents, who would make arrangements for all of the professionals working with their child to meet for interdisciplinary diagnosis and development of therapeutic recommendations.

Regardless of the setting, the interdisciplinary process should minimally consist of a physician, a psychologist, and an educator. Other professionals who may be very beneficial in the process would include any other school personnel familiar with the child (school principal, special education teacher, school psychologist, school nurse, speech-language therapist, occupational or physical therapist, guidance counselor, social worker, and regular classroom teachers), as well as nonschool personnel (physician, psychologists who may have been enlisted independently by the family for evaluation, therapists, social workers from outside agencies, nursery school teachers, community health nurses, and private tutors).

Nonschool professionals must, of course, respect the fact that the school, as the primary service-provider, has regulations and procedures that must be followed. These professionals should assist school personnel in determining whether or not the child meets criteria for diagnosis of learning disabilities by providing information about the child to which the school may not have immediate access (assuming, of course, that the child's parents have agreed to such disclosure). Nonschool professionals should assist in the development of appropriate in-school interventions, again by providing additional information about the child that may be relevant in deciding which strategies will be most effective. Nonschool professionals can play a major role in devising out-of-school interventions that may augment the program provided by the school (e.g., instructing parents in behavior management strategies, providing extracurricular activities that might build the child's self-concept, or suggesting counseling for parents whose expectations are unrealistic). Of course, the physician is a vital member of the team when decisions are being made regarding the need for medication to control AD/HD.

Certain nonschool professionals, especially the child's physician, may be in an excellent position to ensure continuity of appropriate services, even if the child moves from school to school. Because most children have regular contact with their physician and because parents are usually willing to share information freely with the physician, the physician can monitor the child's treatment and progress. Children who might otherwise "fall through the cracks" of the educational system can be assured appropriate ongoing services.

Finally, nonschool personnel should, when necessary, monitor the school's approach to diagnosis and treatment. Unfortunately, some schools are still using outdated methods for identifying children with learning disabilities. Nonschool personnel may need to make certain that the children they represent are not disqualified from service because they do not meet certain inappropriate criteria (e.g., large subtest scatter on the intelligence test). Nonschool personnel may need to monitor the type and amount of special education service the school is planning to provide. For example, if a child needs speech therapy but the school does not employ a speech therapist, the school may not be willing to include the therapy as part of the treatment plan. Nonschool personnel may need to intervene on behalf of the child.

Of course, the primary goal of the interdisciplinary team is to serve the child. Team members, both school and nonschool personnel, should view the interdisciplinary process as an opportunity to educate one another regarding their individual disciplines as well as an opportunity to provide optimal service to the child and family.

How Does the Interdisciplinary Process Work?

The first step in the interdisciplinary process is generally some type of *prescreening*. This may be done by the case manager or by a committee and involves determining whether or not the child is experiencing difficulty that warrants thorough evaluation. The case manager or committee makes this determination usually by talking with the person who initiated the referral (e.g., parents, teacher, physician) to obtain a description of the nature and history of the problems the child is experiencing. When possible, it is beneficial for those conducting the prescreening process to review records or talk briefly with individuals other than the referral source.

The most important aspect of the prescreening process is to determine what types of evaluation are most appropriate and will probably lead to the most fruitful results. Just as a physician determines what types of lab tests to conduct on the basis of the patient's symptoms, the individual(s) conducting the prescreening must determine from a description of the child's problems whether it would be more productive to explore the possibility of learning disabilities rather than other disorders (e.g., serious emotional disturbance). More specifically, the prescreening process will allow the case manager to make arrangements, when necessary, for evaluations from allied professionals (e.g., speech and language therapist, occupational therapist, physical therapist).

Finally, the individual(s) conducting the prescreening process should determine whether any evaluations have already been conducted that will be relevant in the formulation of the diagnoses and therapeutic recommendations. Although it is not necessary that the case manager determine precisely what evaluations will be carried out before the diagnostic process is initiated, some preplanning may reduce the number of visits the family must make to the clinic, reduce redundancy among the evaluations, and ensure that the concerns of the referring party are addressed thoroughly.

After the prescreening team or case manager has determined which evaluations will probably be most productive, individual professionals conduct the appropriate evaluations. These evaluations generally consist of a thorough history (obtained through a review of records and interviews with the parents, teachers, and child) as well as assessment with specific tests. The types of evaluation procedures employed by the physician, psychologist, educator, and allied professionals are described thoroughly in Chapters 3 through 8. Some of the options currently available to identify preschool-age children "at risk" for subsequent learning difficulties are discussed in Chapter 2.

After the individual professionals have conducted their evaluations, a case conference is held during which each professional shares the results of his or her evaluation. By reviewing Chapters 2 through 8, individual team members will have the necessary background to understand the evaluation techniques employed by each of the various disciplines. It is important, for example, for the special educator to understand how the physician arrived at a diagnosis of AD/HD. It is equally important for the physician to understand the nature of the tests used by the psychologist to determine the level of the child's cognitive abilities. By understanding each discipline's evaluative procedures, team members can better understand the data presented and their relationship to members' own data, suggest alternative interpretations to the data, monitor the appropriateness of the evaluation procedures for individual children, and identify areas in which information is incomplete.

After the data have been presented, the case manager will need to summarize the data presented and formulate tentative diagnoses to be discussed by the team. (Chapter 9 describes how the information gathered by each of the team members can be integrated to arrive at appropriate diagnoses.) Following discussion of the data, team members should be able to agree upon a list of the primary and secondary disabling conditions that are interfering with successful performance. On occasion, however, team members may decide that further evaluation is necessary before the diagnoses can be formulated. In this case, final diagnoses are postponed until a later meeting.

After diagnoses have been established, the interdisciplinary team should formulate a general treatment plan. For example, they might determine that the child should receive special education services in math and written language, that a trial on medication for AD/HD should be initiated, and that the parents should be provided with some training in behavior management strategies. Just as individual team members need to understand the evaluation procedures employed by professionals from other disciplines, it is important that they understand the various treatment strategies to be used. The special education teacher, for example, needs to understand what should be expected from a child treated with medication for AD/HD. Similarly, the psychologist needs to understand what types of reading programs are used by special educators to deal with a child who demonstrates language processing difficulties. By understanding the various treatment modalities available to the child, team members can better determine which treatments should be used, when and how they should be employed (e.g., all treatments started simultaneously or various treatments added in increments), how to evaluate their effectiveness, and how to determine when they are no longer needed. Strategies for treatment of primary and secondary disabling conditions are discussed in Chapters 10, 11, and 12. Because we acknowledge the chronic nature of learning disabilities as well as the importance of integrating the young adult with learning disabilities into the community, strategies for effective transition are discussed in Chapter 13.

The team should not attempt at the time of the initial interdisciplinary conference to develop specific goals and objectives, timelines for accomplishing their aims, or criteria for success. Instead, individual team members should be assigned responsibility for ensuring that the general areas of the treatment plan are refined further and implemented. The team should determine, however, what procedures will be used to coordinate and monitor the implementation of the general treatment plan. Procedures for follow-up and reevaluation should also be addressed.

Following this interdisciplinary case conference, the case manager (or other person appointed by the team) will be responsible for sharing the results of the evaluation, the diagnostic formulation, and the general therapeutic recommendations with the parents. Strategies for parent counseling are discussed in Chapter 14. This step is necessary in order to promote the parents' understanding and acceptance of their child's disorders and to elicit their cooperation in treatment. Parents of the school-aged child with learning disabilities are often encouraged to participate in the development of the Individualized Educational Plan (IEP) at the child's school (Chapter 10). With the introduction of P.L. 99-457, Individualized Family Service Plans (IFSPs) are required for outlining appropriate services for "at risk" children and their families. Parents' contribution to the development of these plans will be greatly enhanced if they previously have been presented with information regarding their child's disorders, been given the opportunity to ask the questions necessary to clarify their understanding of the situation, and had a chance to discuss treatment options.

CONCLUSION

The field of learning disabilities has matured tremendously since the term was first introduced in 1962. However, a great deal of confusion and misunderstanding still exists, even among professionals who diagnose and treat children with learning disabilities on a regular basis. Part of the reason for misunderstanding involves the interdisciplinary nature of the disorder. Because the child with learning disabilities often exhibits problems that are generally treated by professionals in different disciplines, it has been difficult for individual professionals to deal effectively with the total child. For this reason, an interdisciplinary approach is vitally important. By better understanding the diagnostic and treatment tools available to each discipline involved with the child, individual professionals can work together more effectively for the *total* well-being of the child and family.

PART I

ESTABLISHING THE DIAGNOSIS

CHAPTER 2

Learning Disabilities in Preschool Children

Barbara K. Keogh
Lucinda P. Bernheimer

Interest in learning disabilities in young children stems in part from the recognition that development is malleable in the early years, that appropriate services may alleviate or at least moderate the severity of problems, and that secondary, compounding problems may be prevented. The importance of the early years in the lives of children with disabilities was explicitly recognized at the federal level with passage of the 1986 and the 1991 Amendments B to the Education of the Handicapped Act (P.L. 99-457). These legislative actions reaffirmed and expanded guarantees of a free, public education as articulated in P.L. 94-142, the Education for All Handicapped Children Act of 1975. The Part H Program for Infants and Toddlers and the Preschool Grants Program for children in the 3–5 year range were part of the 1986 legislation and called for early identification and for programs of treatment and intervention.

These are worthwhile goals. The challenge is to find methods and techniques to implement the policy mandates. Because of the legislative changes, states are grappling with issues relating to eligibility criteria, child find activities, interagency agreements and efforts, training and quality of personnel, quality control and monitoring, and placement and inclusion in least restrictive environments (Thiele & Hamilton, 1991). Federal legislation also emphasizes the importance of providing services for families as well as for children. Indeed, the focus of services has shifted from the individual child and an Individual Educational Plan (IEP) to the family and an Individual Family Services Plan (IFSP). Educators and clinicians must now consider how to productively involve families when they plan interventions with children who have learning and developmental problems, and they must learn to understand and work with the larger family unit.

These policy changes affect all young children with disabilities and their families. Questions about eligibility criteria and procedures for accurate identification are particularly critical for children with learning disabilities at the preschool level, however, as there are a number of ambiguities and unanswered questions about learning disabilities in young children. Questions of primary importance include: How are learning disabilities expressed in young children? How do we recognize or identify learning disabilities in the preschool years? Do we have valid and reliable techniques for assessing learning disabilities before children enter school? Do we have valid and reliable techniques for describing families and family functioning?

A DISCREPANCY DEFINITION OF LEARNING DISABILITIES

Paraphrasing the definition in P.L. 94-142, specific learning disabilities in school-age children and adults describe problems in basic psychological processes or language which impair or affect abilities in higher order literacy and mathematical skills. This component of the definition has led to an emphasis on the expression of learning disabilities in the school age years. It has also led to an operational definition expressed as a discrepancy between IQ (aptitude) and achievement in school subjects (e.g., reading, arithmetic). The discrepancy definition itself has been challenged, and the amount or size of discrepancy is argued, but the notion of an aptitude-achievement discrepancy is still widely accepted as an important definitional criterion of learning disabilities.

A second, and related, criterion has to do with discrepancies or differences in abilities and aptitudes within a given child. A learning disability may be inferred when the "profile" of skills or achievements is inconsistent, when there are highs and lows across ability domains. A child who functions poorly in all domains is likely to be considered developmentally delayed. A child who has an uneven profile, who has unexpected lows in specific ability areas while performing as expected in others, is likely to be considered learning disabled. In the case of school-age children, the discrepant profiles usually reflect adequate performance in some academic areas (e.g., arithmetic) but markedly low and discrepant performance in others (e.g., reading or spelling).

Is a Discrepancy Definition Useful for Preschoolers?

An interesting problem arises when we attempt to use a discrepancy definition to identify learning disabilities in children who have not yet reached school age. Three- and 4-year-old children are not expected to have basic reading or mathematic calculation skills, nor to have well developed abilities in written expression, reading comprehension, or mathematics reasoning, all components of the federal guidelines for identification. Therefore, it is difficult to apply a discrepancy definition using these educational accomplishments or outcomes. Limiting learning disabilities to an educational frame of reference almost precludes identification in the early years.

Nonetheless, the notion of an unexpected discrepancy between expected and actual level of development or performance is appealing when applied to preschool children. The idea that differences occur in patterns or profiles across ability domains is also useful. The difficulty comes in operationalizing these discrepancies. Practical questions include: Which developmental domains or dimensions are important? How can they be measured? How large must a discrepancy be between the expected and actual developmental level to be considered indicative of learning disabilities? Closely related, it may also be difficult to accurately identify discrepancies within developmental profiles, the second major criterion used in identifying children with learning disabilities. An uneven or "spikey" profile of abilities or achievements is characteristic of many school-age children, but delays expressed early on are frequently more generalized, and differences across developmental domains may not be extreme.

In a recent discussion of eligibility issues affecting infants and toddlers with disabilities, Harbin, Gallagher, and Terry (1991) noted little consensus in the magnitude of the discrepancy accepted by states as indicating a significant delay in development. They found that accepted discrepancies ranged from 15 to 50%, and that investigators relied almost exclusively on standardized tests for determining discrepancies, despite the limited number of valid and reliable measures appropriate for assessing young children with disabilities. The discrepancy issue is particularly troublesome when assessing preschool children, as many instruments lack psychometric adequacy; children's motivation and behaviors are often variable and lack stability; and their performance on a given test or at a given time may not accurately reflect their competencies. In identifying young children with learning disabilities, it is difficult to make a clear distinction between general ability and specific developmental accomplishments in the early years. Further, differential diagnosis may be clouded because language or motor delays may be indicators of general cognitive or developmental delay as well as of specific learning disabilities. For these reasons many professionals have adopted a developmental framework for assessing learning disabilities in young children, urging clinicians to consider learning disabilities against a backdrop of expected developmental patterns.

A DEVELOPMENTAL FRAMEWORK

Based on their own experiences, most adults have ideas, although often not formalized, of what children "should be like" at certain ages, and about what kind of behaviors and competencies can be expected of children at different developmental periods. The child development literature contains many rich descriptions of characteristics of "typical" children at different ages. There are also a number of tests and surveys which provide detailed, normative description of behaviors and skills expected of infants and children in the early years. Because these techniques provide a way to describe individual children relative to developmental norms or expectancies, they can be useful in identifying development which is discrepant from normative expectancies.

McCarthy (1989a, 1989b) suggested that the federal definition of learning disabilities found in P.L. 94-142 should be modified for young children so that a severe discrepancy is defined in terms of differences between actual developmental accomplishments and expected developmental milestones, intellectual ability, or both. She proposed that the achievement domains of importance should be the precursors of academic skills, specifically, oral expression, listening comprehension, prewriting, prereading, and premathematical skills. She also suggested that basic processes or abilities of importance in the preschool years "include, but are not limited to, attention, memory, perceptual and perceptual-motor skills, thinking, language, and nonverbal abilities" (1989a, p. 70). McCarthy's approach is similar to that of the National Joint Committee on Learning Disabilities (Leigh, 1986), which proposed that learning disabilities in the preschool years may be expressed as deficits in areas of language, speech, and reasoning, and may co-occur with problems in social interaction and in motor skills or self-regulation.

Implicit in both of these approaches is the notion that the young child with learning disabilities has abilities and behaviors that are different or discrepant from normative expectancies, and that these differences are not explainable by sensory limitations, general cognitive deficits, or disadvantaged environments. This definitional approach is consistent with the one applied to older children and adults except that the discrepancy is based on developmental milestones and preacademic skills rather than on intellectual ability and specific academic accomplishments.

Placing learning disabilities in the preschool years within a developmental framework allows us to consider a broad range of characteristics, including preacademic accomplishments. It also underscores the need to consider a given child's attributes and problems against a backdrop of normal developmental expectancies, as a particular sign or behavior may be age-specific rather than problem-specific. Inability to follow a sequence of verbal instructions is not unusual in 2-year-olds but is surprising in 5-year-olds; copying complex geometric designs is too difficult a task for 3-year-olds but is successfully mastered by most kindergartners. We emphasize that the importance or significance of a particular behavior must be evaluated by taking into account the expected age-related abilities. Thus, a developmental perspective is essential in understanding learning disabilities in children in the preschool years.

Developmental Indicators in Preschool Children

What are the early signs of learning disabilities? How predictive are early indicators? How can we accurately assess and identify children with learning disabilities in the preschool years? These are questions that have important practical implication for services for children and their families. Answers to these questions lead to clinical and educational decisions about who is identified as learning disabled, who receives services, and what kinds of services should be provided.

Haring et al. (1992) identified 11 "clusters of characteristics" which they suggest signal possible risk for later academic problems. These characteristics are delays in concept development, delays in speech, delays in receptive and expressive language, directionality problems, delays in gross and fine motor skills, problems in attention, problems in auditory and/or visual perception, immature reasoning, hyperactivity, poor academic reading skills, and deficits in affective or social skills. These clusters are consistent with findings from a comprehensive review (Keogh, Major-Kingsley, Omori-Gordon, & Reid, 1982) of the research and clinical literature in education, psychology, medicine, and related fields. In that review the most frequently cited symptoms or indicators in the preschool years were in areas of language, visual perception, attention and impulse control, and behavior. These areas of problems deserve more detailed discussion as they provide a potentially useful description of young children with learning disabilities.

Language Problems

It should not surprise us that language problems are considered significant indicators of learning disabilities, given the importance of language in educational and personal-social competence. Language processing abilities are consistently associated with early reading skills and with subsequent reading problems. Phonological awareness and phonological processing skills specifically have been identified as important contributors to reading success or failures (see Felton, 1992, for discussion). Phonological problems range from generalized delay to specific deficits or disturbances, including problems in receptive vocabulary, syntax, phonemic awareness, and phonological production, all problems that can be identified in 2- and 3-year-olds. Scarborough (1990) described children with dyslexia as evidencing vocabulary deficiencies, poor rhyming and recitation skills, and phonemic awareness deficits typically at 3 to 4 years of age, and, at 2 years of age, to have produced shorter and simpler sentences and to have more pronunciation problems than nondyslexic children. Other investigators also find that preschool tests of expressive and receptive syntax and semantics are associated with later problems in reading and spelling, and that children with learning disabilities have particular problems with complex language demands, such as with narratives or in story telling.

Considerable evidence thus suggests that language delay or disturbance may be key indicators of potential learning disabilities in preschool children. A number of developmental tests include assessment of both receptive and expressive language domains (e.g., the Battelle Developmental Inventory [1984], the Gesell Developmental Schedules-Revised [1980]), and there are also language-specific measures (e.g., The Sequenced Inventory of Communication Development [1979], the Utah Test of Language Development [1978]) that are appropriate for preschool children.

We should emphasize, however, that language problems are not necessarily specific to learning disabilities, but may also be indicators of other developmental problems, particularly cognitive delay (see Hecht, 1986, for discussion). We should also emphasize that how and when children achieve early language milestones vary considerably, and that language delay does not necessarily signal problem development. However, given the importance of language in children's intellectual and social development, serious discrepancies from normative expectancies deserve attention as early signs of learning disabilities.

Attention Span/Impulse Control Problems

The clinical literature contains many descriptions of problems involving attention deficits, impulsivity, and excessive motor activity. These problems were often referred to earlier as hyperkinesis or hyperactivity, but are now thought to comprise a condition of attention-deficit/hyperactivity disorder (AD/HD). The major characteristics or "symptoms" of AD/HD (developmentally inappropriate attention span and/or impulse control and excessive motor activity) are not always linked, but the frequency of association has led to the use of the term AD/HD to refer to this complex of problems. The condition is more common in boys than in girls, is identifiable early in life, and is often associated with behavioral and learning problems. It is important to stress that AD/HD and learning disabilities are not the same, that learning disabilities may exist without AD/HD, and that not all children with AD/HD have learning disabilities. Based on their recent review, McKinney, Montague, and Hocutt (1993) concluded that AD/HD and learning disability co-occur in 10–20% of cases, but they noted that prevalence estimates varied from 9 to 63% in the studies. The evidence that the two conditions often co-occur is strong enough to suggest that diagnosis and planning for treatment may be confounded (Zentall, 1993).

Despite the somewhat confusing clinical picture, researchers agree that extreme overactivity and attentional problems are recognizable in the preschool years and that they represent an early warning sign of possible problems, including learning disabilities. Campbell, Szumowski, Ewing, Gluck, and Breaux (1982) found that the "core symptoms" of inattentiveness, hyperactivity, and aggression were identifiable by parents of 2- to 3-year-olds as well as by laboratory measures. Other researchers reported that teachers are also able to reliably identify preschool children who show signs of hyperactivity and distractibility. Inventories and rating scales such as the Preschool Behavior Questionnaire (1974) are often used to gather adults' perceptions of children's activity level and attentional characteristics.

The ability to modulate activity level, to come to attention, to focus, and to sustain attention are all important attributes in children's learning. These are the attributes which appear most affected in children with AD/HD, and which are often found in young children with learning disabilities. There is, thus, considerable support for considering overactivity and attentional problems as possible preschool indicators or signs of at-risk conditions, including learning disabilities.

Behavior Problems

Behavior problems, especially aggression, are frequently associated with hyperactivity and are often viewed as predictors of later problems. The diagnostic significance of behavior problems for learning disabilities is not entirely clear, yet serious problems in socialization and behavioral control suggest possible underlying processing difficulties. A number of checklists or inventories of problem behaviors are available for assessing behavior problems (e.g., The Preschool Behavior Questionnaire [1974], the Child Behavior Checklist-Preschool Form [1984]). We usually think of behavior problems as being externalizing in nature, that is, aggressive, unruly, difficult to discipline, and the like; however, internalizing problems, such as withdrawal, excessive shyness, and the like, may also be associated with learning problems. In a recent meta-analysis of 58 studies, for example, Horn and Packard (1986) found that after distractibility, internalizing problem behavior was one of the best early predictors of reading failure.

Because behavior problems may be expressed in a variety of ways, and because the long-term consequences of early problem conditions are unknown, it is difficult to draw definitive conclusions about direct causal relationships between behavior problems in the preschool years and learning disabilities. Some generalizations, however, follow from a sizeable research literature. Behavior problems may be reliably identified in the preschool years. Parents' and preschool teachers' views of problems agree considerably, suggesting some stability across settings. Children referred for clinical services as learning disabled often have histories of severe behavior problems in the preschool years.

A word of caution is in order about the interpretation of behavior problems and AD/HD in the preschool population as a whole. Overactivity and lack of sustained attention are relatively common characteristics of 2- and 3-year-olds and tend to change with age. Some studies have suggested that as many as 20–30% of preschoolers display externalizing problem behaviors. Thus, the age-related aspect of these indicators must be considered when making clinical decisions about young children. Also, it is important to emphasize that attentional problems, as well as behavior problems, are situationally related, and that the context, including the constraints and characteristics of the environment, comes into play. This is especially important to remember when most of the descriptions of preschool children come from parents' or teachers' reports.

Neuromaturational Indicators

Neuromaturational indicators are often used to identify preschoolers at risk for subsequent learning disabilities. Much of the early work on learning disabilities was based on the assumption of minimal brain dysfunction, and current research suggests a relationship between neuromaturational indices and learning problems. Neurological "soft signs" usually include such specifics as fine and gross motor coordination problems, abnormal or choreiform movements, reflex asymmetries, and or visual-motor abnormalities. Neuromaturation indicators also likely overlap with AD/HD, as both attention and activity problems may be considered primary (neurologically based) disabling conditions (see Chapter 1). In general, hyperactivity and attentional problems are more powerful predictors of subsequent learning problems than are the neurological "soft signs." Yet, neurological symptoms may serve as red flags for a range of problem conditions, including learning disabilities.

The interest in neurological indicators has led to the use of a variety of tests or measures, some included in neurodevelopmental examinations (Chapter 3), others more psychologically (Chapters 4 and 5) or educationally (Chapter 6) focused. Educationally or psychologically focused tests are aimed at behavioral expressions of possible neurological conditions and commonly tap perceptual and motor abilities. Widely used techniques require children to copy or reproduce designs or geometric forms, solve maze puzzles, or perform tasks requiring visual-motor coordination. As with other techniques, an important question when identifying preschool children with learning disabilities concerns the predictive power of these tasks. Few single signs in and of themselves are powerful diagnostic indicators. On the other hand, both the "soft" neurological signs and the behavioral indicators may be part of a pattern that suggests increased vulnerability or risk for the development of learning problems.

A Cautionary Note

Language problems, attention problems, behavioral problems, and delays of early neurodevelopment are all potential indicators of possible learning disabilities in young children. Thus, parents and teachers need to be sensitive to delays or deficits in connected language understanding and usage, speech articulation, attentional focus, impulse control, and behavioral control. Whether these signs are specific to learning disabilities is uncertain, as in the preschool years these signs may also be associated with other problem conditions such as mild retardation or emotional problems. Whatever the specific problem condition, however, such indicators send a message that some children may be at-risk and that special attention is needed.

It is important to emphasize that despite agreement about the domains of importance and about general normative or age-related expectancies for young children's development, children differ in both rate and pattern of growth, so we can anticipate a wide range of individual differences within any developmental period. A visit to any preschool dramatically illustrates the variations among preschoolers in physical size and motor skills, language facility, and social competence.

Some children will be "typical" in most developmental areas, others will be accelerated or delayed in all, and still others will have uneven patterns of skills. Important considerations from a developmental perspective have to do with the significance of these differences as predictors of subsequent problems, and with their stability and continuity over time. These points become particularly important when we attempt to identify learning disabilities early on, as there is some uncertainty about what characteristics are necessary for confident identification and about the long-term significance of many early indicators. Haring et al. (1992) suggested that the early indicators are best interpreted as signaling at-risk status rather than definitively identifying a specific problem condition. Nonetheless, the indicators are useful red-flags that require attention and follow-up.

APPROACHES TO ASSESSMENT

In general, two main types of procedures are used in assessing young children: rating scales and direct assessment or testing. Both types are based on the assumptions that there are early indicators which are valid predictors of subsequent learning disabilities and that those indicators can be identified and measured reliably.

Direct Tests

One area of direct testing targets general ability or developmental level. Thanks to a long tradition of psychometric efforts, a number of well constructed and well studied tests have been developed for assessing the general ability of young children. These include the 1989 version of the Wechsler Preschool and Primary Scale of Intelligence (WPPSI-R), the Stanford-Binet Intelligence Scale (4th Edition, 1986), the McCarthy Scales of Children's Ability (1972), and the Kaufman Assessment Battery for Children (K-ABC, 1983). These scales have been normed on large samples of children and have good reliability and validity. They meet the technical requirements for tests as defined by the U.S. Office of Education Special Education Programs Work Group on Management Issues in Assessment of Learning Disabilities (Reynolds, 1984). They also have been widely used in clinical and educational assessment. These tests, in addition to developmental scales such as the Bayley Scales of Infant Development—Second Edition (1993), the Griffiths Mental Development Scales (1954), and the Gesell Developmental Schedules: Revised (1980), provide ways to estimate general developmental levels.

In addition, several of these tests provide estimates of abilities in specific areas or ability domains. The Gesell Developmental Schedules yields developmental ages in language, adaptive behavior, motor, and personal-social domains. The McCarthy scales are composed of 18 subtests tapping verbal, perceptual, quantitative, memory, and motor abilities. The K-ABC yields scores for simultaneous and sequential processing as well as a mental index composite and a global achievement score. The WPPSI-R is consistent with the Wechsler tradition in providing scores for verbal, performance, and full-scale IQs. Thus, in addition to providing global estimates of ability to be compared to achievement measures, such tests are often used to address the profile component in the discrepancy model. Useful sources of information on testing young children include books by Bracken (1990) and Simeonsson (1986).

Rather than yielding general cognitive or developmental scores, a number of direct tests target basic skills, particularly school readiness or prereadiness skills. Tests differ in focus and scope, in technical and psychometric adequacy, and in predictive validity. They also differ in administrative time and conditions and in cost. Some may be administered to groups of children, others require individual administration; some assess a range of skills, others are aimed at identification of particular skills or problems. The Boehm Tests of Basic Concepts—Revised (1986), assesses children's knowledge and mastery of concepts important for success in kindergarten. A preschool version, designed to be used with children ages 3–5, taps understanding of such concepts as size, direction, and quantity. The Diagnostic Scale of the Bracken Basic Concept Scale (1984) measures children's understanding of over 250 concepts grouped into 11 subsections. Included are items tapping knowledge of colors, numbers and counting, and letter recognition. The Pre-Reading Screening Procedures—Revised (Slingerland, 1980), administered to children individually, assess entering school children's abilities on 12 dimensions related to reading (e.g., visual and auditory skills, auditory-visual association). The Developmental Indicators for the Assessment of Learning—Revised (DIAL-R, 1983) is an individually administered screening test aimed at identifying children at risk for learning problems upon school entrance. The test yields motor, concepts, language, and total scores. Both the Slingerland Procedures and the DIAL-R are lengthy and require a minimum of 30–40 minutes to administer. Many of these tests are useful in that they provide a systematic way of documenting children's competencies across a range of content domains. E. Aylward (personal communication, 1992) notes, however, that the basic concepts important for school success also may reflect general cognitive skills.

Some assessments are focused on specific academic areas or problem areas, such as language, mathematics, or reading. The Test of Early Language Development-2 (TELD-2, 1991) or the Test of Language Development-Primary:2 (TOLD-P:2, 1988) are examples of individually administered tests designed to screen for problems in receptive and expressive language. Group screening measures are also available and often used. The Comprehensive Test of Basic Skills (1981, 1982, 1983) and the Metropolitan Achievement Tests (1984) are well known group readiness tests which are designed to yield information about children's competencies or problems in both language and quantitative areas. The content of possible screening tests is broad, and their technical adequacy varies. Thus, effective and accurate early identification requires careful selection of methods and instruments, and appropriate and sensitive implementation procedures.

As suggested earlier, one of the potential problems in assessing specific abilities or skills in the preschool years is that many of the skills are also included in tests used to infer general cognitive ability or developmental level. In addition, the assessment of specific abilities or aptitudes of preschoolers is limited by measurement considerations. Many preschool tests have face validity (the content looks relevant and appropriate), but they are not psychometrically sound and they lack solid evidence documenting predictive validity or accuracy. In a review of almost 100 tests purported to be appropriate for assessment of kindergarten or preschool children, E. Aylward (personal communication, 1992) found that many were inadequately standardized with questionable reliability and validity, and/or were narrow in scope of material covered. Aylward's review suggests the need for especially careful selection of tests of specific aptitudes when diagnosing learning disabilities in preschool children, as inappropriate or unreliable measurement is a threat to accuracy when used in the discrepancy model.

Influences of Children's Performance on Tests

Although many tests may have good technical or psychometric properties, numerous factors may influence children's performance and thus may distort early identification findings. Possible challenges to the validity of results range from the obvious to the subtle, but, nonetheless, all need to be taken into account when planning and implementing programs for early identification of children with learning disabilities. Two points are particularly important when testing children.

The first has to do with the language and cultural background of children being assessed. Non- or limited-English-speaking children, or children whose home language is dialect based, are clearly at a disadvantage when test material is presented in standard English. Some tests are nonverbal in content and do not require spoken answers and thus are considered "nonlanguage." However, there are many linguistic demands in most tests, including nonverbal tasks, which may distort or reduce children's responses. In addition, cultural differences in interaction styles and in children's behavioral styles may interfere with their performance in a testing setting, lowering their scores and leading to incorrect inferences about their cognitive abilities or their readiness for school.

Closely related, investigators may assume that children come to the testing situation with similar and the necessary experiences, that they have the prerequisite background to perform. Thus, when performance is poor it may be inferred that some deficits in cognition, attention, language, or other ability domains are present. The assumption of prerequisite skills may be inaccurate in many cases, and indeed, there is evidence that poor performance may sometimes be related to lack of experience with the materials and demands of the tests themselves. Experience in schoollike activities, including test-taking skills, affect children's performance on tests, so that poor scores may be related to lack of experience rather than to general or specific deficits or delays. This, of course, emphasizes the need to exercise caution when attributing poor scores to child deficits.

Rating Scales

Rating scales and developmental inventories completed by adults who know a child well are alternatives or supplements to direct testing of children. The number of published rating scales attests to their utility and popularity. Many scales are aimed at gathering information from parents, teachers, or others close to the children being studied. Scales tap a range of child characteristics, some focusing on specific preacademic behaviors and aptitudes, others covering a broad range of content. The System to Plan Childhood Services (SPECS, 1991) integrates the views of parents and professionals regarding 2- to 6-year-old children's abilities in six domains: physical, communication, sensorimotor, self-regulation, self-social, and cognition. The Vineland Adaptive Behavior Scale (1984), also based on interviews with parents, covers communication, daily living, and motor skills, as well as adaptive behavior. The Child Development Inventory (1994) provides a comprehensive picture of children's development, also based on their parents' report.

Some rating scales are focused on problem behaviors or indicators of potential problems. The Preschool Behavior Questionnaire (1974), a widely used rating system, is aimed specifically at identifying emotional and behavioral problems in children 3 to 6 years of age. Teachers or child care workers are asked to rate children on 36 items tapping three domains: anxious-fearful, hyperactive-distractible, and hostile-aggressive. The Behavior Problem Checklist—Revised (1987) contains items appropriate for children ages 5 to 12 years, and consists of 89 items to be rated by teachers or parents. The scale yields six scores: conduct disorder, socialized aggression, attention problems and immaturity, anxiety-withdrawal, psychotic behavior. The Pre-School Form of the Child Behavior Scale (1990), a downward extension of the Child Behavior Problem Checklist (1984), covers externalizing and internalizing behaviors likely to be observed in young children.

Some rating scales used for screening are focused more specifically on school-related learning and classroom behaviors. The Rhode Island Profile of Early Learning Behavior (1982) is a 40-item scale to be completed by classroom teachers of kindergarten to Grade 2. The ratings yield scores about classroom behavior, written work, and a total score. The Pupil Rating Scale—Revised: Screening for Learning Disabilities (1981) was designed to gather teachers' and counselors' views of children 5 to 14 years of age. The kindergarten to Grade 6 form consists of 24 items tapping verbal and nonverbal skills, auditory comprehension and memory, spoken language, and motor coordination.

In addition to published rating scales of the kinds described above, many scales have been developed within school districts or for particular research projects. When used by professionals who have had an opportunity to become well acquainted with the children, many of these rating scales have been found to be effective in identifying children with learning problems. However, whether standardized and published or locally developed and unique, all rating instruments must be evaluated in terms of their predictive validity and appropriateness. Issues of reliability of measurement must be considered, especially when ratings provide the basis for placement or instructional decisions. Professionals' expectations, attitudes, values, and prior experiences may bias their ratings and lead to erroneous decisions regarding a child's status as at risk for learning disabilities. On the positive side, parents and teachers who work with children on a daily basis are an important and useful source of information and may well serve as the "first screen" to identify young children with learning disabilities.

ADDITIONAL DIAGNOSTIC CRITERIA

In addition to a developmental framework, signs or symptoms in the preschool years may usefully be evaluated in terms of other criteria: intensity, chronicity, breadth, and stability. Sometimes the most diagnostic information is gained from understanding not just what a child does, but how, how often, and under what conditions the problem behaviors occur. Information relevant to these criteria is not necessarily gathered from tests or direct assessment of children but may be gleaned from interviews with parents and teachers and from naturalistic observations of children.

Quite obviously, the severity or intensity of a problem behavior is of real concern, and adults are usually well aware of this aspect of a problem. All preschoolers have outbursts of frustration and temper and may have episodes of sulking or withdrawal; most preschool children are physically active. The intensity of expression will vary, however, and some behaviors go considerably beyond expected bounds. Inappropriately intense or severe misbehavior thus may be an indication of learning problems.

Closely related, the frequency of expression or the regularity of problem behavior is also a useful diagnostic sign. Occasional inappropriate, ineffective, or maladaptive behaviors are to be expected in preschool children. Young children are learning new skills and are trying out new strategies; thus, it is not surprising that their efforts are sometimes discrepant or disruptive. When such behaviors occur frequently or typically, however, they suggest a lack of adequate coping skills, and thus may signal problems.

Particular behaviors also need to be evaluated relative to the settings or situations in which they occur, as the diagnostic significance of a particular behavior is related to its breadth of expression. Is the behavior evident in many situations or is it situation-specific? Is the child overly active at home and at school? When playing outside and when watching television? With most children or only with particular children? Maladaptive or negative behaviors evident in only one situation are likely not as serious as behaviors evident across a range of settings.

Finally, the stability of problem behaviors over time is another important diagnostic indicator. The preschool years are a time of rapid change, and problem behaviors early on are often replaced by more adaptive and mature skills, so that many behavior or learning problems are transitory. A 2-year-old may have brief periods of difficulty in sustaining attention such that he or she appears distractible and impulsive. A 3-year-old may stammer or reverse words for a few weeks or months. These are not necessarily signs of learning disabilities but may represent transition periods in development or be responses to stress. On the other hand, a learning disability may be present if the same behaviors or indicators are maintained over long periods of time and if they are not replaced by more effective and age-appropriate behaviors.

Parents as Sources of Information

Traditional approaches to assessment of children's development placed heavy emphasis on direct testing and on professional's clinical impressions. Relatively little weight was given to parents' views, as the assumptions were that parents' perceptions were biased, that parents tended to overestimate their children's levels of development and competence, and that they overlooked or minimized problems and deficits. Indeed, when parents and professionals held different views of a child, the professional view was considered the "standard" and deviations from that standard (e.g., a different perception by the parents) were viewed as error. This view is changing, and there is increasing recognition of the benefits of parents' reports in the assessment process (Sexton, Thompson, Perez, & Rheams, 1990; Diamond & Squires, 1993). This shift parallels the conceptual shift in thinking about early intervention, as the focus is no longer exclusively on the child, but on the child in the context of the family. Importantly, too, P.L. 99-457 mandates the inclusion of parents in the development of the Individual Family Service Plan, and assessment is a key component in this plan.

We agree with Diamond and Squires (1993) that information from parents enhances the validity of assessment based on other approaches. Parents' reports often provide information that cannot be obtained during direct testing, as parents' perceptions have been gathered over a longer time period and are based on experiences with the child in many situations. Parents can provide information about behaviors that are difficult for the clinician or examiner to observe (sleeping and eating behavior, relationships with family members) and can provide insights about a child's unique behavioral competencies or problems. Parents' reports often address the diagnostic characteristics described earlier (intensity, frequency, breadth, and stability), as their descriptions of life with a given child provide information about how often, in what situations, and under which circumstances particular behaviors occur. By including parents' report in the assessment process, professionals can compose a more accurate picture of a child's abilities and problems, because data from several environments are taken into account (Sexton et al., 1990; Dinnebeil & Rule, 1994).

While parents' information is beneficial in the assessment of all young children with disabilities, it may be particularly important in the case of young children with learning disabilities. As previously noted, in the absence of academic indicators, other child status variables play a significant role in assessment. These include motor skills and language skills as well as attention span and activity level. Parents are often keenly aware of inconsistencies, even discrepancies, in children's behaviors and skills and thus can supplement the findings from direct assessments.

Information from parents can be collected in a variety of ways, including developmental questionnaires, behavior checklists, and structured interviews. Many of the rating scales described earlier (e.g., Vineland Adaptive Behavior Scales; Child Development Inventory) can be completed by parents. A joint observation of the child by parent and professional may also be helpful in determining the representativeness of a particular behavior or characteristic. There is also increasing interest in the use of semistructured or open-ended interviews, in which the parents are asked to tell their "story" with a focus on the way in which the child influences the day-to-day life of the family (Bernheimer, Gallimore, & Kaufman, 1993). The advantage of this method is that it yields information about what is important to the family, and hence, information that will be critical in the development of a treatment plan.

Bailey and Wolery (1989) note that parents and professionals often hold different views about behavior and that they may have different criteria for determining competence; they also interact with children in different contexts. Thus, agreement between parents and professionals increases confidence that what is observed is a reliable estimate of the child's abilities (Diamond & Squires, 1993). On the other hand, it is not surprising that professional and parental judgments sometimes differ. Bailey and Wolery pose an interesting and important question when they ask whether parent-professional agreement is always to be desired. The reason for using both sources of information is to uncover the basis for differences: Is the child just beginning to develop a particular skill? Are the skills evident in some settings but not in others? Finally, including parents in the assessment process lays the groundwork for a parent-professional partnership, a concept inherent in the spirit and letter of P.L. 99-457. This partnership is critical if the Individual Family Service Plan (IFSP) is going to be a meaningful reflection of parents' priorities and concerns. The more the IFSP reflects parents' priorities for the child, the more likely it is that parents will support, implement, and sustain professional recommendations for treatment and intervention.

CONCLUSION

We underscore the importance of early identification and intervention services for young children with learning disabilities. We also emphasize that an increasingly large literature demonstrates that it is possible to accurately and reliably identify preschool children who are at risk for subsequent developmental and learning problems, including learning disabilities. We caution, however, that identification is not just a matter of testing. A number of instruments and behavior surveys are available and are useful in identification procedures. Yet, the information provided by such measures, while useful and relevant, is not sufficient for diagnostic decisions or intervention planning. Sensitive and accurate identification of young children with learning disabilities requires consideration of a range of attributes and conditions, including the severity, chronicity, breadth, and stability of problems. Evaluating behaviors and symptoms within a developmental perspective ensures an age- and gender-appropriate framework. Gathering information from multiple sources (tests, clinical evaluations, parents' and teachers' perceptions) provides a more complete and accurate picture of children's competencies and problems.

CHAPTER 3

Neurodevelopmental Evaluation (The Physician's Diagnostic Role in Learning Disabilities)

Frank R. Brown, III

The diagnosis of learning disabilities for school-age children has traditionally depended upon measurement of, and establishment of a discrepancy between academic achievement and cognitive functioning levels. In Chapter 2 Keogh and Bernheimer noted some of the difficulties in using discrepancy definitions to identify preschool-age children at risk for subsequent learning disabilities, and they discussed the utility of a neurodevelopmental/behavioral approach to facilitate early identification of children at risk for subsequent poor academic achievement. The physician plays a vital role in the interdisciplinary approach to the identification and remediation of learning disabilities. In the case of preschool-age children, the physician is frequently the first professional resource consulted regarding questions of neurodevelopmental/ behavioral progress. When questions arise about learning disabilities in school-age children, the physician can contribute both in the diagnostic process and in ensuring a balance of professional perspectives when establishing a remediation program. To make these contributions to the diagnostic and prescriptive process for both preschool and school-age children, the physician must expand the traditional role of medical history taking and examination to include a *neurodevelopmental history* and *neurodevelopmental examination*. Components of the physician's expanded neurodevelopmental history and examination process for the preschool and school-age child are the focus of this chapter.

IDENTIFICATION OF PRESCHOOL-AGE CHILDREN AT RISK FOR LEARNING DISABILITIES

Unfortunately, a reliable method for identifying children with learning disabilities at an early age (before first grade, and usually not until beginning second grade) does not yet exist. One approach to early identification of preschool-age children "at risk" for subsequent learning disabilities is to identify patterns of neurodevelopment that correlate with subsequent learning difficulties, looking especially for delays in language understanding and usage, visual perception, attention and/or impulse control, and for the presence of any associated oppositional, noncompliant, and avoidant behaviors. The physician has a vital role to play in this approach to early identification, and the physician's assessment begins with the neurodevelopmental history.

Neurodevelopmental History

The neurodevelopmental history, that is, the history of the temporal sequence of development, is an important element of the physician's evaluation of the preschool child at risk for subsequent learning disabilities. The importance and utility of the neurodevelopmental history is underscored by the following:

1. The neurodevelopmental history affords the physician multiple "windows" on the course of neurodevelopment to date. Consistencies observed within the neurodevelopmental history and between the history and neurodevelopmental examination improve reliability and validity of conclusions regarding levels of neurodevelopmental function.
2. The neurodevelopmental history affords the physician an opportunity to compare present and past rates of neurodevelopment. Such comparisons assist the physician in determining whether developmental delays manifest as a constant, albeit slower than normal rate of development ("static encephalopathy") or as a progressive deterioration in neurodevelopment ("progressive encephalopathy" or "neurodegenerative disorder").
3. The neurodevelopmental history can assist the physician in determining additional diagnostic tests to perform. A history suggesting a constant, albeit slower than normal rate of development may disincline the physician from performing elaborate studies to establish causation. The yield of such efforts, from the standpoints of both establishing causation and identifying treatable disorders, is usually limited. On the other

hand, a history consistent with neurodegeneration should alert the physician to perform a variety of additional diagnostic tests, such as computer assisted tomography, nuclear magnetic resonance scans, electroencephalograms, urine metabolic screens, serum and urinary amino acid screens, and biochemical evaluations of cultured skin fibroblasts. By restricting use of these diagnostic studies to those progressive neurological processes identified in the neurodevelopmental history, the physician can optimally identify those children whose course is expected to be altered by this information.

4. The neurodevelopmental history affords the physician a temporal accounting of developmental progress and can serve as a guideline to the appropriate level at which to begin the neurodevelopmental examination.

5. Comparison of the parents' accounting of the neurodevelopmental history with developmental findings observed in the neurodevelopmental examination affords the physician and interdisciplinary team insight into how realistic the parents are in their understanding of the extent of their child's problems. This information can help guide subsequent parent conferences and counseling sessions.

The first part of the neurodevelopmental history is the ascertainment of any pre- and/or perinatal risk factors (Table 3–1) that might place the child at increased risk for subsequent developmental disabilities, including specific learning disabilities. The physician and interdisciplinary team must appreciate that many affected children may not have obvious histories of pre- and/or perinatal risk factors. In fact, although a significant number of children with a high-risk pre- or perinatal course will manifest subsequent neurological deficits, the majority of children with neurological deficits do not have histories which we would identify as high risk. This may reflect the fact that many of the risk factors listed in Table 3–1 can manifest in subtle, sometimes undetectable fashion, or that current technologies are not sophisticated enough to detect more subtle insults. For example, although the effects of high maternal alcohol consumption on the fetus and the full-blown fetal alcohol syndrome are obvious (intrauterine and postnatal growth retardation, physical abnormalities, and impaired cognitive development), the effects of lesser degrees of alcohol and cigarette consumption as well as other factors, such as subclinical maternal viral infections on the developing fetus, are less obvious. Certainly the presence of risk factors in the pregnancy, labor, and delivery should alert the physician to carefully monitor subsequent neurodevelopment. We

TABLE 3–1
Prenatal and Perinatal History—Risk Factors Associated with Learning Disabilities

Pregnancy	Labor and Delivery (cont'd)
Maternal age	Problems:
Paternal age	premature rupture of membranes
Parity	maternal fever
Length of gestation	toxemia
Maternal weight gain	abnormal bleeding
Fetal activity	fetal monitoring
Previous maternal obstetrical	failure of labor to progress
problems	labor induced
Problems:	Caesarian section
bleeding/spotting	forceps/instrumentation
medications	resuscitation
trauma	abnormalities at birth
toxemia	abnormal placenta
radiation	**Neonatal**
rash/infection	
fluid retention	Duration of hospitalization
abnormal fetal movements	Problems:
alcohol	respiratory distress syndrome
tobacco	cyanosis
Labor and Delivery	seizures
	oxygen therapy
Hospital	feeding problems
Duration of labor	infections
Birth weight	jaundice
Apgars	metabolic
Analgesia/sedation	congenital abnormalities
Presentation	apnea

hope in the future that the ability to identify milder (and more frequently occurring) insults will improve.

In addition to the historical questions used to identify high-risk pre- and perinatal situations, the physician should elicit a careful neurodevelopmental history, that is, a history of temporal development in four areas:

1. Motor—including gross, fine, and oral motor function.
2. Visual Perception and Problem Solving—including concepts such as size, shape, and spatial relationships.
3. Language—including expressive and receptive language abilities.
4. Social-Adaptive—including self-help skills such as dressing and feeding.

As the physician elicits the temporal sequence of development in these four areas, it is important that he or she be aware that parents frequently have difficulty recalling neurodevelopment in those areas in which the physician has most interest, especially receptive language and visual perception/problem solving. Parents usually have an easier time relaying historical information regarding events that they perceive as major events in their child's life (e.g., age at which the child took his or her first steps or uttered first words). As the physician initiates the neurodevelopmental history, it is advisable that he or she build the parents' confidence as historians by asking them to recount their child's development in those areas where they are anticipated to be the best observers. In most instances this proves to be in gross motor (Table 3–2) and expressive language development (Table 3–3) (i.e.,

TABLE 3–2
Gross Motor Developmental Milestones

Age	Skill Attained
2 mo	Lifts head in face down (prone) posture
3 mo	Up on forearms in prone
4 mo	Up on wrists in prone Rolls over, face down (prone) to face up (supine)
5 mo	Rolls over, supine to prone
6 mo	Sits without support, anterior propping
8 mo	Lateral propping in sitting Lateralizes (reaches to side) in sitting
9 mo	Pulls to standing, cruises holding on
12 mo	Walks independently Posterior propping in sitting
18 mo	Runs
27 mo	Walks up stairs ("marking time")
3 yr	Pedals tricycle Walks up stairs alternating feet, down "marking time"
3.5 yr	Walks up and down stairs alternating feet
4.5 yr	Balances briefly (5 sec.) either foot
5 yr	Skips

TABLE 3–3

Language—Expressive and Receptive Milestones

Age	Skill Attained
2 mo	Spontaneous smile
3 mo	Cooing (vowel) sounds
4 mo	Turns to voice
5 mo	Lateralizes to bell "Raspberry" or "Bronx Cheer"
6 mo	Babbling (consonant) sounds
7 mo	Orients to bell (2 planes)
8 mo	Ma-Ma/Da-Da, non-specific
9 mo	Gesture language (bye-bye, point to wants) Orients to bell (directly)
10 mo	Ma-Ma/Da-Da, specific
12 mo	First word other than ma-ma/da-da
14 mo	Follows 1-step command with gesture
16 mo	Follows 1-step command without gesture
18 mo	Indicates 1 body part 12 word vocabulary
21 mo	Combines 2 words 20 word vocabulary

24 mo	Follows 2-step command without gestures
	   e.g., "Put the ball on the table and give the pencil
	   to me"
	50 word vocabulary

30 mo	Concept of "just one" Prepositions "on" & "under"
3 yr	Asks for word meanings Answers "What do you do when you're hungry?" Identifies sex Concepts of "big" & "little" Prepositions "behind" & "next to" 250 word vocabulary
4 yr	Tells stories using complex syntax Answers "What do you do when you're cold?" Concepts of "longer" & "shorter"
5 yr	Follows 3-step command in correct order Vocabulary too numerous to count

"walking" and "talking"). After building the parents' confidence in their ability to recall historical details, the physician can proceed to elicit the neurodevelopmental history in those important, but more difficult, areas to recall, such as receptive language (Table 3–3) and visual perceptual/fine motor performance (Table 3–4).

Because the parents will not be as accurate in recalling details regarding receptive language and visual perceptual/fine motor development, the physician will sometimes have to be creative and persistent in the history-taking process, asking questions in a proper sequence to maximize accuracy of the parents' recollections. For example, questions regarding visual perceptual/fine motor development need to be asked in a fashion which the parents appreciate, that is, in terms of tasks that relate to everyday living. This might mean that visual perception would be evaluated through a history of development of skills such as dressing and feeding, skills that depend on a combination of visual perception and problem solving. Again, milestones relating to visual perceptual/fine motor development are listed in Table 3-4. The physician should appreciate that the items listed also represent "social-adaptive" development, and depend on the parents' willingness to allow the child to express developmental capabilities.

TABLE 3–4
Visual Perceptual/Fine Motor Milestones

Age	Skill Attained
3 mo	Unfisted hands Active reaching
6 mo	Transfers hand-to-hand
8 mo	Holds 2 objects simultaneously
9 mo	Pincer grasp Finger feeds
12 mo	Drinks from cup Intentional release
14 mo	Spoon feeds
18 mo	Scribbles spontaneously
27 mo	Imitates horizontal/vertical stroke
3 yr	Unbuttons
4 yr	Buttons up
5 yr	Ties Shoes

The physician should conclude the neurodevelopmental history by asking the parents to state their perceptions of their child's overall level of neurodevelopmental function in terms of age equivalents. This question can be as simple as "At what age level do you see your child functioning overall?" If the parents show any resistance in formulating a response, they should be further encouraged to "Give me your best guess." If both parents are present, the question should be asked separately in order to determine concurrence (this concurrence may be of import later during the parent conference). Further clarification is afforded if the parents are asked to describe age equivalents for areas of "best function" and "worst function." Parents' willingness and concurrence in estimating an age-equivalent of their child's development may indicate the degree to which parents will be able to accept later diagnostic formulations. In addition, the physician may find that parents are better able to accept diagnostic conclusions if they have initially acknowledged that their child is delayed in one or more areas.

The physician should resist simple conclusions that parents are "poor" or "bad" historians, and instead make a concerted effort to become a more effective history taker. "Bad" historians, meaning parents who provide misinformation because they are not prepared to accept their own suspicions of delay, are extremely rare. Numerous factors can contribute to a poor history-taking process. When a child exhibits significant delays in an area of neurodevelopmental function, not only will development of the process be protracted over time (and therefore its precise time of evolution be somewhat blurred), but also the quality of the process will be affected, and therefore the parents may have difficulty recalling specific ages of attainment. The physician should also be careful to avoid giving parents the perception that he or she views the child's neurodevelopment as a rote compendium of deficits. The physician should develop the history via questions focused exclusively on age-equivalent descriptors, for example, "At what age did your child walk independently?" The physician should avoid questions that imply perceptions of delay, for example, "When did you appreciate your child's delay in walking?" Terms that imply delayed development, such as "slow," "delayed," or "disabled" should be assiduously avoided because they result in miscommunication. These summary descriptors serve no purpose other than to potentially offend and distort the history-taking process.

Having obtained estimates of current neurodevelopmental functioning (i.e., age equivalents) through the neurodevelopmental history, the physician will progress to the second component of the physician's process, the neurodevelopmental examination. If the history and examination are properly performed, the examination should simply confirm levels of neurodevelopmental function inferred in the history, and the combination of the two will produce a reliable and valid assessment.

Neurodevelopmental Examination

Physicians typically have utilized "screening instruments" as a basis for neurodevelopmental examination and in making decisions regarding referrals for more detailed evaluations. Reliance on any single screening instrument is problematic for the following reasons:

1. These instruments often result in significant false positives and negatives, and referral decisions based on them are apt to be inaccurate.
2. Their design and use affords a limited perspective on neurodevelopment, that is, at only one point in time. This contrasts with and ignores the important utility of the developmental history and leads to the false positives and negatives described previously.
3. Their design affords no reliability or validity of observation unless another instrument is administered.
4. Overreliance on screening instruments translates into "test scores" with poor appreciation of the process utilized by the generalist in looking at neurodevelopment.

I believe that assessment and referral decisions regarding preschool-age children at risk for subsequent learning disabilities are best made on the basis of appreciation of normal and abnormal development, the depth and breadth of training of the physician, and the reliability and validity inherent in the neurodevelopmental history and examination gathering process. The neurodevelopmental assessment tools described are not intended to replace more detailed evaluations by allied health professionals, but they can help the generalist develop appropriate schema for subsequent referrals.

The neurodevelopmental examination is the physician's detailed examination of a child's development in the four areas discussed previously: motor (gross/fine/oral), visual perception and problem solving, language (expressive/receptive), and social-adaptive function. Social-adaptive function, for example, self-help skills such as dressing and feeding, usually is not directly assessed in the neurodevelopmental examination because of time constraints and lack of efficiency.

Because the child's cooperation is essential for accurate assessment of cognitive function, and because cognitive function is deemed to be particularly germane to the prediction of future school success, I recommend that the neurodevelopmental examination of the preschool-age child commence with cognitive assessment and proceed subsequently to analysis of motor skills. I recommend initiating cognitive assessment with visual perceptual problem solving, then proceeding to language. A good reason for conducting the examination in this order is to take into account the child who may have disproportionate delay in language functioning relative to other cognitive abilities. This approach is particularly advised when the neurodevelopmental history provided by the parents suggests that such problems in language exist. If such children are approached initially with any significant language demand, further cooperation in the examining process may be impaired. Rapport will, of course, be further enhanced by careful selection of initial areas and levels of assessment so as to avoid challenging the child in areas of relative weakness.

Assessment of Visual Perceptual/Problem Solving Abilities

Assessment of visual perceptual/problem solving for preschool-age children involves analysis of playlike skills with simple toy items of the type described in Table 3–5. Many of these test items involve high-interest tasks and are similar to children's play. As a result, for many children, visual problem solving is an ideal starting point in the neurodevelopmental examination. Assessment of visual problem solving for children is dependent upon a combination of their cognitive ability to visually conceptualize the task and their fine motor skill to respond. The interdependency of these two processes points up the need to dissociate inability to perform a task into its requisite parts.

Several of the toy items used to assess visual problem solving, especially one-inch cubes and pencil or crayons and paper, cover a fairly broad range of developmental abilities. The one-inch cubes, for example, cover a visual perceptual/fine motor neurodevelopmental age range of approximately 3 months to 7 years, and pencil/crayons and paper approximately 16 months to 12 years. Because they are useful in assessing visual perception/visual problem solving across such a breadth of developmental age range, and because they represent very simple test procedures that the physician may incorporate in the neurodevelopmental assessment battery, these two items have particular utility.

When assessing a child's visual perceptual abilities with one-inch cubes, the examiner first builds the block constructs out of the child's field of view (typically by concealing the assembly process with the examiner's hand). The child is then given the appropriate number of blocks to build a duplicate of the examiner's model, and the model is left in place for visual imitation by the child. The two exceptions to this procedure are the staircase assemblies (Table 3–5, f and g), where the

TABLE 3–5

Assessment of Visual Perception/Problem Solving

One-Inch Cubes (3 months to 7 years)

3 mo	Regards (visually tracks) cube
5 mo	Reaches up to obtain cube in supine (lying face up)
6 mo	Reaches out to obtain cube in sitting Transfers cube hand-to-hand
8 mo	Holds two cubes simultaneously
9 mo	Releases cube into a cup (over side of cup)
12 mo	Intentional (precise) release of cube into a cup
14 mo	Holds three cubes simultaneously
18 mo	Vertical tower of 3 cubes (a)
24 mo	Train of 3 cubes (b)
27 mo	Train of 4 cubes with smoke stack (c)
36 mo	3 block bridge (d)
4 yr	5 block gate (e)
5 yr	6 block staircase (f)
7 yr	10 block staircase (g)

Pencil and Paper (16 months to 12 years)

16 mo	Scribbles in imitation
18 mo	Scribbles spontaneously
27 mo	Imitates horizontal/vertical stroke
30 mo	Copies circle as circular motion
3 yr	Copies circle
3.5 yr	Copies cross
4 yr	Copies square
5 yr	Copies triangle
6 yr	Copies "Union Jack"
7 yr	Copies diamond
8 yr	Copies Maltese cross
9 yr	Copies cylinder
12 yr	Copies cube

Gesell Drawings (see Figure 3–1)

model is built out of sight, shown to the child, and destroyed, and the child is then asked to build the assembly from visual memory.

The drawing tasks listed in Table 3–5 are suitable for testing visual perceptual development over a wide age range. The Gesell figures (Figure 3–1) are a series of increasingly complex figures that the child is asked to replicate with crayon or pencil and paper. These drawings are presented to the child in a completed, predrawn fashion and the child is asked to draw a likeness of the figures. It is imperative that the physician observe the child in the process of replicating the figures, as satisfactory replication is not the only information to be obtained. It is also important to analyze the child's approach to replicating the figures, noting issues such as time to complete the figures and omission of key elements. The child who does not understand the gestalt of the figures may, for example, approach the "Union Jack" in a fragmented fashion, perhaps drawing it as a series of small triangles. Unless the child is observed in the drawing process these qualitative deficits in performance may not be appreciated.

Assessment of Language Functioning

As discussed earlier, several aspects of neurodevelopmental function in the preschool-age child are particularly suggestive that a child is at increased risk for subsequent learning difficulties. Of all neurodevelopmental domains, receptive language is perhaps most predictive of future developmental course. Particular attention should be paid to the elucidation of the neurodevelopmental history and in the neurodevelopmental assessment in this domain.

Assessment of language functioning does not depend on specific test items of the type described for assessment of visual perceptual abilities. When assessing language development in the preschool-age child, the examiner should be most concerned with connected language understanding and usage. This most meaningful aspect of the preschooler's language development can be assessed simply and appropriately by the examination of the ability to manipulate familiar objects upon command (i.e., follow simple directions, with and without gestures, and of increasing complexity) and ability to answer simple comprehension questions as exemplified in Table 3–3. Instruments such as the Peabody Picture Vocabulary Test-Revised (PPVT-R, 1981) assess more limited aspects of language development (picture identification) and, therefore, are less informative of meaningful language development. In other words, the generalist might well attach more meaning to the child's ability to comprehend the direction "put the book in the drawer" than the ability to identify pictures in the book, PPVT-R.

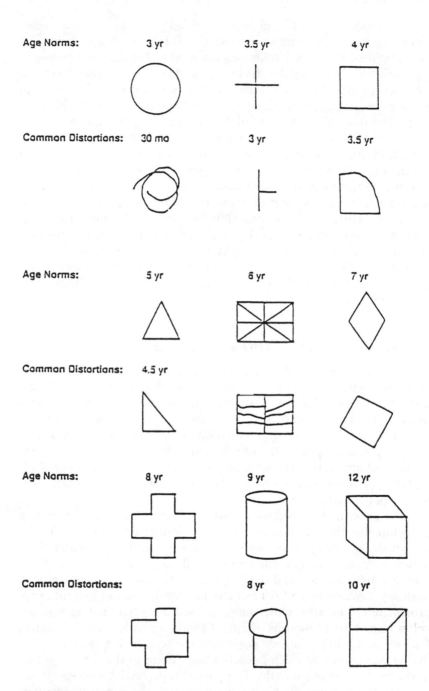

FIGURE 3-1. *Assessment of Visual Problem-Solving Abilities (Gesell Drawings)*

An important red flag in identifying language delay is the persistence of echolalia beyond approximately 30 months of age. Echolalia, as exemplified by the repetition of a question rather than responding to the question, or echoing the last thing heard (e.g., Question—"Are you a boy or a girl?" Answer—"boy or girl"), represents a failure to comprehend language. Presence of echolalia beyond 30 months is tantamount to saying that the child is delayed in the language sphere.

In an office setting it is unrealistic to expect a child to exhibit a reasonable facsimile of his or her expressive vocabulary and mean length of utterance. To estimate expressive language the examiner will have to rely in significant part on the parents' history. This need not be a major deterrent to the assessment of expressive language, as long as the examiner recognizes that it is impossible for receptive language to lag behind expressive language development. On the other hand, expressive language, at least in the usual restricted evaluative setting, may well appear to lag behind receptive language development. Receptive language is therefore usually considered a far better indicator of inherent language capabilities.

Assessment of Gross/Fine/Oral Motor Abilities

Having completed the cognitive (visual perceptual and language assessment) portion of the neurodevelopmental examination, the examiner will proceed with assessment of motor function. This domain is reserved for the last part of the examination because it represents a more invasive aspect of the examination process; that is, the child is actually approached physically. In addition, it is more effective to assess cognitive domains before the child becomes tired, and it is more likely that the physician can continue to elicit cooperation in motor tasks that may be perceived as fun.

The gross motor milestones listed in Table 3–2 can be used as a guideline for the examination of gross motor development in the preschool-age child. It is important to appreciate that many gross motor skills, for example, the ability to sit independently and to function in sitting, are attained over significant intervals of time. Children normally develop the ability to sit independently without support at approximately 6 months. Other more refined aspects of sitting may develop from 6 to 12 months of age. The ability to lateralize in sitting (i.e., to reach out to the side in sitting) and to exhibit a lateral protective response (i.e., to catch oneself when falling to the side in sitting) normally develop at 8 months. The posterior protective response in sitting (i.e., to catch oneself in a rearward fall with the arms) emerges normally at 12 months of age. In summary, sitting does not develop at a single age, but rather develops over an age range of at least 6 to 12 months, and some aspects of sitting are still developing at a time when a child is normally beginning to walk independently.

A child's ability to perform on stairs (see Table 3–2) can be a tool for assessing gross motor development for children at an approximate 2.5- to 3.5-year level. At 2.5 years, a child should be able to ascend stairs with alternating feet. At 3 years, a child will ascend stairs with alternating feet and will descend stairs "marking time." Also, at about 3 years, a child normally will have developed the ability to pedal a tricycle. By 3.5 years a child will ascend and descend stairs with alternating feet.

As mentioned previously in the section on visual perceptual/problem solving, an important antecedent to the assessment of visual perceptual abilities is in ascertaining the extent of any intercurrent difficulties in fine motor performance. Assessment of fine motor abilities is typically inferred from observing a child's performance on visual problem-solving tasks. An exact level of fine motor function is not derived from this process. Rather, the extent to which fine motor difficulties might represent an interfering factor is inferred.

Oral motor functioning is inferred from the neurodevelopmental history and observation in such areas as feeding and speech articulation. Certainly a history of feeding difficulties and/or persistence of drooling suggests significant delays. An additional manifestation of oral motor dysfunction is delayed speech articulation. In general, children's speech should be nearly 100% intelligible to the parents by age 30 months and to strangers by 36 months.

NEURODEVELOPMENTAL HISTORY AND EXAMINATION FOR THE SCHOOL-AGE CHILD

The neurodevelopmental history and examination process described previously serves well for children under 5 years of age and permits identification of preschool children at risk for subsequent learning difficulties based on delays in neurodevelopment. When the physician is asked to evaluate school-age children for possible learning disabilities the evaluative task will be different. The physician's role in identifying preschool-age children "at risk" for subsequent learning difficulties is described here as involving primarily early recognition of children with delays in neurodevelopment, especially in the areas of language understanding and usage, and visual perception/problem solving. Subsequent chapters will discuss the physician's role in the early identification of developmentally inappropriate attention span and/or impulse control (Chapter 11) and behavioral disturbances including oppositional, noncompliant, and avoidant behaviors (Chapter 12).

The physician plays a role in identifying learning disabilities in school-age children by performing a neurodevelopmental evaluation that will at least screen whether discrepancies exist between cognitive expectation and academic achievement. The physician has some tools available to assess developmental functioning and academic achievement levels for these older, school-age children. However, because of the older age and the possibility of overlap with more specific testing performed by the psychologist or special educator, the physician more typically will defer to these colleagues and ask that precise levels of cognitive functioning be established on the basis of more detailed psychological and special education assessments, as described in Chapters 4, 5, and 6. The physician evaluating the school-age child is looking for neurodevelopmental findings that, although not pathognomonic for identification of learning disabilities, nevertheless correlate highly with and are risk factors for the subsequent development of learning disabilities.

Neurodevelopmental History

The physician's history for the school-age child with learning difficulties begins in the same format employed with the preschool child; that is, the history will begin with a review of the pregnancy, labor, and birth history to identify pregnancies that represent high risks for subsequent developmental problems (Table 3–1). The physician will next elicit a neurodevelopmental history, that is, a history of temporal patterns of development. Historical questions will be asked in the developmental areas discussed previously for the preschool child, especially detailing the parents' conception of the preschool developmental course in motor (gross/fine) and language (expressive/receptive) areas. The history to this point then identifies risk factors in the pregnancy, labor and delivery, and slowness in early (preschool) development for the child.

The remainder of the history will be somewhat similar to that elicited by the psychologist and educational specialist. Questions will be asked typically regarding present educational placement (including the current type of class and present attempts at remediation), past educational placements and attempts at remediation, the parents' conception of present levels of academic achievement and developmental (cognitive) functioning, presence of attention deficits and behavioral problems (and whether these are occurring more at home or in school), family history of learning disabilities and related developmental problems, and psychosocial circumstances of the family. A flow sheet for this history-taking process is shown in Table 3–6.

The history described previously is obtained in major part directly from the parents. Supplementary information can be obtained through

TABLE 3-6
History Taking—School-Age Child

EDUCATION—CURRENT PLACEMENT
School
Grade
Type of class
Description of specific remedial assistance
Problems:
  Academic—present academic achievement levels
  Behavior—problems occuring in school setting

BEHAVIOR
Disposition
Interpersonal relationships
Group activities
Hobbies/interests
Behavior problems:
  Short attention span
  Attention seeking
  Distractibility
  Impulsivity
  Hyperactivity
  Noncompliance
  Oppositionalism
  Avoidance
  Truancy
  Fire Setting
  Cruelty to animals
  Lying
  Stealing
Parental management of behavior

FAMILY/PSYCHOSOCIAL HISTORY
Family History (for both mother and father)
  Age
  Education
  Academic problems—including family history of learning disability
  Illness
  Occupation
  Marital Status
Social History
  Marital problems
  Caretakers
  Financial problems
  Medical insurance

phone conversations with school personnel and review of materials submitted by the school, as well as through the team staffing conference (Chapter 9). Comparison of the school's information with the parents' history can be very instructive of the depth and accuracy of the parents' understanding of issues relevant to their child's learning difficulties. This insight will be of great value in subsequent counseling with the family.

Neurodevelopmental Examination

Because of the complexities of cognitive functioning and academic achievement in school-age children, the physician does not directly assess abilities in these areas, but rather defers to colleagues in psychology and education. Similarly, language is generally assessed by the speech/language pathologist. The physician's examination of the school-age child with learning difficulties should focus on delineation of the neurodevelopmental history and examination of other neurodevelopmental factors that are often associated with learning disabilities. The physician should assess visual perceptual development (using drawing and block assembly tasks), short-term memory deficits, laterality, hand dominance, and soft neurological signs. The relationships between these factors and learning disabilities, and their utility in the remediation process remains unclear. Although deficits in these areas are not pathognomonic of learning disabilities, they are frequently observed in conjunction with learning disabilities. For that reason, the physician's assessment of these factors contributes to the diagnosis. The remainder of this chapter will focus on methods for examining performance in these areas.

Assessment of Visual Perceptual Development—Gesell Figures

A variety of drawing tests may be appropriately used by the physician or allied personnel to assess visual perceptual/motor development. The Gesell figures, again, a series of increasingly complex figures that the child is asked to reproduce, represent the most generally useful (Figure 3–1). As with the preschool-age children, it is mandatory that the physician observe the child in the drawing process, as satisfactory completion of the drawings is not the only information to be gleaned. For example, the child with attention-deficit/hyperactivity disorder (AD/HD) may execute the figures in a driven fashion, omitting key elements of the drawings (e.g., omission of component lines in the "Union Jack" figure). Additionally, the child who does not understand the gestalt of the figures may, although producing a satisfactory final representation of the figures, assemble the drawings in an abnormal fashion (e.g., composing the "Union Jack" figure from a series of small triangles). As noted earlier, quite often these errors of approach or assembly of drawings would be missed if the drawing process were not observed and only the completed figure inspected.

Common distortions of the Gesell drawings are shown under each of the drawings in Figure 3–1 and include the following:

1. Circle—at an approximate 30-month level, a child will imitate circular motions but will not finish with satisfactory completion of a circle.
2. Intersecting lines—at an approximate 27-month level a child will imitate horizontal and vertical strokes. The most common distortion in copying intersecting lines is shown in Figure 3–1.
3. Square—the most common distortion of a square includes partial replication of a square with the remainder of the figure completed with a circular motion as shown in Figure 3–1. This distorted figure represents a synthesis of the circle and square and is at an approximate 3.5-year level.
4. Triangle—the most common distortion of the triangle includes a right angle with the remainder of the figure completed with a sloping line. The resultant drawing looks more like a right triangle.
5. "Union Jack"—the most common distortion is drawing the figure in a fragmented fashion (as a series of pie slices or with spokes radiating out from a central focus). Another common distortion is shown in Figure 3–1.
6. Vertical diamond—the most common distortion is drawing the figure as a square tipped on its side rather than as a diamond.
7. Maltese Cross—distortions include unequal arm heights and widths.
8. Cylinder—this is the first figure in the series that is three-dimensional. The most common distortion of the figure is a drawing with a circular top or flat bottom, missing the concept that the figure has depth into the page.
9. Opaque three-dimensional cube—this again is a three-dimensional figure, and the most common distortion is to draw it as a series of flat squares or with poor perspective. Quite often, when one observes a child who has extreme difficulty in copying this last figure, one may also observe comparable difficulty in the parent's replication of this same figure. If this process can be conducted in a tactful fashion it may help the parents better understand their child's visual perceptual diffi-

culties. The parents may have learned to rationalize their own perceptual difficulties by defenses of the type, "I never liked art." In effect what they may well share with their child is an unrecognized visual perceptual deficit.

Assessment of Visual Perceptual Development—Block Performance

Earlier in this chapter, the use of one-inch cubes was discussed in the assessment of visual perceptual abilities for preschool children. Two of the block constructions presented in Table 3–5 (staircase assemblies f and g) may be useful for assessing visual problem solving for early school-age children (5–7 years).

The relationships among visual perceptual deficits, the type of learning disabilities encountered, and the most effective modes of remediation are unclear. It is still taken on faith that children with visual perceptual deficits will have more substantial difficulties with letter and shape recognition and in perceiving whole words visually as gestalts. Intuitively it seems reasonable to suppose that a careful evaluation of a child's strengths and weaknesses would be useful in remediation planning, although sadly this has not been a very straightforward process.

Short-Term Memory Assessment

Short-term memory is tested with digits forward, digits reversed, and sentence memory (Table 3–7). Qualitative deviance may be noted when a child remembers the digits but does not get them in the correct order (sequential memory deficit rather than a rote auditory memory deficit). Additionally, the child with AD/HD frequently exhibits an inconsistent performance with digit recall, doing somewhat better when attention is carefully focused and distractions minimized. The child with AD/HD may also exhibit better ability to reverse digits than to perform them forward.

Handedness, Laterality, and Dominance

A number of researchers have observed developmentally inappropriate right-left confusion, failure to establish hand preference at an appropriate age, and problems with laterality (child's awareness of the two sides of the body and ability to identify them as left and right) in dyslexic children. Tests of right-left discrimination and laterality are included in Table 3–8. However, no conclusive evidence supports the proposition that these developmental problems are related to a failure to establish asymmetrical functions of the two brain hemispheres. Furthermore, neither mixed dominance (e.g., preference for the right hand

TABLE 3–7
Auditory Memory

Digits Forward—Digits spaced approximately 1 second apart

2.5	yr	47 _____	63 _____	58 _____
3	yr	641 _____	352 _____	837 _____
4.5	yr	4729 _____	3852 _____	7261 _____
7	yr	31589 _____	48372 _____	96183 _____
10	yr	473859 _____	429746 _____	728394 _____
Adult		72594836 _____	47153962 _____	41935826 _____

Digits Reversed

7	yr	295 _____	816 _____	473 _____
9	yr	8526 _____	4937 _____	3629 _____
12	yr	81379 _____	69582 _____	52618 _____
Adult		471952 _____	583694 _____	752618 _____

Sentences—Read at a normal rate

4 yr   We are going to buy some candy for mother.
           Jack likes to feed the little puppies in the barn.

5 yr   Jane wants to build a big castle in her playhouse.
           Tom has lots of fun playing ball with his sister.

8 yr   Fred asked his father to take him to see the clowns in the circus.
           Billy made a beautiful boat out of wood with his sharp knife.

11 yr   At the summer camp the children get up early in the morning and go swimming.
           Yesterday we went for a ride in our car along the road that crosses the bridge.

13 yr   The airplane made a careful landing in the space which had been prepared for it.
           Tom Brown's dog ran quickly down the road with a huge bone in his mouth.

Adult   The red headed woodpecker made a terrible fuss as they tried to drive the
           young away from the nest.
           The early settlers had little idea of the great changes that were to take place in
           this country.

TABLE 3–8
Left-Right Discrimination Testing

Show me your *left* hand Show me your *right* eye }	4.5 yr
Put your *left* hand on your *left* eye Put your *right* hand on your *right* ear }	4.5 yr
Put your *left* hand on your *right* eye Put your *right* hand on your *left* ear }	5.5 yr
Touch my *right* hand Touch my *left* knee }	7.5 yr
Put your *left* hand on my *right* hand Put your *right* hand on my *left* knee }	7.5 yr
Put your *left* hand on my *left* knee Put your *right* hand on my *right* hand }	7.5 yr

but the left eye) nor left-handedness per se seems to be related to learning disabilities in children.

Several red flags of underlying significant pathology relate to the issue of handedness with preschool children:

1. Establishment of handedness below 1 year of age is an abnormal finding, and until proven otherwise should be construed as equivalent to a hemiparesis (relative motor disability on one side of the body).
2. Failure to develop hand preference by 2 years of age should be considered equally suspect.

Soft Neurological Signs

The classical neurological examination looks at what are termed *hard neurological signs*, that is, neurological findings that are either present or absent and do not appear to be modified by maturation of the child's nervous system. In this context the presence or absence of neurological findings is used to identify the presence of and permit localization of pathology in the nervous system. In the child's developing nervous system, however, things are not so simple. The physician performing a neurological examination with a child's developing nervous system is faced with neurological findings that are on a developmental continuum; that is, they appear and disappear with development and maturation of the nervous system. Pathology here does not equate simply with the presence or absence of physical findings, but rather will depend on the extent of their presence and the timing of their appearance and disappearance. This fact has led to a great deal of confusion in interpreting the significance of these *soft neurological signs*. It has been demonstrated that, despite some variability on serial examination, soft signs can have a reasonably high interexaminer reliability and their presence may correlate significantly with learning disabilities. Between one third and one half of children with learning problems demonstrate significant soft neurological signs. Mirror movements and synkinesias (associated movements) represent the most commonly encountered soft neurological signs. Mirror movements are associated movements of the opposite extremity that arise when a specific request is made for isolated movements of one of the extremities. Synkinesias represent an overflow or overshooting of muscle movements into other surrounding muscle groups when a request is made for performance with an isolated muscle group. Both mirror movements and synkinesias are commonly encountered in children with learning disabilities, but the presence of these movements is not pathognomonic.

CONCLUSION

The physician, because of early and ongoing contact with the child, is in an opportune position to identify early delays that may portend subsequent learning difficulties. This chapter has described how the physician, through an expanded neurodevelopmental history and neurodevelopmental examination, can make an individual contribution in this early identification process. With older children, and with further progression of learning disabilities, the physician can be a valuable participant in the interdisciplinary diagnostic and therapeutic process. The role of the physician in the interdisciplinary process will be discussed in subsequent chapters.

CHAPTER 4

Neuropsychological Evaluation

Douglas R. Bloom
Jack M. Fletcher

Neuropsychological assessment has a long and time-honored tradition in psychology and behavioral neurology. Although the origins are diverse, neuropsychological assessment arose as a set of standardized methods for assessing human abilities that were thought to be more directly related to brain function. Early applications involved adults with brain injury and were subsequently expanded to children with known brain injury or suspected problems related to the integrity of the brain, including disorders of learning and attention.

Over the past 25 years, neuropsychologists have devoted increasing amounts of attention to children with learning disabilities. The early interest stemmed from observations that children with learning disabilities had problems that were not obviously related to academic problems. These difficulties included problems such as finger agnosia, right-left discrimination, color naming difficulties and other deficiencies that clearly relate to brain injury in adults (Benton, 1975). It was hoped that evaluation of these types of deficiencies would provide information concerning the neurobiological bases of learning disabilities. From these early interests, neuropsychological assessments of children with learning disabilities have expanded into comprehensive assessments of ability, achievement, and psychosocial factors. Over the past 10 years, several approaches and models have evolved. The purpose of this chapter is to review these approaches and models in relation to children with learning disabilities.

APPROACHES TO NEUROPSYCHOLOGICAL ASSESSMENT IN CHILDREN

Three general approaches to neuropsychological assessment of children are frequently described in the literature: fixed battery, flexible battery, and process-oriented assessment (Fennell, 1994; Mattis, 1992; Tramontana & Hooper, 1988). Following a brief summary of these three general approaches, the five distinct assessment models developed by Rourke; Pennington; Holmes-Bernstein and Waber; Wilson; and Taylor and Fletcher, will be described.

Fixed Battery Approach

A fixed battery approach to child neuropsychological assessment is one in which each child of a given age receives the same set of neuropsychological instruments regardless of the nature of the child's presenting difficulties. Fixed batteries generally utilize a broad range of instruments designed to evaluate basic neuropsychological functions. Examples of fixed batteries include the Halstead-Reitan Neuropsychological Test Battery for Children 9–14, Reitan-Indiana Neuropsychological Test Battery for Children 5–8 (Reitan & Davison, 1974), and the Luria-Nebraska Neuropsychological Battery—Children's Revision for children aged 8–12 years (Golden, 1986; 1989; Tramontana & Hooper, 1988).

Fixed batteries have been particularly useful when employed in research studies (Fennell & Bauer, 1989). The use of a standard set of tests with all subjects facilitates interpretation of test results across research groups over multiple follow-up evaluations, providing a large normative base of information, and the opportunity to test developmental hypotheses of interest to the researcher.

Disadvantages of the fixed battery approach generally stem from the inflexible nature of the battery. Although a fixed battery generally provides a consistent, broad-based assessment (Tramontana & Hooper, 1988), there may be a loss of efficiency because of the number and type of tests used for specific kinds of presenting problems. In addition, component neuropsychological processes of particular importance to an understanding of a child's specific learning problem may be inadequately assessed. For example, the Halstead-Reitan Battery provides a limited assessment of memory and component language skills that would contribute to accurate diagnosis and useful recommendations for a child with suspected reading disability. Finally, the inflexible nature of the fixed battery does not readily lend itself to the introduction of new test measures that reflect the most recent knowledge regarding child development and advances in test development with children (Taylor & Fletcher, 1990; Tramontana & Hooper, 1988).

Flexible Battery Approach

The use of a flexible neuropsychological test battery appears to be a popular choice among many clinicians. The flexible approach is one in which a core battery of standardized tests are used to screen the general spectrum of neuropsychological functions. Additional tests are employed to more fully evaluate functions relevant to the referral question, or other areas of potential deficiency identified by the core test battery. Actual tests used in a flexible battery are selected from among the body of standardized tests and published experimental instruments that provide a reliable, valid assessment of the neuropsychological functions of interest. Unlike the fixed battery, the flexibility inherent in this approach permits additions or deletions from the test battery as refinements in neuropsychological evaluation procedures become available (Tramontana & Hooper, 1988).

Process-Oriented Approach

A third general approach to neuropsychological assessment has been termed a process-oriented approach. In this approach, the examiner seeks an in-depth understanding of the child's cognitive and motor deficiencies by using active hypothesis-testing procedures to identify the nature of specific deficits in component processes of complex neuropsychological functions (Milberg, Hebben, & Kaplan, 1986; Tramontana & Hooper, 1988; Mattis, 1992). Initial evaluation of complex cognitive abilities is followed by formal or informal procedures to more precisely delineate specific areas of impairment that led to breakdowns on complex tasks. For example, difficulties on a task suggestive of memory impairment might result in more specific assessment of memory functioning involving recall versus recognition memory, verbal versus nonverbal memory, memory for contextually related versus unrelated verbal information, immediate versus delayed recall, or use of strategies to aid recall. The examiner may use standardized tests, modifications of standardized tests (e.g., adjustments in instructions, removal of time limits, additional instructions or examiner assistance), or procedures developed by the examiner to test specific hypotheses related to problem solving in a child with learning disabilities. The Boston Process Approach (Milberg, Hebben, & Kaplan, 1986) and Wilson's branching hypothesis model (1992) are examples of process-oriented approaches to neuropsychological assessment.

Process approaches have the advantage of providing an in-depth analysis into the nature of the deficits in the child with learning disabilities that can be very helpful in developing remedial recommendations. However, this approach also requires an experienced, skillful examiner with considerable knowledge of normal and abnormal development. The examiner must thoroughly understand and be able to judge the adequacy of task performance associated with the relationship between task demands of modified procedures and the underlying cognitive processes of interest, in the absence of normative data on these types of tasks.

SPECIFIC METHODS OF NEUROPSYCHOLOGICAL ASSESSMENT IN CHILDREN

Specific approaches to neuropsychological assessment outlined by Rourke, Pennington, Holmes-Bernstein and Waber, Wilson, and Taylor and Fletcher generally represent variants of the flexible and process-oriented approaches to assessment. Each of these assessment models can be utilized with a broad range of childhood disorders, including the evaluation of children with learning disabilities. In addition, one of these models, Wilson's process-oriented approach to assessment, is particularly pertinent to the evaluation of preschool children at risk for later academic learning problems (see Mattis, 1992, for a similar approach with school-age children).

Despite variations in specific test instruments employed and different emphases in the evaluation process, the basic assessment goals in each approach are similar. Each model provides a broad-based assessment of cognitive skills that takes into account relevant environmental and CNS factors in an attempt to accurately portray the multiple influences on children with learning disorders. In addition, the ultimate goal of assessment in each approach is to provide information relevant to the development of a workable, effective remedial plan that benefits the child.

Rourke: Treatment-Oriented Approach

Byron Rourke and his colleagues (Rourke, Fisk, & Strang, 1986) have described a seven-step "treatment-oriented approach" to neuropsychological assessment. A fixed battery approach is utilized in Rourke's model, which provides a framework for developing a set of individualized short- and long-term predictions and treatment plans for the child with learning disabilities. These predictions and plans are based on assessment findings that detail the child's neuropsychological strengths and weaknesses, and that consider environmental demands on the child. The first step in Rourke's model attempts to identify the interaction of the child's neuropsychological ability structure and status of the central nervous system (CNS). At this stage of the assessment process, formal neuropsychological assessment is conducted and findings are integrated with information from the medical history that potentially relates to brain function. The effect of these factors on current patterns and levels of educational performance and other areas of adaptive functioning are also identified. However, it is worth noting that there are significant limitations in the current understanding of the relationship of observational and test findings to brain status in children with learning disabilities (Fletcher & Taylor, 1984; Taylor & Fletcher, 1990). Consequently, inferences regarding the CNS status of individual children derived solely from these sources of information would be potentially misleading and unwise.

The second step in Rourke's model involves an evaluation of the short- and long-term environmental demands placed on the child. These demands, which generally change with the child's age and response to interventions, might include the child's ability to maintain attention and appropriate behavior at school, complete academic assignments at a reasonable level of accuracy, and maintain good relationships with peers and teachers. Outside the school environment, demands might include parental expectations regarding school achievement, or social pressures by peers. A consideration of these types of environmental demands is of considerable importance for intervention planning.

The third step involves the process of developing written predictions of short- and long-term behavioral outcomes based on what is known from outcome studies related to the specific learning disorder. These predictions are helpful in developing sets of ideal short- and long-term remedial plans (step four), and in assessing the effectiveness of treatment programs relative to predicted outcomes. The fifth step in Rourke's model involves investigation of the availability of remedial resources to the child within the family, school, and community. For example, the family's ability to afford needed treatments outside the school (e.g., private tutoring, therapy), community availability of tutors and therapists for the learning disabled child, and family acceptance and support for recommended intervention programs (e.g., resource room reading instruction), would be considered in step five.

The sixth step in Rourke's model deals with the development of a realistic remedial plan that strives to achieve ideal goals developed in step four, but tempered by limitations imposed by available resources (step five) to the child with learning disabilities. The last step (step seven) provides for follow-up neuropsychological assessments designed to yield ongoing information from which to evaluate effectiveness of interventions, and to furnish information from which to recommend adjustments in treatment programs that reflect the needs of the child over time. As is true of all the assessment approaches presented in this chapter, neuropsychological assessment using Rourke's approach provides information on the strengths and deficiencies of the child with learning disability that are relevant to developing an effective treatment program.

Pennington: Neuropsychological Assessment Approach

Pennington's (1991) approach to neuropsychological assessment stems from the hypothesized relationship between five major domains of cognitive function, the cortical structures believed to mediate these functional domains, and five primary learning disorders of childhood that are believed to result from deficits in these systems. Specifically, reading disorders are believed to represent dysfunction in left hemisphere (perisylvian) language systems, particularly involving phonological processing difficulties. Learning disorders in math and some cases of handwriting deficiency are believed to stem from deficits in spatial cognition (e.g., object localization, analysis of extrapersonal space, short- and long-term visual/spatial memory) subserved primarily by posterior right hemisphere structures. As pointed out by Pennington and a number of other investigators (Bryant & Bradley, 1985; Vellutino, 1979), the majority of developmental reading disorders result from deficient linguistic processing skills (i.e., deficient phonological processing), which contrasts with traditional theories of reading disability which hypothesized deficits in visual-spatial processes.

The last three types of learning disorders identified by Pennington do not correspond specifically with traditional categories of learning disabilities, but do represent important childhood disorders. Attention deficit disorder is hypothesized to correspond to deficiencies in attentional regulatory functions (i.e., one aspect of executive functions) believed to be mediated by frontal lobe systems. The fourth type of disorder involves problems with social cognition (i.e., autism spectrum disorder). This disorder is hypothesized to be mediated by limbic, orbital frontal, and some aspects of right hemisphere structures. The fifth learning disorder identified by Pennington concerns memory difficulties related to medial temporal lobe structures.

Pennington's model of neuropsychological assessment advocates an active process of hypothesis testing that refines diagnostic decisions over four levels of data collection (i.e., presenting symptoms, history, behavioral observations, and test data). New information collected at each stage is evaluated against potential cognitive and emotional diagnoses until final diagnoses are obtained. Neuropsychological tests are selected so that diagnostic hypotheses generated prior to the evaluation are adequately assessed. Pennington uses a variety of assessment measures to thoroughly evaluate important functional domains typically associated with the suspected learning disorder, and to screen for associated areas of deficiency. This model is a good example of a flexible battery approach.

Holmes-Bernstein and Waber: Systemic Approach

The Systemic Approach is a theoretical framework developed by Holmes-Bernstein and Waber (1990) to guide neurospychological assessment of the child from a process-oriented assessment perspective. This approach focuses on the dynamic interaction of neurological and psychological processes as the child develops and interacts with his or her environment. The neuro facet of neuropsychology conceptualizes behavior as emanating from the dynamic interplay of three neuroanatomical axes (i.e., anterior-posterior, left-right, and cortical-subcortical) in conjunction with environmental influences on the developing child. "Psychologically," cognitive processes related to the three CNS axes are also seen in terms of their dynamic interaction from a developmental perspective. The qualitative aspects of a child's performance (e.g., strategies used, error type) are carefully observed and evaluated in the assessment process to help identify appropriate intervention programs based on the specific needs of the child with learning disabilities. In addition, the effect of environmental factors (e.g., language spoken at home, additional services available) on the child's behavior and academic performance are considered in the evaluation and diagnostic processes.

The assessment process used by Holmes-Bernstein and Waber consists of three components: evaluation, diagnosis, and management. Three sources of information are used in the evaluation process. These include historical information (e.g., health, development, educational), observation of the child in various contexts (e.g., during testing, natural settings), and through formal test procedures. Testing provides both quantitative and qualitative information related to specific cognitive skills and processes. A particular emphasis is placed on qualitative information obtained not only from a careful observation of the child's behavior and interactions during the evaluation, but also from analysis of the processes and strategies used to solve novel or difficult problems. Formal test procedures used by Holmes-Bernstein and Waber sample functional domains similar to other batteries described in this section: general cognitive level, memory, language, visual/nonverbal processing, executive control processes, sensory/motor, academic achievement, attention/vigilance, and emotional status.

Information from these sources is integrated to generate a diagnostic formulation of the child's difficulties. An intervention plan is then developed for the child that provides a better match between environmental demands and available services, and the child's abilities.

Wilson: Neuropsychological Assessment Approach

Wilson's (1992; 1986) approach to neuropsychological assessment provides a useful framework for conceptualizing the evaluation of preschool children. Wilson employs a process-oriented branching, hypothesis-testing model of assessment. In addition to formal testing procedures, the neuropsychologist reviews the child's prenatal, birth, neonatal, developmental, medical, and family histories and observes the child in a variety of settings with peers and parents when possible. Initial test procedures are selected to evaluate major domains of complex neuropsychological functions, with emphasis on areas of potential difficulty based on analysis of the history, clinical observations, and initial test results. Deficiencies revealed in complex neuropsychological functions (e.g., observation of possible auditory semantic comprehension difficulties) are followed up with additional tests that are more narrowly focused (e.g., auditory discrimination, auditory memory of words and sentences) to identify more specifically the nature of the difficulty. Assessment instruments selected are often subtests of standardized instruments that careful task analysis has shown to tap the component process of interest. Due to factors such as variable attention or differences in temperament and cooperation in preschoolers, the reliability of assessment measures at these age levels may be reduced. To deal with this problem, Wilson recommends assessment with multiple measures or repeat testing as a check on test reliability when possible. Correspondence among test results measuring similar processes generally enhances diagnostic confidence, whereas a check of the psychometric properties (e.g., norms, reliability) of individual tests may help to make interpretive decisions in the context of inconsistent test results (Wilson, 1992). Finally, data from the history, clinical observations, and test findings are integrated to identify patterns of strengths and weaknesses, which guide recommendations for appropriate interventions for the child.

Taylor and Fletcher: Biobehavioral Systems Approach

Taylor and Fletcher's "biobehavioral systems model" (Taylor & Fletcher, 1990; Fletcher, Taylor, Levin, & Satz, in press) separates assessment into four dimensions for evaluation:

1. The first involves a detailed examination of the presenting problems for which the neuropsychological assessment was requested. These difficulties represent the "manifest" form of

the disability (e.g., reading difficulty, behavioral or attentional problem).

2. The second step involves assessment of child traits that influence the expression of the manifest disability. Assessment of
child traits involves formal neuropsychological evaluation of
cognitive abilities and assessment of psychosocial factors that
may be contributing to the child's problems. Cognitive and
psychosocial traits are often interrelated.

3. The third variable involves an evaluation of environmental
factors that influence the relationship between the child's
traits and the manifest disability (i.e., presenting complaints).
Environmental factors would include a variety of family, cultural, and social variables as well as educational opportunities.

4. The fourth component of investigation involves the direct or in-
direct influence of neurological and genetic influences on the
child's traits. This is accomplished by reviewing factors such as
the child's medical history from the prenatal period to the present, and the family history of learning and attentional problems.

The Taylor and Fletcher model encourages three levels of analysis
related to the four components described above based on a flexible
battery approach. The first level of analysis comprises efforts to discern
the relationship between the child's presenting problems (i.e., manifest
disability) and the cognitive and psychosocial traits (i.e., child traits).
This is followed by a second level of analysis where an attempt is made
to discover the mutual impact of cognitive and psychosocial factors on
each other and on the manifest disability. For example, poor language
skills may contribute to social withdrawal, but poor motivation or a low
tolerance for frustration (psychosocial) may contribute to a diminished
capacity to benefit from speech therapy to improve language functioning. The third level of analysis involves efforts to understand the influence of environmental and neurological variables on the child's traits
and the manifest disability. It is assumed that both environmental and
CNS variables significantly affect underlying traits and thus expression
in behavior. Consequently, this model posits that neurological factors
are just one of several influences on the traits, learning problems, and
other symptoms of the child being evaluated (Taylor & Fletcher, 1990).
Taylor and Fletcher note that attempts to analyze the relative contribution of neurological variables to the manifest disability begin with in-
vestigating the child at the behavioral level, then proceed to considering CNS variables, while simultaneously analyzing the potential
moderating effect of the environment on the relationship of neurological and cognitive/behavioral domains. Therefore, this approach emphasizes analysis of the multidimensional relationship of the four compo-

nents described above at both behavioral and neurological levels of analyses. In this regard, this model encourages evaluation of the "whole child" when assessing learning difficulties and discourages unwarranted inferences regarding brain status solely from behavioral measures in children (Taylor, 1988). This caveat is of importance in the case of children with learning disabilities where cerebral dysfunction is presumed but direct evidence of CNS involvement is generally lacking for individual children seen for assessment.

GENERAL MODEL FOR NEUROPSYCHOLOGICAL ASSESSMENT

This section will provide a more detailed description of the use of the Taylor and Fletcher model of neuropsychological assessment with children with learning disabilities. In this model the components of the assessment process consist of (a) an examination of the presenting problems (manifest disability), (b) neuropsychological assessment of cognitive traits, (c) evaluation of psychosocial functioning, (d) assessment of environmental and (e) biological factors that influence cognitive traits, and (f) interpretation and remedial recommendations.

Assessment of the Manifest Disability

Assessment of a child with learning difficulties generally begins with efforts to obtain information that will lead to a clearer understanding of the child's presenting difficulties. Four sources of information that are of particular value in this process are (a) review of educational and medical/health histories, (b) behavioral checklists and questionnaires, (c) parent interview (and others working with the child where needed), and (d) academic achievement evaluation.

Relevant educational and medical records should be requested of the parent for review prior to the evaluation session if possible. Requested records might include report cards, disciplinary records, reports of previous individual evaluations, and group achievement test scores. In addition, medical records should be requested when there is a history of treatment for attention deficit disorder, Tourette's syndrome, head injury, epilepsy, primary sensory disorder, or any other neurological, psychiatric, or chronic medical disorder.

Parents also complete a child history form which provides information regarding basic family information (e.g., parent occupation, children in the family), schools attended, prenatal and birth history, emergence of early developmental milestones, health history of childhood illnesses, surgeries, hospitalizations, and injuries, and medications the child is taking. In addition, the parent is asked to complete behavior checklists such as the Child Behavior Checklist (CBCL; Achenbach, 1991a) for children aged 4–18 years. The CBCL is useful in providing a parental perspective regarding the child's academic progress as well as the internalizing and externalizing behaviors associated with the child's social, behavioral, attentional, and emotional functioning. Similar information can be obtained from the child's teacher(s) by requesting that the teacher complete the Teacher's Report Form (TRF; Achenbach, 1991b) for children aged 5–18 years. A brief descriptive summary by the teacher of the child's academic performance, behavior, and inclusion in special instructional or behavioral programs can also be helpful.

A third source of background information is obtained through interview with a parent. The interview helps to clarify information from the child history form and CBCL and to obtain the following types of information: family history of similar problems; parent disciplinary philosophies; description of the child's strengths and talents; and parental perception of the scope, duration, and causes of their child's learning, behavioral, or other problems. A phone interview with the teacher, school counselor, pediatrician, or other professional working with the child can also be helpful in clarifying referral questions and obtaining additional information.

Direct assessment of a broad range of academic difficulties is a fourth means of obtaining information related to the child's presenting difficulties. In some instances, the school will have completed a recent academic evaluation that will provide needed information regarding the child's level of academic performance. A number of popular individual academic achievement tests evaluate basic reading, spelling, and arithmetic skills. These include the Woodcock-Johnson Psychoeducational Battery: Tests of Achievement (Woodcock & Mather, 1989), the Wide Range Achievement Test-Revised (WRAT-R; Jastak & Wilkinson, 1984), and the Peabody Individual Achievement Test—Revised (PIAT-R; Markwardt, 1989). Differences in the format and type of skills evaluated by these tests should be taken into consideration when selecting tests for children with different learning problems. For example, each of these tests includes a word identification subtest. However, the Woodcock-Johnson and PIAT-R assess reading comprehension and provide an evaluation of written language in different ways, whereas the WRAT-R samples written spelling of single words, but not reading comprehension. Assessment of real and nonwords is a key area of assessment for suspected reading disability due to the frequent difficulty these children experience with decoding skills (Fletcher et al., 1994). A number of other reading tests also are available that provide a more in-depth analysis of reading skills (e.g., Stanford Diagnostic Reading Test; Karlsen, Madden, & Gardner, 1984).

A more informal, but often very revealing evaluation of reading proficiency can be obtained by asking the parent to bring one of the child's school texts and having the child read from a current lesson. In this manner, the child's ability to read and comprehend grade-level material can be assessed in a more ecologically valid manner. These observations may provide useful information regarding the child's reading speed, reading fluency, error types, differential reading and error rates over longer units of text, and frustration tolerance in the context of reading difficulties.

Computational arithmetic skills are evaluated by the WRAT-R and Woodcock-Johnson in a paper-pencil format. This type of written test format can be especially difficult for a child with suspected arithmetic difficulty. These tests permit some capacity for analyzing factors such as the child's knowledge of basic arithmetic facts and math procedures, spatial alignment of columns, and attention to detail, whereas the multiple choice format of the PIAT-R is less conducive to such analysis. Other tests, such as the KeyMath Revised test (Connolly, 1988) may be preferred when assessment of a broader range of math skills is desired.

Work samples from schoolwork (e.g., seatwork, writing samples, test papers) may also provide clues regarding the child's consistency of performance on and between assignments, work completion, and quality of written assignments (e.g., penmanship, grammar usage, punctuation and capitalization, vocabulary usage, writing fluency, complexity of thematic content). For a more thorough coverage of academic assessment issues and procedures, the reader is directed to Chapter 6.

Assessment of Child Traits

Once a better understanding of the child's presenting difficulties has been attained, a battery of neuropsychological tests is administered typically to identify patterns of cognitive strengths and areas of impairment that contribute to the child's academic deficiencies or behavioral problems. Although neuropsychologists vary considerably in their choice of specific test instruments, most employ a battery of tests that assesses a broad spectrum of important domains of neuropsychological functioning. The emphasis given to each domain in the assessment process usually depends on the type of learning disability or behavioral difficulty suspected (e.g., more language tests for suspected reading disability). In addition to academic achievement, a comprehensive neuropsychological evaluation of a child with suspected learning disability will generally include assessment of the following domains: (a) intelligence, (b) language, (c) memory and learning, (d) attention, (e) visual-spatial processing/constructional skills, (f) sensory and motor functions, (g) problem solving/concept formation, and (h) psychosocial adjustment.

Intelligence

Intelligence tests are included in child neuropsychological test batteries by most clinical neuropsychologists, especially when the child is being evaluated for school-related problems. The Wechsler Intelligence Scale for Children-Third Edition (WISC-III; Wechsler, 1991), for example, is a widely popular, well-standardized measure of general cognitive functioning for school-aged children 6 through 16 years. The WISC-III evaluates a number of verbal and nonverbal performance abilities that contribute to Verbal and Performance IQ scores and four factor scores (i.e., Verbal Comprehension, Perceptual Organization, Freedom from Distractibility, Processing Speed). These scores provide important diagnostic information regarding individual cognitive strengths and weaknesses when assessing a child for possible learning disabilities.

Other tests of general intellectual ability that evaluate somewhat different cognitive functions in both preschool and school-aged children include the Stanford-Binet Intelligence Scale (4th Edition; Thorndike, Hagen, & Sattler, 1986) and the Kaufman Assessment Battery for Children (KABC; Kaufman & Kaufman, 1983). Tests designed primarily for preschoolers include the Wechsler Preschool and Primary Scale of Intelligence-Revised (WPPSI-R; Wechsler, 1989) and the McCarthy Scales of Children's Abilities (McCarthy, 1972). A detailed description of these and other tests of intelligence used in identifing children with learning disabilities can be obtained in Chapter 5.

Intelligence tests scores are widely used in conjunction with achievement test results to identify discrepancies between IQ and academic achievement. Under current federally mandated special education eligibility guidelines, a significant discrepancy between IQ and achievement test scores generally must be obtained to identify a child with learning problems and thereby qualify him or her for placement in a remedial education program. Although current realities require a significant IQ-achievement discrepancy in the identification of children with learning disabilities, several recent research articles have identified a number of shortcomings in the use of discrepancy criteria as the primary basis for identifying children with learning disabilities. These problems are as follows: (a) cognitive problems underlying the learning disability may affect both IQ scores and academic performance; (b) intelligence tests do not assess all significant cognitive functions; (c) statistical limitations in use of discrepancy formulas; and (d) the meaning of aptitude as measured by intelligence tests. Most important, there is little evidence that nonmentally deficient children whose poor reading skills are consistent with IQ levels differ from children with poor reading skills relative to their higher IQ in cognitive skills, developmental outcomes, and response to treatment. A more detailed discussion of these issues may be found in Chapter 5 and in Siegel, 1992; Fletcher, et.al., 1993; Hurford et al., 1994; and Taylor & Fletcher, 1990.

Language Functions

Assessment of language functions is of particular importance for children with significant reading difficulties. There is a growing consensus that the vast majority of children who experience significant problems in acquisition of decoding skills have impairment in several aspects of phonological processing skills, particularly phonological awareness and phonological recoding (Bradley & Bryant, 1983; Mann, 1985; Liberman, 1973; Wagner & Torgeson, 1987; Stanovich, 1988; Fletcher, et al., 1994). Young children with severe reading and spelling disabilities have been reported to have deficient phonological awareness involving the ability to segment or blend the component parts of spoken words (Bradley & Bryant, 1983; Mann, 1985; Liberman, 1973), and difficulties in rapidly retrieving names of familiar stimuli such as objects or letters from memory (Wolf, Bally, & Morris, 1986; Fawcett & Nicolson, 1994; Denkla & Rudel, 1976; Denkla, 1972). These phonological processing skills can be assessed with the Auditory Analysis Test (Rosner & Simon, 1971) and the Rapid Automatized Naming Test (Denkla & Rudel, 1976). The Auditory Analysis Test is a phonological segmentation task that requires the child to form a new word by deletion of phonemes from a spoken word. The Rapid Automatized Naming Test is sensitive to disruptions of efficiency of word retrieval from memory. The Word Fluency Test (Gaddes & Crockett, 1975), requiring rapid retrieval of words beginning with specific alphabet letters, is sensitive to phonological processing difficulties in reading disabilities (Fletcher, 1988). For younger children, alternative word fluency tasks requiring rapid word retrieval from specific semantic categories, such as types of food or animals, may be more appropriate (Halperin, Zeitchik, Healy, Weinstein, & Ludman, 1989).

A number of other tests are available to assess additional aspects of language functioning (i.e., syntax, semantics) that may be deficient in children with learning disabilities. For example, the Token Test for Children (DiSimoni, 1978) assesses syntactic and semantic comprehension skills by requiring the child to follow verbal commands of increasing syntactic complexity. Comprehension of single words (i.e., receptive vocabulary) is assessed by the Peabody Picture Vocabulary Test—Revised (PPVT-R; Dunn & Dunn, 1981). The ability to define words (i.e., expressive vocabulary) is evaluated by the WISC-III Vocabulary subtest (Wechsler, 1991). The Boston Naming Test (Second Edition; Kaplan, Goodglass, & Weintraub, 1983) is a popular test of confrontation naming under untimed conditions. Disturbances in these types of language functions may contribute to the sparse output, poor vocabulary usage and grammar, and reduced complexity in thematic content on written language assignments observed in many children with learning disabilities. Valuable information regarding the child's speech and language functioning (i.e., phonology, syntax, semantic, pragmatic functions) is also frequently available from the speech therapist at the child's school. This information should be integrated with language-based neuropsychological assessment results to provide a clearer understanding of the child's language functioning.

Memory and Learning

Disruption of learning and memory processes are frequently noted in children with learning disabilities. For example, children with severe reading disabilities often experience difficulty on working memory tasks (e.g., memory span tasks for letters, digits, words), suggesting inefficient encoding of the phonological features of stimuli in working memory, potentially disrupting other aspects of phonological processing (e.g., sound blending) during reading (Wagner & Torgeson, 1987; Mann, 1985). In addition, Fletcher (1985) found disturbances in learning and memory processes for word lists administered to groups of reading disabled students using selective reminding procedures (Buschke, 1974) that separate verbal learning and memory performance into storage and retrieval processes. Of particular interest in the Fletcher study were the contrasting results obtained in children with reading versus arithmetic disabilities on verbal and nonverbal (i.e., memory for dot localizations) selective reminding tests. The performance of students with reading disabilities was significantly poorer on verbal compared with nonverbal memory tasks. In contrast, children with arithmetic disabilities achieved the opposite pattern of results. These children performed normally on the verbal memory task but demonstrated impaired nonverbal memory performance. Results from these investigations support the contention that children with learning disabilities are a heterogeneous group who differ along several important dimensions of neuropsychological and academic functioning.

As noted above, the Verbal Selective Reminding (Buschke, 1974; Spreen & Strauss, 1991) and Nonverbal Selective Reminding (Fletcher, 1985) tests have been helpful in discriminating between contrasting types of academic learning disorders. In addition, they allow the examiner to more closely examine deficiencies in memory related to storage and retrieval processes. The Continuous Recognition Memory Test (CRM; Hannay, Levin, & Grossman, 1979) has been beneficial in evaluating visual recognition memory functioning in children with learning disabilities. This test requires the child to identify recurring visual stimuli in a series of 120 line drawings. Misidentification of a nonrecurring picture as having been previously viewed results in a false positive error. High rates of false positive errors may suggest impulsive response tendencies (Fletcher, 1988). The Story Memory subtest of the Wide Range Assessment of Memory and Learning (WRAML; Sheslow & Adams, 1990) provides an evaluation of prose recall in immediate and delayed conditions. In addition, the WRAML Design Memory subtest and the Benton Visual Retention Test (Fifth Edition, 1991; Sivan, 1992) can be used to assess nonverbal recall of geometric figures within a paper-pencil format. Verbal memory for sentence length material can be assessed with the Sentence Repetition Test (Spreen & Benton, 1969, 1977). This test evaluates the child's memory for tape-recorded sentences of increasing length that must be repeated without error.

Investigators have found differences between children without and children with learning disabilities in the utilization of strategies for remembering (e.g., rehearsal, semantic clustering) (Torgeson, 1980; Torgeson & Goldman, 1977). The recent introduction of the California Verbal Learning Test-Children's Version (CVLT-C; Delis, Kramer, Kaplan, & Ober, 1994) can aid in analyzing the child's ability to utilize semantic clustering or serial order memory strategies in remembering a 15-word list during learning and delayed recall trials. The CVLT-C also provides information on susceptibility to retroactive and proactive interference effects, as well as encoding, retrieval (immediate and delayed), and recognition memory processes.

Attentional Functioning

Disturbances in attentional functioning are common in children with learning disabilities. Estimates of comorbidity of learning disability and attention-deficit/hyperactivity disorder (AD/HD) vary. Shaywitz and Shaywitz (1988) reported a 33% comorbidity rate between children with dyslexia and/or arithmetic disability and AD/HD, where each disorder was independently defined. Difficulties in focusing and maintaining attention can influence the quality of performance on any academic task, contributing to decreased efficiency in academic learning and greater inconsistency in performance within the same task and across tasks.

It is important to recognize that attention as a disorder and as a psychological construct are not the same (Barkley, 1994). Assessment of AD/HD (see Chapter 10) is typically accomplished through a combination of direct observation of the child, parent and teacher behavior rating scales, and formal assessment of the child on tasks reputed to be sensitive to disturbances in attentional functioning. Parents and teachers provide valuable information regarding a child's ability to pay attention, withhold impulsive responses, remain undistracted, follow instructions and rules of behavioral conduct, sustain effort, complete tasks efficiently and on time, and monitor the quality of his or her performance. Observations during the evaluation session related to these same behaviors are also important in assessing attentional functioning (and more generally in evaluating the reliability of test results). Parent and teacher rating scales such as the CBCL and TRF (Achenbach, 1991a, 1991b), are useful because the child's attentional functioning can be compared to a normative group of same-aged children. In addition, the child's attention and behavior can be assessed in different settings by separate observers.

Formal assessment of attentional skills can provide important information but should be analyzed in the context of observational sources of information due to limits in the current understanding of important underlying constructs related to attention in childhood (Barkley, 1994). Several versions of continuous performance tests are available to assess sustained attention/vigilance (monitoring) and inhibition of impulsive responding over a prolonged time period. For example, a computer-based self-pacing continuous performance test (CPT; Buchsbaum & Sostek, 1980) can be employed, where the rate of stimulus presentation is related to response speed and accuracy. Another nine-minute version of the CPT has been developed by Gordon (1983). Several assessment procedures appear to assess selective attention, psychomotor efficiency, and freedom from distractibility, including WISC-III subtests associated with the Freedom from Distractibility factor, the Underlining Test (Rourke & Gates, 1980), Symbol Digit Modality Test (Smith, 1982), and the Trail Making Test (Reitan & Davison, 1974; Spreen & Strauss, 1990). As noted above, a high rate of false positive errors on the Continuous Recognition Memory Test (CRM; Hannay, Levin, & Grossman, 1979), is suggestive of difficulty in inhibiting impulsive responses. In general, the greater the number of positive findings suggestive of attentional difficulties that are noted across settings on these tasks and observational procedures, the greater the confidence the examiner is likely to have in the significance of the attentional disturbance.

Visual-Spatial Processing/Constructional Skills

The assessment of visual-spatial and constructional skills has considerable value in identifying children with particular types of learning disabilities. For example, Pennington (1991) identified a learning disability in spatial cognition (e.g., spatial imagery, spatial construction, spatial memory, math disorder) that was attributed primarily to posterior right cerebral hemisphere dysfunction. Similarly, Rourke (1989, 1993) has delineated subtypes of reading and arithmetic disabilities with contrasting profiles of neuropsychological strengths and weaknesses. Germane to the current topic, Rourke's research has revealed a nonverbal learning disability subtype characterized by well-developed automatic language and word identification skills, but with primary impairment of a number of nonverbal cognitive skills (e.g., visual-spatial processing, constructional skills, fine motor coordination, tactile-perception), computational arithmetic and handwriting, and psychosocial (particularly social) adjustment. In contrast, children with an academic disability in reading and spelling (and variable arithmetic skills) exhibited poor language-based skills, but normally developed nonverbal cognitive abilities. These findings again emphasize the heterogeneous nature of learning disabilities and the need to broadly assess neuropsychological abilities, including visual-spatial and constructional skills.

Assessment procedures should evaluate motor-free tests of visual-spatial skills as well as procedures requiring integration of visual and motoric abilities. Tests that assess visual-spatial skills with reduced motor output requirements include the Recognition-Discrimination Test (Satz & Fletcher, 1982), Judgment of Line Orientation (Lindgren & Benton, 1980; Benton, Sivan, Hamsher, Varney, & Spreen, 1994), and the Test of Visual-Perceptual Skills (Gardner, 1988). Tests that also involve active motoric involvement include the Developmental Test of Visual-Motor Integration (Third Revision; Beery, 1989), Benton's Three-Dimensional Block Construction Test (Benton, Sivan, Hamsher, Varney, & Spreen, 1994), and the Block Design and Object Assembly subtests from the WISC-III (Wechsler, 1991). Results from these tasks should be analyzed to distinguish problems more specific to visual-spatial functioning compared with difficulties produced by the introduction of motor output requirements. It is also important to assess the contribution of attentional problems and deficiencies in problem solving/executive functions to performance on these types of tasks.

Somatosensory and Motor Functions

Performance on tests of somatosensory and motor functions are sensitive to lateralized neurological disorders and have been shown by Rourke (1989) to help in differentiating children with subtypes of learning disabilities. From this perspective, children with nonverbal learning disabilities demonstrate bilateral deficiencies in tactile-perceptual functioning, and fine motor speed and dexterity. Deficiencies in both domains are generally more prominent on the nondominant left hand, particularly in younger children. Educationally, deficits in fine motor speed and coordination may require recommendations for further occupational therapy evaluation as well as curriculum modifications, such as reduced length of written assignments, fewer paper-pencil seatwork assignments for young children, provision of extra time for tests, or modified expectations for standards of performance in word processing or other academic or prevocational activities requiring rapid, well-coordinated bimanual movements and sensory feedback to guide fine motor activities.

Assessment of sensory-perceptual functioning includes finger localization, graphesthesia, stereognosis, and sensory extinction testing. Reitan (Reitan & Davison, 1974; Reitan, 1985) and Benton (Benton, Sivan, Hamsher, Varney, & Spreen, 1994) have described administrative procedures and interpretive guidelines for evaluating performance on these sensory-perceptual functions. The child's level of attention should be carefully monitored during these tasks as attentional lapses contribute to the appearance of impaired performance on sensory-perceptual tests. Benton's Tactile Form Perception Test (Benton, Sivan, Hamsher, Varney, & Spreen, 1994) is a more complex test of bilateral tactile discrimination and recognition.

Assessment of fine motor function commonly involves tests of both simple and complex fine motor speed and dexterity. The Finger Tapping Test (Reitan & Davison, 1974; Finlayson & Reitan, 1976) provides a measure of relatively pure finger tapping speed. Performance with each hand (i.e., index finger) is assessed over multiple trials. These tasks also lend themselves to observations of neurological "soft signs" such as motor steadiness and precision of finger movements, motor overflow and mirror movements, or susceptibility to fatigue. The Grooved Pegboard Test (Klove, 1963) assesses more complex fine motor skills involving both fine motor speed and dexterity. In this test, the child must place a number of keylike pegs in slotted holes as quickly as possible with each hand. The Purdue Pegboard Test (Gardner & Broman, 1979) also evaluates finger dexterity and speed of performance in placing round pegs in holes with each hand separately and simultaneously. The child's performance on each of these motor tests can be evaluated against age-based normative data for each hand with regard to speed of performance. In addition, the relative proficiency of the child's right versus left hand performance is compared for exaggerated asymmetries in completing the motor tasks with the two hands.

Problem Solving/Concept Formation

Evaluation of problem solving and conceptual skills in children has received increased attention in recent years (e.g., Welsh & Pennington, 1988; Passler, Isaac, & Hynd, 1985; Levin, Mendelson, Lilly, & Fletcher, 1994), but remains an area that is difficult to define much less directly assess, particularly in children. As Taylor and Fletcher pointed out (1990), difficulties in evaluating a child's problem-solving skills may result from deficiencies in component skills that are brought together to solve more complex problems. Consequently, a child's difficulties on a problem-solving task may result from deficiencies in component skills, or other confounds, such as reduced motivation, rather than in more complex cognitive regulatory functions, often referred to as executive functions. Cognitive activities such as goal formulation and planning, organizational skills, self-monitoring of performance, inhibition of impulsive responses, regulation of attention, use of strategies, cognitive flexibility, and set maintenance are among the constructs encompassed by this term. Another problem in testing in this area relates to what these concepts mean in their application to the cognitive skills and behavior of children and what constitutes normal development in these areas. Further research is clearly needed.

Despite these problems, several tasks may be of help in evaluating a child's problem-solving skills. The Category Test (Reitan & Davison, 1974), with separate versions for 5- to 8- and 9- to 14-year-olds, is a measure of abstraction, concept formation, and the ability to flexibly use ongoing feedback in solving problems. In this test, the child is shown a sequence of geometric figures (or colored figures in the younger-children's version). From this information, the child is to infer an underlying principle based on feedback regarding the correctness of each response. The Wisconsin Card Sorting Test (Chelune & Baer, 1986) assesses concept formation and the ability to either maintain or shift cognitive set in sorting a set of cards according to specific concepts in response to environmental (examiner) feedback regarding response accuracy. The Trail Making Test (Reitan & Davison, 1974; Spreen & Strauss, 1990) for 9- to 14-year-olds, is a popular paper-pencil test that involves visual attention and scanning ability, and the ability to shift attention flexibly between alphabet and number sequences (Trails B) under timed conditions. The Progressive Figures Test and the Color Form Test are somewhat similar tests developed by Reitan for children 5–8 years of age. Children with difficulties in these tasks may require more structure, step-by-step procedural guidelines, and increased teacher monitoring and explicit feedback regarding performance accuracy to achieve success in complex problem-solving activities in school. Specific test scores and observation of behavior on many of the tests described in previous sections may also be helpful in evaluating problem- solving functions. For example, the ability to inhibit impulsive responses on the Continuous Performance Test and the Continuous Recognition Memory Test, or utilization of semantic clustering strategies as an aid to memory on the CVLT-C, may also provide useful information for purposes of educational recommendations.

Assessment Of Psychosocial Functioning

Many children with learning disabilities experience difficulties involving social, behavioral, and emotional problems. As a group, children with learning disabilities tend to be less popular and experience lower social status among peers, demonstrate poorer social perception and communication skills, engage in increased levels of off-task behavior and negative interactions at school than nondisabled peers, and exhibit lower self-esteem than peers, often internalizing responsibility for their academic failures (Bloom, 1993). Looking at psychosocial adjustment in learning disability subtypes, Rourke (1991) demonstrated that children with arithmetic disabilities (i.e., specifically, nonverbal learning disabled) often exhibit reduced social competence and increased internalized (e.g., anxiety, dysphoria) psychosocial dysfunction compared with children with reading disabilities, who generally experience fewer difficulties. Bloom generally confirmed these findings using parent and teacher psychosocial instruments; self-report measures were less likely to reveal significant concerns among children with learning disabilities. In light of these factors, it is important that test results not be viewed in isolation, but that the influence of psychosocial factors be considered not only on the child's academic disability, but also on neuropsychological test performance (Taylor & Fletcher, 1990).

Evaluation of psychosocial functioning is generally accomplished through interviews, behavior checklists, and direct assessment of the child. Interviews with the parents, teacher, and child often provide crucial information regarding the nature, breadth, and intensity of concern over adjustment difficulties the child is experiencing. In addition, the child's strengths and talents can be explored and potentially capitalized upon later in the process of developing recommendations.

Parent and teacher behavior checklists and inventories can provide nonredundant information regarding social, behavioral, and emotional adjustment from different perspectives. The Personality Inventory for Children—Revised (PIC-R; Wirt, Lachar, Klinedinst, & Seat, 1984) and the Child Behavior Checklist (Achenbach, 1991a) are parent-report instruments that are helpful in understanding the child's adjustment issues. The Teacher's Report Form (Achenbach, (1991b) provides the perspective of the teacher(s) regarding social, behavioral, attentional, and emotional adjustment within the school setting. Interview of the child and use of a self-report instrument such as the Personality Inventory for Youth (PIY; Lachar & Gruber, 1995), the Youth Self-Report (Achenbach, 1991c), or the Perceived Competence Scale (Harter, 1985) may reveal personal feelings or information that is unknown to the parent or teacher and provide the child's perspective on areas of difficulty and how they are being handled. In addition, these procedures may help in judging the child's awareness of identified psychosocial difficulties and the extent to which these difficulties may relate to academic, family, or other frustrations.

Influence Of Environmental Factors

It is important to consider the potential impact of environmental factors that interact with other child characteristics to influence the child's academic and behavioral adjustment. Influential environmental factors that must be considered in the process of interpreting assessment results relate to child and family characteristics and background, school, and community variables (Fletcher, 1988). In most instances, this type of information can be obtained from interviews of the parent and teacher. Several examples of child-based factors that should be considered in formulating conclusions regarding the child's difficulties are level of motivation, self-esteem, child attitudes toward school—including the relevance of specific academic subjects and of past academic performance, frustration tolerance, child perceptions of parental expectations and support within the family, and child impressions of relationships with peers, family members, and teachers. The influence of family variables must also be considered when examining children's learning and behavior problems. Among the many family influences that might be considered are family stresses such as marital instability or financial problems, language background, cultural influences, parental ability to advocate for their child's academic needs at school, parent behavior management skills, parental ability to help with academic lessons and homework, and parental attitudes regarding the importance of education and their child's learning difficulties. If it is concluded that these types of variables significantly contribute to a child's learning or behavioral difficulties, recommendations such as school counseling, individual and/or family therapy, or parent behavior management training may be appropriate. As the primary provider of educational services to children, the school system plays a crucial role in enhancing the educational adjustment of children with learning disabilities. Consequently, it is important that the neuropsychologist be familiar with grade level curriculum, and available remedial programs, therapies, and specialized services at the child's school. With this information in mind, the neuropsychologist can work with the child's parents, teachers, and other education professionals to explore the child's service needs based on strengths and weaknesses identified in the neuropsychological assessment.

Influence of Genetic Factors

Neuropsychological assessments of children with brain injury make extensive attempts to relate test results to indices of brain damage. This process is more difficult in children with learning disabilities who (by definition) do not have brain injury. More relevant than, for example, electrophysiological or neuroimaging studies, are the child's developmental history and the family history of learning disability and related disorders. A careful developmental history is important. In addition, learning disability is clearly a familial disorder. Evidence is emerging that learning disabilities have a genetic basis, particularly disorders involving reading (Pennington, 1995).

CONCLUSION

A naive view is that the sole purpose of a neuropsychological evaluation is to determine brain status. Although test results can be relevant for this determination, most neuropsychologists conduct evaluations of children with learning disabilities and brain injury in order to develop treatment plans for the child. The five different approaches reviewed in this chapter vary in their emphasis on conclusions concerning brain function in children with learning disabilities. What they have in common is an emphasis on ability assessment in order to evaluate strengths and weaknesses relevant for treatment. In the coming years, it is likely that this emphasis will continue. Particularly important will be the question of interactions of treatment with different neuropsychological profiles. It is hoped that neuropsychological assessments will continue to be characterized by a broad, comprehensive approach to the child from ability, CNS, and psychosocial perspectives.

CHAPTER 5

Psychological Evaluation

Robert D. Annett
Elizabeth H. Aylward

As mentioned previously, the diagnosis of learning disabilities is based on evidence of a discrepancy between the child's cognitive abilities and academic achievement, when other disabling conditions (e.g., sensory impairment, mental retardation, social and emotional disturbance) or environmental influences (e.g., cultural differences, insufficient or inappropriate instruction, psychogenic factors) have been ruled out as primary reasons for the discrepancy. The psychologist plays an important role in making the diagnosis by providing information regarding the child's cognitive functioning. Additionally, the psychologist provides information that helps rule out other conditions and information that helps to explain the nature of the disabilities. Finally, the base of knowledge about the child is used by the psychologist to provide input regarding appropriate remediation.

There are five components in the complete psychological evaluation of a child. These include the clinical interview with the parents, a review of the child's school and medical records, psychological testing of the child, integration of these components with information gained from other professionals evaluating the child, and development of a written report. The first four of these components will be detailed in the following pages.

CLINICAL INTERVIEW OF THE PARENTS

History Taking

Like the physician, the psychologist is in an excellent position to gather important information from the parents that assists in understanding the child's school difficulties. Some of the questions will necessarily overlap with those included in the physician's interview and in the special educator's information-gathering process. It is not a waste of time to have questions repeated by various professionals, as it will provide each professional with a clearer understanding of the parents' perception of the problems. Furthermore, parents are bound to share different bits and pieces of the puzzle with different professionals, even if the questions asked are identical. This will allow for a clearer view of the "big picture" when the team gets together to share information.

The psychologist will want to gather information from the parents either before or after testing the child. The psychologist may want to ask about the child's school history, if this information is not already available from the special educator's report. Included in the school history will be information regarding number of years at the current school, previous schools attended and years of attendance, preschools attended and years of attendance, regularity of attendance, reasons for excessive absences, problems noted by teachers throughout the grades, special education services provided in previous years, any repetitions of grades or specific courses, types of remedial efforts attempted, and the outcome of these efforts. The psychologist will want to ask parents about their perceptions of current behavior problems at school and perceptions of strengths and weaknesses in the various subject areas. The psychologist will also want to explore issues that relate to the child's success and satisfaction with school, including the ability to interact with peers (both at home and at school), involvement in extracurricular activities, and self-concept. Important also are the sociocultural variables that may be affecting the child's performance at school.

In order to determine if problems observed in school are unique to the school situation or more pervasive, the psychologist should ask about behavior problems at home (e.g., excessive activity level, tantrums, inability to listen to and follow instructions, lying, stealing, refusal to do what is asked). The psychologist should ask about homework: how much is assigned (in the parents' estimation), how long it actually takes the child to complete the work, whether parental supervision is required, and particular problems with completion of homework (e.g., procrastination, whining, distractibility, need for assistance). The child's ability to carry out other responsibilities (e.g., regular daily chores) should also be discussed.

The psychologist should question the parent regarding the presence of symptoms of depression or other emotional disturbance in the child (e.g., unusual fears, sleeping problems, eating problems, mood swings, difficulty separating from parents). The psychologist needs to ask questions regarding any learning, emotional, or behavior problems in other family members. Finally, the psychologist should ask whether the child is currently taking any medication which might affect testing (e.g., psychostimulants, antihistamines) and, if so, whether the medication was administered on the day of psychological testing.

An interview form that the psychologist might want to use with parents is included in Appendix A. Of course, the psychologist will want to modify the form to suit individual needs.

Behavioral Questionnaires

An important component in the psychological evaluation of the child is the completion of standardized behavioral questionnaires by parents and teachers. Broad-based questionnaires, such as the Child Behavior Checklist (CBCL; Achenbach, 1991a) and the Behavioral Assessment System for Children (Reynolds & Kamphaus, 1992), provide valuable quantitative and qualitative information about the child. These questionnaires are important for several reasons. First, they provide the psychologist with standardized information that assists in making a judgment about the degree to which the child's behavior is "normal." This occurs through comparing the parent's rating with the ratings of over 4,000 other parents in the reference group. Ratings about the extent of internalizing (e.g., anxiety and depression) and externalizing (e.g., hyperactive and aggressive) behaviors can serve to focus subsequent interviewing and testing on specific dimensions of interest. Teacher observations can also be quantified through their completion of a parallel form of the questionnaire (i.e., Teacher Report Form). Obtaining information directly from the teacher is frequently time consuming and difficult, with a completed teacher questionnaire allowing for a direct sampling of the teacher's observations. Questionnaires ask about information that may not be covered in the typical clinical interview process (e.g., does the child speak of suicide), thus allowing for further inquiry with parents and teachers about other behaviors that may not have been previously discussed. Finally, behavioral questionnaires such as the CBCL also help define areas of the child's competency, an important element in understanding the total child.

Medical and School Records

The child's previous medical and school records are critical sources of information about the child which may not have been sufficiently disclosed in the clinical interview. Reviewing a child's medical records can provide insight into the child's developmental course, history of medication usage, and in the case of a medically complex child, specific information about the medical condition (e.g., the results of electroencephalography, brain imaging, etc.). Similarly, examining academic records yields valuable information regarding the child's academic and social development. Specifically, report cards depict the child's progress in academic areas and contain information regarding the development of study skills, peer relationships, and motivation. Finally, the results of annual standardized academic achievement tests reveal how the child performs on group tests in academic areas relative to a national reference group. This information is vital in tracking how the child's skills in specific academic areas have progressed over time.

Defining Sociocultural Context of the Family

With the burgeoning awareness of the multicultural nature of our society, defining the sociocultural context of the family has been increasingly emphasized when interpreting data. The sociocultural context, including the child's ethnic group, socioeconomic status, primary language, and culture, serves as a foundation to interpret psychological testing results. For example, information pertaining to the child's development of both his or her primary and secondary language is essential to understanding patterns of strengths and weaknesses in language processing abilities (e.g., when and how the child began acquiring English as a second language). Further, cultural expecations (e.g., the family's values regarding education) may affect the child's pattern of social development. Cultural expectations may relate to the expression of certain behaviors such as independence and the maturation of impulse control that can influence the child's performance on psychological testing. Other sociocultural factors to consider in an assessment include the family's socioeconomic status, stresses associated with immigration, the extent of acculturation, gender-related variations in expectations for academic achievement and behavior, and the child's past and present school context.

Obtaining Informed Consent

During the initial parent interview the psychologist determines the nature of the assessment needed and this information is discussed with the parents. If the parents agree to have the child evauated, the psychologist obtains informed consent for the proposed testing. Informed consent is essential to the assessment process as it provides the parents with information that might reasonably be expected to affect their decision on behalf of their child. The informed consent should entail a detailed explanation of the psychological evaluation process, including the necessity of parent and child interview, the selection of psychological instruments, and the mechanisms for sharing the child's results with other members of the evaluation team and the parents. Further, parents should be provided with a description of the ways potential conflicts will be managed. Explaining the evaluation process to the parents and obtaining their informed consent ensures cooperation in the procedures and satisfaction with the results from the evaluation. In addition, the parents and, subsequently, the psychologist will need to explain the reason for the evaluation to the child. While parents typically provide consent for the assessment process, it is useful to elicit the child's consent in order to optimize his or her compliance with test procedures. The child's consent can usually be obtained in the clinical interview, yet occasions will arise when the child is unwilling to participate in the evaluation process. When noncompliance occurs, the psychologist must consult with the parents about managing the child's refusal to participate in the evaluation process.

CLINICAL INTERVIEW OF THE CHILD OR ADOLESCENT

In the psychological evaluation of the child or adolescent, there is a clear necessity to interview the youngster before beginning any testing. The primary purpose of this clinical interview is to begin developing rapport, which is essential to ensuring optimal motivation for test performance and candidness in responses. In addition, obtaining the child's perspective of academic difficulties, peer and family relationships, and potential areas of stress is essential. Further, it is important that the psychologist explain to the child that psychological testing data will be employed in his or her best interest to help with the concerns expressed by the family.

Elements in the Clinical Interview

The clinical interview process with the child and adolescent has a variety of dimensions. Researchers such as Greenspan and Greenspan (1991) have described useful dimensions that should be examined in the course of the clinical interview. The clinical interview process provides a means of sampling spontaneous behavior, including observations about the child's physical and neurological development and how he or she relates to a novel situation and modulates emotions. In the context of this interview, the psychologist asks the child about his or her own worries or concerns with respect to school, peers, and family members. Questions about the specific details in each of these areas leads to a more complete understanding of the youngster's insight, emotional adaptation within these areas, and coping strategies. With younger children the context of this interview occurs through play, with the resulting exploration of each of these areas requiring a different amount of time and effort. Equally as important as the emotional themes that emerge in the clinical interview process, the psychologist has an opportunity to make observation about the development of cognitive structures. For example, the child's use of language pragmatics, ability to understand and manipulate concepts such as emotions, ability to modulate impulses, and responsiveness to limits become important areas that can affect subsequent interpretation of psychological testing performance.

PSYCHOLOGICAL TESTING OF THE CHILD OR ADOLESCENT

Basic Assumptions in Psychological Testing

Several basic assumptions are in place at the beginning of any psychological testing. These assumptions are meant to ensure valid and reliable test results and if left unquestioned may jeopardize any test results. As mentioned previously, the clinician desires to ensure that the child is motivated to perform to the best of his or her abilities, and this assumption underlies test interpretation. The tests themselves have built in other assumptions about the child and these need to be considered. For example, a basic assumption to most psychological tests is that the child's vision and hearing are normal or adequately corrected. This should be verified before any testing takes place. It is also assumed that the child is physically healthy at the time when testing occurs. Acute illness can impede the child's attention, motivation, and persistence, and should not be overlooked as a contributing factor to test performance. Perhaps overlooked at times are the gross and fine motor skills of the child. Impairment at either the gross or fine motor level can impact quite negatively on the child's speed and accuracy of performance, thus detrimentally affecting measures like intelligence, which relies to a significant degree upon speed of performance in some nonverbal tasks.

Language competence is another critical variable that is assumed in the normative data associated with all psychological tests. There are substantial numbers of children and adolescents for whom English is a second language. This raises a concern for the psychologist who must consider the role that another language (and likely another culture) may be playing in test performance. When circumstances like this arise it is not always possible to have a bilingual examiner administer the psychological testing, so the psychologist must be extremely careful in selecting assessment measures and be considerate in making judgments about the child's test performance.

Recent Legal Issues in Psychological Testing

Psychological tests have been the basis of several landmark legal decisions in recent years. The psychologist needs to be aware of the impact these cases have had upon the process of psychological testing with children. The two major issues addressed in recent litigation are the child's right to receive an appropriate education and the overrepresentation of ethnic minority children in classes for the mentally retarded.

Public Law 94-142 and other legislation have guaranteed the right of all children to receive a free and appropriate education. Subsequent litigation has resulted in confusion about the role of intelligence tests in determining eligibility for special education services. In the Larry P. v. Riles (1979) case in California the court determined that intelligence tests were culturally biased and could not be used in assessing black children for placement in classes for educable mentally retarded children. In the P.A.S.E. v. Hannon (1980) case in Illinois the court determined that intelligence tests were not culturally biased and did not discriminate against black children. Thus these cases have not resolved the issue of whether intelligence tests are culturally fair, though they have led to a greater understanding and appreciation of the complex issue of using intelligence tests, and thus other psychological tests, to make decisions about the best interests of the child. These cases serve as a reminder to the psychologist that factors such as the sociocultural context of the family plays an important role in interpreting results from any psychological test. Thus test results cannot be simply interpreted in an actuarial manner, but require the training and experience of the psychologist in order to reach accurate conclusions.

Cultural Differences in Testing

Interpretation of the effects of culture on test performance is a complicated process. Language may well be the most salient expression of culture that is discerned through psychological testing. Perhaps the simplest manner for examining language differences would be through the process of testing limits of a particular psychological test. This typically occurs at the psychologist's discretion and entails asking more detailed questions of the child or adolescent about his or her responses. Testing of limits is a manner of clinical inquiry about the child's response and is meant to clarify the psychologist's understanding of the child's capabilities. Typically testing limits occurs at the completion of standardized administration of the particular test. Based upon clinical experience and observation of the child's performance on particular items, the psychologist would redirect the child to items of interest and begin the process of inquiry. For items requiring a verbal response, the standardized prompting question may be restated or rephrased. For example, it may be necessary to discern if the child can recite all of the days of the week before proceeding to a more difficult recalling of specific information. Nonverbal responses may be examined in a similar manner or, where performance time is a vital element of the response, the child may be provided with additional time so the psychologist can observe the process for solving the problem.

Ideally the psychologist should be bilingual and be able to administer verbal items in both the dominant and the secondary language of the child. In addition, the psychologist should be able to interpret colloquialisms that the child may use. Yet having a bilingual psychologist is often not possible; thus, other procedures may be employed in testing limits. Some of the procedures that may be used include using a bilingual translator to ask questions, having the child's parent repeat questions, or having another professional (e.g., speech pathologist) observe and test limits together with the psychologist. Under these circumstances the child's responses in the other language must be considered in interpreting test results. A bilingual translator may be in the best position to provide the examiner with insights about the child's sociocultural background.

Considerations for Children with Multiple Disabilities

Children with significant developmental differences pose another challenge for the psychologist. Handicapping conditions seriously impact test performance and must be considered in the process of testing limits, to see what the child is capable of achieving on the particular measure, and in the process of test interpretation. For example, with cerebral palsy, the impairment in motor coordination impacts performance in the areas of speech intelligibility as well as motor skills, such as the time tasks from the Performance items on the WISC-III. While standardized administration is the hallmark of all psychological tests, the process of testing limits is typically required in evaluating children with multiple disabilities so that the psychologist can determine the child's real capabilities. Testing of limits helps describe the child's capabilities as well as gather useful information about the child's learning process, including how the handicapping condition(s) may be impeding learning.

Test Selection

The most popular basis for a diagnosis of learning disabilities is performance on individually administered tests of intelligence and academic achievement. As explained previously, a learning disability exists when academic achievement in one or more areas is significantly lower than the level that would be predicted from the child's cognitive profile, assuming that other conditions (e.g., emotional disturbance, excessive school absences, vision or hearing problems, inappropriate educational techniques) are not present. It is clear, then, that reliable assessments of both academic achievement and intellectual abilities are essential for accurate diagnosis. The psychologist is generally responsible for assessing intellectual abilities, whereas the educator is responsible for assessing academic achievement.

Because reliable assessment of intelligence is essential to the accurate diagnosis of learning disabilities, it is imperative that the psychologist select a valid and reliable instrument to measure the child's intellectual abilities in a manner that is not biased by the child's potential lack of academic achievement. There is, of course, no single, correct definition of "intelligence." Therefore, there is no single, correct way of measuring this construct. The examiner must be aware of the types of cognitive abilities assessed by the various intelligence tests in order to select the measure(s) that will provide the most valid estimate of intellectual functioning for the child.

Individually Administered IQ Tests

Although most school systems have adopted programs for assessing children at regular intervals throughout the elementary and secondary school years, the tests are typically administered to students in large groups consisting of 20 or more students. Although these tests provide fairly accurate evaluations of academic skills (and sometimes general intellectual ability) for many students, they are inappropriate for children suspected of having learning disabilities. First, many children with learning disabilities have concomitant attention deficits. As a result, they are at a disadvantage in a group-testing situation, particularly if the tests are administered with a time limit. Group testing may inadvertently penalize children who have difficulties with inattention, impulsivity, and overactivity. Second, most group tests require the student to independently read the test items. Although poor reading abilities will be reflected in reading subtest scores on group tests, they may impede the accurate assessment of other academic abilities and knowledge in content areas (e.g., social studies, applied math, study skills) as well as of overall cognitive abilities. Third, group testing does not provide the examiner with an opportunity to closely observe many of the behaviors that interfere with testing and similarly interfere with classroom learning (e.g., limited attention span, impulsivity, excessive frustration). For these reasons, individual testing is essential for correct diagnosis of learning disabilities.

Selection of a Test of Intellectual Functioning

In making a diagnosis of learning disabilities the minimum information necessary is an accurate assessment of intelligence (often in the form of an "IQ" score) and an accurate assessment of academic achievement in one or more areas. Although many currently available intelligence tests claim to provide an IQ or other score reflecting overall cognitive ability, few are appropriate in making the diagnosis of learning disabilities.

In a 1984 report from the United States Department of Education, Special Education Programs Work Group on Management Issues in the Assessment of Learning Disabilities (Reynolds, 1984), 11 considerations were presented for selection of instruments used in the diagnosis of learning disabilities. These are presented in Table 5–1. Basically, these standards require tests used for the diagnosis of learning disabilities to meet generally accepted criteria for reliability (i.e., ability of a test to consistently measure what it measures) and validity (i.e., ability of a test to actually measure what it purports to measure). Furthermore, the normative data must be based on a sufficiently large sample that reflects the demographic characteristics of the national population. The test norms should allow the examiner to compare the child with other children of the same age. The degree to which different ethnic and cultural populations perform differently on the test should have been studied and reported. The test of cognitive abilities should measure "general" intelligence. Another primary consideration is the need for the test of cognitive ability and the test of academic achievement to be normed on the same or similar populations.

In addition to these important criteria, it is desirable to use an intelligence test that allows the examiner to observe the child over a range of response modes (e.g., single-word responses, elaborated oral responses, paper-and-pencil tasks, manipulation of materials, identification by pointing, imitation of the examiner, timed and untimed responses). The test should also tap various aspects of intelligence.

TABLE 5–1
Essential Characteristics of Tests Used in Making the Diagnosis of Learning Disabilities

1. Tests should meet all requirements stated for assessment devices in the rules and regulations implementing Public Law 94-142.

2. Normative data should meet contemporary standards of practice and be provided for a sufficiently large, nationally stratified random sample of children.

3. Standardization samples for tests whose scores are being compared must be the same or highly comparable.

4. For the purpose of arriving at a diagnosis, individually administered tests should be used.

5. In the measurement of aptitude, an individually administered test of general intellectual ability should be used.

6. Age-based standard scores should be used for all measures and all should be scaled to a common metric.

7. The measures employed should demonstrate a high level of reliability and have appropriate studies for this determination in the technical manual accompanying the test.

8. The validity coefficient r_{xy}, representing the relationship between the measures of aptitude and achievement, should be based on an appropriate sample.

9. Validity of test score interpretations should be clearly established.

10. Special technical considerations should be addressed when using performance-based measures of achievement (e.g., writing skill).

11. Bias studies on the instruments in use should have been conducted and reported.

Adapted from Reynolds, C. (1984–1985). Critical measurement issues in learning disabilities. *Journal of Special Education, 18*(4), 451–476.

WISC-III, Stanford-Binet, K-ABC, and KAIT

Four intelligence tests that generally meet the technical criteria described (validity, reliability, adequate norming samples) and that are most commonly used are the Wechsler Intelligence Scale for Children-Third Edition (WISC-III, 1991), the Stanford-Binet Intelligence Scale (Fourth Edition, 1986; hereafter, "Stanford-Binet" refers to the Fourth Edition), the Kaufman Assessment Battery for Children (K-ABC, 1983), and the Kaufman Adolescent and Adult Intelligence Test (KAIT, 1993). There is, of course, much debate regarding the nature of intelligence and much debate regarding the types of tasks that should be used to measure intelligence. The K-ABC, KAIT, Stanford-Binet, and WISC-III differ considerably in their conceptualizations of intelligence. None of these tests can be considered "right" or "wrong" in their approach to intellectual assessment. The examiner will have to consider the nature of the individual subtests comprising these tests of intelligence to determine which is the best choice for each child being evaluated.

The two major aspects of intelligence measured by the WISC-III are verbal (language) and nonverbal (primarily visual-spatial) skills. In addition, this newest version of the WISC can be analyzed in four factors: Freedom from Distractibility, Verbal Comprehension, Perceptual Organization, and Processing Speed. The Stanford-Binet conceptualizes intelligence as "crystallized abilities" (verbal reasoning and quantitative reasoning), "fluid-analytic abilities" (abstract/visual reasoning), and short-term memory. The K-ABC is based on a theory that views intelligence as a composite of "simultaneous" and "sequential" information processing. On tasks measuring Sequential Processing, stimuli are manipulated in serial or temporal order to solve problems; in contrast, on tasks measuring Simultaneous Processing, stimuli are integrated in a holistic, gestalt, or parallel fashion to solve problems. Intelligence, as measured by the K-ABC, is considered to be "an individual's style of solving problems and processing information" (Kaufman & Kaufman, 1983, p. 2). Further, the K-ABC attempts to "minimize the role of language and acquired facts and skills" (Kaufman, 1983, p. 206) by including language and culturally based tasks in an Achievement Scale that is not utilized to compute the child's Mental Processing Composite.

The KAIT, appropriate for ages 11-85, has been designed as a comprehensive intelligence measure with two major dimensions, "crystallized" and "fluid" intelligence, that are combined into a composite score. The Crystallized Scale "measures acquisition of facts and problem-solving ability using stimuli that are dependent on formal schooling, cultural experiences, and verbal conceptual development" (Kaufman & Kaufman, 1993, p. 7). The Fluid Scale was developed to assess "a person's adaptability and flexibility when faced with new problems" (p. 7). The KAIT was not designed to be an upper extension of the K-ABC, but rather a measure appropriate for assessment of intelligence in learning disability evaluations and as part of a vocational battery.

Although many of the subtests on the WISC-III, Stanford-Binet, and KAIT are similar to K-ABC subtests in measuring problem-solving and information-processing styles, these tests also include other subtests that definitely rely on learned material for successful performance. The type of learning required on these subtests is, however, the type that is generally picked up in day-to-day living (e.g., vocabulary, understanding of social situations, general information), rather than that which relies on direct school learning.

Because the WISC-III, Stanford-Binet, K-ABC, and KAIT all have distinct advantages and disadvantages in different applications, we recommend that the psychologist on the interdisciplinary team be familiar with these four major tests of intelligence. The psychologist may find it more appropriate to use one or the other in various situations. Although it is impossible to identify the K-ABC, KAIT, Stanford-Binet, or WISC-III as the "best" test for measuring intelligence as part of the diagnostic process, the psychologist should consider certain factors in each individual case:

1. One of the major advantages of using the K-ABC or WISC-III instead of the Stanford-Binet is the availability of the K-ABC Achievement Scale subtests, the Kaufman Test of Educational Achievement (K-TEA, Kaufman & Kaufman, 1985), and the Wechsler Individual Achievement Test (WIAT, 1992). The K-ABC Achievement subtests were normed on the same sample as the K-ABC Mental Processing subtests. In a similar manner, the WIAT and the WISC-III have been administered to the same "linking sample" so as to ensure that the measures can be compared for purposes of discerning a meaningful discrepancy. This allows the examiner to confidently compare results of the intelligence measure and the academic achievement measures, which is essential in making the diagnosis of learning disabilities. However, a number of clinicians think the K-ABC Achievement subtests do not adequately test several important academic skills (e.g., application of phonic skills, written calculations) that are commonly measured by achievement tests.

2. Both the K-ABC and the WISC-III included in their norming sample exceptional children (e.g., learning disabled, mentally retarded, gifted children) in some proportion. The K-ABC had 7% of its sample from special classes, including speech impaired, learning disabled, mentally retarded, emotionally disturbed, physically impaired, or Chapter I reading program students. In addition, 5% of the sample comprised students in gifted programs. The Stanford-Binet norming sample included some exceptional students, but it is not clear what types and what proportions of exceptional students were involved. The KAIT does not report the inclusion of exceptional adolescents or adults in the standardizations. Inclusion of exceptional students in the norming sample increases validity of the scores for the individual exceptional student.

3. Because the WISC-III represents a continued updating of normative information on children in North America, the children in the standardization sample may be more similar to children currently being evaluated than the children in the K-ABC and Stanford-Binet standardization samples, thus increasing the chance for validity. The KAIT was recently standardized and closely corresponds with 1990 U.S. census information. An important point to be noted in the use of tests for diagnosing learning disabilities is the necessity for a high degree of comparability of standardization samples for tests whose scores are being compared. That is, when the scores from two tests (e.g., an intelligence test and an achievement test) are compared, the samples on which those two tests were normed should be highly similar. The most widely used tests of achievement have been standardized within the past ten years.

Notable is that measures such as the K-ABC and the WISC-III have been developed in conjunction with academic achievement tests. This represents the state of the field in test development, as discrepancies between scores represent true differences in the individual and not differences between the normative groups. Thus comparisons between scores from a test of intelligence and scores from a test of academic achievement are likely to represent a true discrepancy between intellectual ability and achievement.

4. Racial and ethnic differences are less pronounced on the K-ABC than on the other tests. For example, Kaufman (1983) reported a 7-point average difference between the scores of black children and white children on the K-ABC. A similar trend is reported for the differences between scores of Hispanic and white children. There are no indications of racial differences in the WISC-III or KAIT manuals. The developers of the Stanford-Binet had a large staff representing various minority groups review all of the test items for the possibility of racial, ethnic, or gender bias. This procedure resulted in some items being reviewed or dropped. Test developers for the Stanford-Binet, WISC-III, and KAIT do not provide information regarding differences in scores among various racial and ethnic groups or sexes. Thus examiners cannot be certain of the nature or extent of any racial or ethnic differences on these measures.

5. All K-ABC Mental Processing subtests and KAIT Core Battery subtests include teaching or training items. These allow the examiner to use various means to make certain that the child understands the task. Although the WISC-III and Stanford-Binet provide sample items for most subtests (which allow the examiner to correct mistakes, using a clearly prescribed protocol), these sample items do not always clearly ensure that the child understands what is expected. This, of course, is a

more serious problem with younger, less intelligent, or culturally different children. The K-ABC and KAIT teaching items allow the examiner a
greater degree of latitude to be certain that a low score reflects a true
weakness in a skill area rather than an inability to understand directions.

6. The K-ABC provides a Nonverbal Scale, made up of subtests
that can be administered in pantomime and responded to motorically.
This is designed for children who are hearing impaired, who have serious speech or language disorders, or who use English as a second language. The KAIT makes teaching allowances for bilingual and hearing-
impaired children by allowing the examiner to present materials in
another language. Although many of the WISC-III Performance subtests require no verbal response, it may be difficult to communicate instructions for the task to a child with hearing impairment. This could
result in PIQs that underestimate visual-spatial skills. Furthermore, any
nonverbal communication of instructions could be considered "non-
standard" procedure for administration of the WISC-III subtests and
thus somewhat jeopardize interpretations from the normative sample.
Yet the WISC-III Manual (Wechsler, 1991) reports that a sample of
hearing-impaired subjects demonstrated a higher PIQ than VIQ (106
versus 81, respectively), suggesting that differences in administration,
or perhaps cultural differences, may affect the performance of hearing-
impaired individuals on the WISC-III. The Stanford-Binet suggests alternate batteries that can be given to students with limited English proficiency or hearing deficits, but special norms for these batteries are not
provided.

7. The K-ABC provides a variety of supplementary norms, including sociocultural norms (based on a cross-tabulation by race and by
parental education). Also important, children can, when desired, be
compared with peers from similar sociocultural backgrounds.

8. The K-ABC provides specific strategies for teaching reading,
math, and spelling, based on the child's profile of strengths and weaknesses on the Simultaneous versus Sequential Mental Processing tasks.

9. Although the K-ABC intentionally omitted tasks that require
extensive verbal expression, it cannot be denied that this is an ability
that contributes greatly to school success. The examiner may want information comparing verbal and nonverbal skills, which can be obtained much more directly and thoroughly from the WISC-III and
Stanford-Binet, and to a lesser extent from the KAIT.

10. Just as the K-ABC and KAIT may be useful for testing children who are hearing impaired or who have serious speech or language
disorders, the WISC-III Verbal subtests may be useful for assessing
cognitive abilities of children who are visually impaired. These children
would be seriously disadvantaged on the K-ABC tests, although sev-

eral of the KAIT subtests could be administered to adolescents and adults with visual impairment. The Stanford-Binet suggests alternative batteries for children who are blind or visually impaired. None of these tests provide special norms for children with visual impairment.

11. The WISC-III, KAIT, and Stanford-Binet allow the examiner to observe the child over a greater range of response modes than the K-ABC. Manipulation of objects, paper-and-pencil skills, single-word responses, elaborated oral responses, identification by pointing, and imitation of the examiner are all required by the various WISC-III, KAIT, and Stanford-Binet tasks. Although individual scores are not obtained for each of these response modes, the experienced examiner can use his or her observation to formulate some fairly sophisticated hypotheses regarding certain factors that will interfere with the child's learning. Most of the responses on the K-ABC require identification by pointing, although a few require single word responses, manipulation of objects, or imitation of the examiner. Responses on the KAIT generally require simple verbal responses.

12. The WISC-III and Stanford-Binet employ more manipulative materials than the K-ABC and KAIT. Although this makes the administration of the WISC-III and Stanford-Binet somewhat more cumbersome, it may be more effective in maintaining the child's attention (especially at younger ages). Additionally, the use of manipulatives can provide behavioral data for the examiner about handedness, lateralized sensory deficiencies, and fine-motor coordination that can be subsequently explored with additional tests.

13. Because of its "adaptive-testing" procedure, the Stanford-Binet is definitely the most difficult of the three tests to learn to administer. The WISC-III is generally considered to be a more difficult test to learn to administer than the K-ABC and KAIT. Also, because scoring on several of the WISC-III and Stanford-Binet subtests is somewhat subjective, examiners with less testing experience may have more difficulty scoring these tests as accurately as the K-ABC and KAIT.

14. The four tests are designed to cover different age ranges, with the WISC-III covering ages 6 to 16, the K-ABC covering ages 2 years 6 months to 12 years 6 months, the KAIT covering ages 11 through 85, and the Stanford-Binet covering ages 2 through adult. Younger children or those with significant delays are often unable to reach basal level on several of the Stanford-Binet subtests. For very young children, the K-ABC would be an appropriate test to use, although examiners might wish to supplement it with some measure of verbal ability. The Wechsler Preschool and Primary Scale of Intelligence—Revised (WPPSI-R, 1989), which provides norms for children ages 3 through 7 years, is also an excellent test for preschool children. For individuals

above age 16, the Wechsler Adult Intelligence Scale—Revised (WAIS-R, 1981) should be considered, as the norms for older individuals on the Stanford-Binet only go up through age 23 years 11 months and are based on a large single sample for individuals between 18 and 24.

The Kaufman Adolescent and Adult Intelligence Test (KAIT) was developed in 1993 and covers the adolescent and adult age groups, extending the ability of the examiner to developmentally follow a child into adolescence and adulthood with a measure that is conceptually consistent with the K-ABC. It is important to note that the KAIT manual reports moderate correlations in a sample of 11-year-olds who completed both the KAIT and K-ABC, suggesting that the KAIT may be useful for following children into adolescence. The KAIT provides a Mental Status subtest which can be particularly useful for screening children and adults who are suspected of being unable to adequately participate in the assessment process (e.g., due to confusion or brain injury).

Appropriate Tests of Intelligence for Preschool Children

As discussed in Chapter 2, early identification of children with learning disabilities is desirable, as emphasized under P.L. 99-457. As part of this early identification procedure, it is essential that the psychologist obtain a measure of overall cognitive function. The K-ABC and Stanford-Binet can provide measures of cognitive abilities for children as young as 2 years 6 months. As noted earlier the WISC-III is designed for children who are at least 6 years old. The Wechsler Preschool and Primary Scale of Intelligence—Revised (WPPSI-R) is similar to the WISC-III and is designed for children between the ages of 3 and 7 years. The WPPSI-R is fully described by Aylward (1991). Assessment of preschool aged children is a special area of expertise that involves more than simple test administration. Many more influences on behavior must be considered. The psychologist should have additional training and supervised experience with infant measures, such as the Bayley Scales of Infant Development (Second Edition, 1993), as well as the preschool measures listed above.

Appropriate Tests of Intelligence for Older Children

The K-ABC cannot be used with children over 12 years 6 months, and the WISC-III cannot be used with children over 16 years 11 months. With the recent development of the KAIT, a person older than 11 years who had been evaluated with the K-ABC can be followed with an instrument that emphasizes problem solving like the K-ABC. An examiner wishing to assess or follow up an adolescent with the KAIT will be well advised to review the literature in the manual about the reliability and validity of this newest measure of intelligence. The Wechsler Adult Intelligence Scale—Revised (WAIS-R) is similar to the WISC-III and WPPSI-R in its conceptualization of intelligence and is designed for individuals 16 years or older. It contains the same six Verbal subtests as the WISC-III; the Mazes subtest is omitted from the Performance subtests. Of course, items are more difficult.

Inappropriate Tests of Intelligence for the Diagnosis of Learning Disabilities

As mentioned previously, it is important that the intelligence test selected for use in making the diagnosis of learning disabilities have a strong and comprehensive theoretical base, be individually administered, have adequate validity and reliability, include tasks that tap a variety of aspects of intelligence, and provide the examiner an opportunity to observe the student over a range of response modes. Several commonly used "intelligence" tests do not meet these criteria and are, therefore, inappropriate for making the diagnosis of learning disabilities. Among this group of inappropriate, but commonly used, tests is the Slosson Intelligence Test—Revised (1990, SIT), which is inappropriate because it was inadequately normed on an unrepresentative sample and contains too few items at each age level. The Peabody Picture Vocabulary Test—Revised (PPVT-R) is inappropriate because it measures only limited aspects of receptive vocabulary skills. As described previously, the diagnosis of learning disabilities requires scores based on individually administered tests that allow the examiner to closely monitor the child's test behavior and to ensure maximum attention. For this reason, group-administered tests of intelligence (e.g., the Otis-Lennon Mental Ability Test, 1982) would be inappropriate.

Although some of these "inappropriate" tests may be useful as screening tools for identifying children with possible learning disabilities, they should certainly not be used as the measure of intelligence for making a final diagnosis. Similarly, a child who does not show a significant discrepancy between academic achievement and intellectual ability, as measured by one of these tests, should not necessarily be assumed to be free of learning disabilities if other indications of learning disabilities are observed.

The Role of Personality Testing for Children with Learning Disabilities

As part of a comprehensive psychological assessment of a child there is often a need to assess social and personality functioning. It is imperative that the child's emotional status, including coping style, emotional responsiveness, and self-esteem be represented in the assessment. Children with learning problems often have concomitant difficulties in functioning related to learning experiences, such as anxiety and depression. The psychologist is the one professional who is perhaps best qualified to assess the child's emotional state and self-esteem, integrating this with findings from other test sources, such as performance on tests of intelligence, to arrive at a holistic understanding of the child.

The child's emotional status can be adequately evaluated in a variety of useful ways. As discussed previously, behavioral questionnaires completed by the parent or teacher provide one source of valuable information. The clinical child interview provides another source of information, yet may often take many sessions to discern complex social and emotional problems. Personality tests provide a relatively quick and meaningful source of information directly about the child. These tests take a variety of forms and can include traditional questionnaires, such as the Revised Children's Manifest Anxiety Scale (for children above age 6 years), projective drawings as in the House-Tree-Person Technique-Revised (Buck, 1981), projective story-telling tasks as in the Roberts Apperception Test (Roberts, 1994), and intrapsychic projective tests such as the Rorschach Psychodiagnostic Test (1981; Exner & Weiner, 1994). Psychologists generally have their preference for these measures, as each reveals distinctly different characteristics about the child. Like the tests of intelligence, greater emphasis has been placed in recent years on developing normative data for each of these measures. Yet, for the psychologist, to accurately employ these measures in clinical practice, it requires many years of supervised training and experience.

Supplemental Tests Useful in the Diagnosis of Learning Disabilities

A growing number of useful tests for children have demonstrated clinical utility in the diagnosis of learning and other developmental disorders. Generally speaking these tests are classified as pediatric neuropsychological tests (see Chapter 4) and may comprise a traditional battery of tests (e.g., the Halstead-Reitan) or may consist of individual tests selected by the psychologist for a specific purpose. The purpose of pediatric neuropsychological testing is to evaluate, in a comprehensive manner, the cognitive processes underlying specific neurologic functions. For example, language skills are sampled in a brief manner by measures such as the WISC-III. Pediatric neuropsychological tests examine a child's language competencies and deficiencies more intensively, providing useful information regarding comprehension, processing, and expression. The pediatric neuropsychologist also examines the contribution of a child's perceptual, motor, memory, and executive functioning (e.g., organization, learning-to-learn, planning) to his or her learning disabilities. The role of a pediatric neuropsychological assessment is more fully examined in Chapter 4.

Test Administration

Appropriate Test Conditions

As outlined in any introductory text of assessment or any manual for an individually administered test, a proper test environment is essential for accurate assessment. This is especially true for the child with learning disabilities who is often easily distracted. The testing room must, of course, be quiet, free from excessive visual distractions, properly ventilated, of comfortable temperature, and equipped with furniture that allows the child to be seated comfortably at a table or desk. Several of the tests most useful in diagnosing learning disabilities will not provide reliable results if such conditions are not maintained.

If possible, the child should be tested in the morning when well rested and alert. Tests should be administered in sessions no longer than 2 hours (or shorter for younger children). If tests must be administered in one session, the student should be allowed a short break in the middle of the session.

The examiner needs to make a special attempt to build rapport with the child being evaluated for possible learning disabilities. This can best be accomplished as discussed earlier, in a clinical interview with the child before testing. Many of these children, after years of poor academic achievement, have poor self-esteem, are easily frustrated, poorly motivated, or overly anxious. In order to obtain an accurate assessment of the child's abilities, the examiner must take into account these emotional interferences and must attempt to overcome them.

Behaviors To Be Observed During Intelligence Testing

The psychologist administering the test of cognitive abilities should include in the report a section on behavioral observations of the child in the testing situation. Some of the behaviors that should be addressed in this section of the report are discussed.

General Observations
☐ Is the child oriented?
☐ How does the child physically appear? Is the child dishev-

eled in his appearance? Are there any physical asymmetries apparent?

☐ How does the child orient to the examiner? Does the child greet the examiner with appropriate eye contact and responses?

☐ What is the child's mood? Does the child demonstrate a range of affect?

☐ Is the child motivated to perform?

☐ Describe the child's thought process. Can the train of thought be easily followed?

Distractibility

☐ Did the student have difficulty paying attention and staying on task? Did the student appear to be daydreaming or off in his own world?

☐ Did he often ask to have items repeated?

☐ Did she often comment about or seem attuned to unavoidable visual or auditory distractions (e.g., the squeaking of a chair, the examiner's clothing)?

☐ Did he make irrelevant comments or attempt to relate personal experiences that were brought to mind by the various test stimuli? Did she often talk to herself, especially on tasks that required manipulation of materials rather than a verbal response?

☐ Did he seem to "lose track" of the task presented? For example, on the "digits reversed" section of the WISC-III Digit Span subtest, did he begin to repeat digits forward after several successful trials of repeating digits in reversed order? On the WISC-III Coding subtest did the student stop in the middle of the test, seeming to have forgotten instructions to work as quickly as possible? Did the student frequently lose his place on the Coding subtest?

Restlessness, Fidgetiness

☐ Did the student have difficulty staying seated, especially on the subtests that did not require manipulation of materials?

☐ Did restlessness increase as testing proceeded or stay at a constant level?

☐ Did the child engage in excessive purposeless movement (e.g., squirming, tapping fingers, swinging feet, kicking the table leg?)

Were the child's hands overly "busy" (e.g., repetitively rolling his hands in his shirt tail, twirling his pencil, picking at himself)?

☐ Did he chew on his pencil, shirt collar, cuffs, or other objects?

Rushed, Careless, Impulsive Approach

☐ Did the child appear to give the first answer that came to mind?

☐ Did the child attempt to begin tasks before instructions were complete?

☐ Did the child attempt to turn pages before adequately attending to the material on the current page?

☐ Did he grab for materials before the examiner was ready to present them?

☐ Did the child appear totally oblivious to obviously incorrect responses?

☐ Did she noticeably increase her speed of responding when she was aware that performance was being timed? Did this result in careless errors?

Slow, Obsessive Approach

☐ Did the child take excessive time before responding?

☐ Did he meticulously check and recheck work, resulting in penalties for slow performance?

☐ Were her verbal responses more complete than necessary (especially on vocabulary and comprehension subtests)?

☐ Did he often come up with correct responses *after* time was called?

☐ Did she spend excessive time "planning" before responding (especially on WISC-R Mazes or K-ABC Photo Series)?

☐ Were tasks done with excessive precision (e.g., were blocks on the WISC-R Block Design or triangles on the K-ABC Triangles subtests lined up exactly, lines drawn extremely neatly, or overworked on Stanford-Binet Copying)?

Anxiety

☐ Did the child have difficulty separating from his parent or teacher?

☐ Did she appear nervous? Did this subside or increase as testing proceeded? Did it diminish with positive reinforcement and reassurance?

☐ Did anxiety appear to increase when tasks were timed?

☐ Was more anxiety observed on certain types of tasks (e.g., those requiring a verbal response, those that were timed) than on other types of tasks?

Confidence

☐ Did the child often ask if his responses were correct?

☐ Was the child reluctant to guess at an item he did not know?

☐ Could the child be encouraged to take a guess, and, if so, were guesses often correct?

☐ Did she start to give answers and then change her mind and refuse to respond?

☐ Did the child qualify many responses (e.g., by saying, "I don't know, but..." or "This is just a guess.")?

☐ Did he often comment on the difficulty of items (e.g., "These are so easy" or "I'll never get this one.")? Were these assessments of difficulty congruent with the child's performance?

☐ Did the child often say "I can't" or "I don't know" without putting forth good effort?

☐ Did the child often ask for assistance on items or look to the examiner for reassurance that he was "on the right track"?

Frustration, Perseverance

☐ Did the child often stop working on a task before time was called, claiming an item was too difficult? Could he be encouraged to continue and, if so, was he able to successfully complete the item?

☐ If unable to succeed on an item within the time limit, did the child request "just a little longer" to complete the task?

☐ Did she ever scatter materials in frustration?

☐ Did he act disgusted with himself or make disparaging comments when he could not succeed on an item?

☐ Did she ever ask to complete remaining items after failing the prescribed number of items for discontinuing the testing?

Distortions in Spatial Orientation

☐ Did the child have many rotations on WISC-III Block Design, Stanford-Binet Pattern Analysis, or K-ABC Triangles?

☐ Did he work from right to left when sequencing WISC-III Picture Arrangement cards or completing the WISC-III Coding task?

Pencil Grasp
- ☐ Did the child exhibit an immature or awkward pencil grasp on the WISC-III Coding and Mazes subtests or on the Stanford-Binet Copying subtest?

Avoidance Behavior
- ☐ Did the child ask for excessive breaks (e.g., for bathroom visits, drinks)?
- ☐ Did she complain of stomachaches or other ailments in an apparent attempt to discontinue the session?
- ☐ Did he complain of being tired?
- ☐ Did she often ask how much longer the testing would last?
- ☐ Did he complain about the testing?

Hearing and Vision
- ☐ Were there any indications that the child had difficulty seeing materials or hearing questions (e.g., squinting, holding materials close to his face, often saying "huh?" or asking to have questions repeated)?

Speech and Language
- ☐ Did the child often ask to have verbal items repeated?
- ☐ Was the child slow to begin giving verbal responses?
- ☐ Did the child often appear to not understand verbal directions, but "catch on" quickly after a few demonstration items?
- ☐ Did the child have "word finding" problems? For example, did the child often refer to objects on the WISC-III Picture Completion subtest as "those things" or "what-cha-ma-call-its"? Did she often give a long verbal explanation to describe something for which more concise terminology would have been more appropriate?
- ☐ Were verbal responses extremely limited? Did the child resist your encouragement to elaborate on verbal responses?
- ☐ Did the child give totally inappropriate responses to verbal questions and then, upon repetition of the question, provide an accurate response?
- ☐ Did the child give responses which related only to a portion of the question?
- ☐ Did the child have any observable speech impediments (e.g., stuttering, lisping, poor articulation)? Did they interfere with testing?

Personality Characteristics
- ☐ Was the child friendly, pleasant, well-mannered, cooperative?
- ☐ Did the child appear well motivated?
- ☐ Did she appear to enjoy the testing and the individual attention of the examiner?
- ☐ Did he offer spontaneous conversation?
- ☐ Did she make eye-contact with the examiner?
- ☐ Did he appear to take pride in his successes? Did he respond to praise?
- ☐ Did she respond to the examiner's attempts to build rapport?
- ☐ Was the child overly affectionate with the examiner?

Health
- ☐ Was the child on any type of medication that might have affected performance (e.g., Ritalin, antihistamines)?
- ☐ Were there any other health conditions that might have affected performance?

Although this list of behavioral observations may seem quite lengthy and detailed, it is important that each area be considered. The psychologist may even want to make a checklist to use during testing to facilitate reporting of these characteristics. Some of the child's major difficulties may be reflected more in these behavioral traits than in any test score. Recommendations for remediation of school difficulties will certainly need to take these traits into account.

Models for Interpretation of a Learning Disability

While up to this point we have discussed learning disability as a discrepancy between intelligence and academic achievement, how this discrepancy is ascertained has not been addressed. Before the issue of discrepancy can be addressed, however, it is important to note that by definition a learning disability cannot be accounted for by environmental factors, such as inadequate instruction. In fact, this is often not directly addressed by learning disability examiners except in a gross manner. With the burgeoning of home schooling in certain parts of the United States, the problem of defining adequate instruction is again raised. At this time definitive criteria for how to address the adequacy of a child's school instruction apparently do not exist. The clinical interview process with the parents and, specifically, ascertaining the child's school history are the most useful places to start, but we are lacking in operational criteria for defining adequate instruction.

The controversial topic of measuring the discrepancy between intelligence and achievement has a long history. The arguments have been essentially that there are notable conceptual and measurement assumptions that underlie the notion of a discrepancy. These will not be discussed here, yet interested readers may examine Stanovich's concise review (1992) for further information on this topic. The psychologist examining a child with a learning disability is often left with a significant problem in operationalizing a discrepancy for an individual child. In some states discrepancy is defined by school officials to be a difference between intelligence and achievement of greater than or equal to one standard deviation, actually ranging from 17 to 20 "points" depending on the state and the school district. Other methods have been employed, such as requiring a child to be two or more grade levels behind. These hard-and-fast rules neglect statistical problems, such as the less-than-perfect correlation between intelligence and achievement. Additionally, these means of calculating a discrepancy fail with younger school-aged children and in children with lower levels of intelligence. Thus, these measures underidentify younger children and children with lower intelligence for special education assistance.

Test Interpretation

WISC-III VIQ-PIQ Discrepancy and Subtest Scatter

Many attempts have been made to identify "the learning disability profile" of subtest scores on the WISC-III. Despite the fact that no consistent profile has been found, some psychologists and educators may attempt to make a diagnosis of learning disabilities based on the WISC-III profile alone. This is not appropriate. Most commonly, these inappropriate diagnoses are based on an extreme amount of subtest scatter or on a significant discrepancy between VIQ and PIQ. Although students with learning disabilities often show great subtest scatter (i.e., differences in performance among the various subtests) and VIQ-PIQ discrepancies, many children without learning disabilities also show these "abnormal" patterns, and many students with learning disabilities do not show these patterns.

Compounding the problem, many professionals who work primarily with children exhibiting school difficulties are unaware of the amount of subtest scatter and VIQ-PIQ discrepancy found in the profile of the "normal" child. In examining the standardization data for the WISC-III (Wechsler, 1992) a 15-point difference between Verbal and Performance IQ scores was found to occur in 24% of the standardization sample. The values for determining whether a particular VIQ-PIQ discrepancy is significant (i.e., not due to chance) are 10 points (p < .10 level), 12 points (p < .05), and 16 points (p < .01). Most psychologists consider a VIQ-PIQ discrepancy of 12 points or more (regardless of direction) worthy of explanation. It is important to note, however, that a discrepancy of 12 points or more was found in 36% of the normative sample. Table 5–2 reports the percentage of normal children who have VIQ-PIQ discrepancies of various magnitudes.

Substantial scatter among the ten WISC-III subtests is also not unusual. Sattler (1992) reports that the median scaled score range (the difference between the highest and lowest subtest score) was 7 points for Full Scale IQ, 4 points for VIQ, and 5 points for PIQ. Sattler cautions that the scaled-score range may be helpful to know, yet interpretation is difficult due to the relative lack of research in this area at present.

TABLE 5–2
Percentages of the Standardization Sample Obtaining Various VIQ-PIQ Discrepancies

Amount of VIQ-PIQ Discrepancy	Percentage of Standardization Sample
9	49.3
10	44.5
11	40.5
12	35.8
13	31.7
14	28.2
15	24.3
16	21.6
17	19.4
18	17.0
19	14.5
20	12.3
21	10.9
22	9.3
23	7.7
24	6.2
25	4.9
26	4.0
27	3.1
28	2.7
29	2.3
30	1.9
31	1.5
32	1.0
33+	<1.0

Because VIQ-PIQ discrepancies and the amount of subtest scatter in normal populations are larger than many examiners would suspect, and because these intratest comparisons cannot accurately identify children with learning disabilities, examiners should be careful not to over-interpret WISC-III profiles.

K-ABC Simultaneous-Sequential Processing Differences and Subtest Scatter

Because the K-ABC contains both a measure of intellectual ability (represented by the Sequential Processing, Simultaneous Processing, and Mental Processing Composite scores) and a measure of academic achievement (represented by the Achievement subtest scores), examiners using the test are more likely to rely on the discrepancy between intellectual ability and academic achievement to make the diagnosis of learning disabilities. It is unlikely that an examiner would make the mistake of relying solely on cognitive subtest profiles or on the discrepancy between Simultaneous and Sequential Processing scores in making a diagnosis of learning disabilities. Examiners using the K-ABC should, of course, be aware of the amount of difference needed between the Simultaneous and Sequential Processing scores to reach statistical significance (i.e., the level needed to be confident that differences are not due to chance). A table in the K-ABC Administration and Scoring Manual provides standard score differences required for significance at each age level. The average difference required for significance for children between 2 years 6 months and 5 years is 14 points ($p < .05$), whereas an average difference of 12 points is required for statistical significance in children between 5 and 12 years 6 months. As with the WISC-III VIQ-PIQ discrepancy, a statistically significant discrepancy is not necessarily a clinically meaningful one. The average difference between Simultaneous and Sequential Processing standard scores is 12.3 points. Kaufman and Kaufman (1983) suggest that a 22-point discrepancy between Simultaneous and Sequential Processing "is unusual and denotes marked scatter" (p. 194).

As described earlier, research has provided inconsistent data regarding the size and direction of VIQ-PIQ discrepancies for children with learning disabilities. Research conducted so far with the K-ABC has been more consistent in demonstrating a difference between the Sequential and Simultaneous Scales for children with learning disabilities, with Sequential Processing standard scores averaging 2 to 5 points higher than the Simultaneous Processing scores. Further analysis has shown that children with learning disabilities "performed consistently well on Gestalt Closure, one of the purest measures of Simultaneous

Processing" and "tended to score most poorly on the Sequential Processing subtests" (Kaufman and Kaufman, 1983, p. 139).

KAIT Subtest Scatter and Profile Interpretation

The recent development of the KAIT makes interpretation uniquely difficult. Kaufman and Kaufman (1993) have proposed a method of interpretation primarily based upon clinical observation and clinical analysis of the subtest groupings. The examiner is advised to group subtests according to high and low scores, yet further details about how this procedure should be completed is not provided. The manual does provide several tables that classify subtests by shared abilities among the subtests and unique abilities of each of the subtests, which may be useful to the examiner experienced with the clinical interpretation of psychological testing data.

At present there are no research findings that would assist the clinician in determining a "learning disability profile" for adolescents or adults. The test manual does report on a small validity study with adolescents with reading disabilities. These subjects did not differ statistically from controls on any of the subtest scaled scores, though it is reported that this was the only clinical group study which exhibited a trend toward a difference between the fluid and Crystallized scales (about 8 points). While the KAIT has a number of clinically meaningful subtests, interpretation is currently made difficult by the limited amount of research information available.

Stanford-Binet Subtest Scatter and Discrepancy Among Areas

As is the case with the WISC-III, the Stanford-Binet does not appear to result in a "learning disabilities profile." While the developers of the test do not discuss this issue, results from a sample of 227 children with learning disabilities is presented in the *Technical Manual* (Thorndike, Hagen, & Sattler, 1986). The largest mean difference between any of the four areas measured (Verbal Reasoning, Abstract/Visual Reasoning, Quantitative Reasoning, and Short-Term Memory) was between Verbal Reasoning and Short-Term Memory, and was only 4.4 points. For an individual, a 4.4-point discrepancy between these two areas would not be significant. Thus, the differences among area scores does not appear to be useful in distinguishing children with learning disabilities from other children. The test developers do not discuss whether a greater amount of subtest scatter is obtained by children with learning disabilities versus other children.

Common Subtest Patterns Among Children
with Learning Disabilities

As described earlier, data obtained from cognitive profiles alone are not sufficient to make the diagnosis of learning disabilities. However, several patterns often show up in test protocols of students with learning disabilities. These patterns are not, however, sufficient to make a diagnosis of learning disability, attention deficit disorder, or other developmental disabilities. They are described here simply to help professionals understand possible difficulties that may underlie or exacerbate the condition of learning disability, and perhaps guide them in the selection of additional neuropsychological measures.

In looking for patterns within the subtest profile, one must keep in mind that, because of error of measurement, a subtest score that is one or two points below another subtest score may not represent a meaningful difference in abilities on the two tasks. Sattler (1992) suggests guidelines for determining significant strengths and weaknesses within an individual's WISC-III profile (pp. 1108–1122). A similar method for determining significant strengths and weaknesses within the K-ABC profile is described thoroughly in the K-ABC Manual. Examiners using the K-ABC should rely on this method for interpreting K-ABC results. The Stanford-Binet's *Examiner's Handbook* (Delaney & Hopkins, 1987) includes a chart for interpreting strengths and weaknesses within the profile (p. 87). The "inferred abilities and influences" identified within the profile are, however, based on "the judgment of the authors of this *Handbook* and their interpretation of research literature" (p. 85), and the validity of these interpretations remains questionable. Delaney and Hopkins recommend that inferences based on subtest strengths and weaknesses be confirmed or denied using qualitative data regarding the child.

In reviewing the WISC-III profile, the examiner should first make a comparison with the normative group by examining the child's scaled scores with respect to the normative data. A scaled score of 1 to 7 represents below normal performance, whereas a scaled score of 13 to 19 represents an above-normal level of performance. Following this procedure, the psychologist should find the mean of the Verbal subtest scores. Next, any Verbal subtest scores that are 3 or more points above this mean should be identified (these are the relative strengths) as well as any subtest scores that are 3 or more points below the mean (these are the relative weaknesses). This procedure should be repeated for the Performance subtest scores. In using this approach, it is clear that, for example, a subtest score of 10 may indicate a strength for one child but may indicate a weakness for another child. It is only the relative position of the subtest scores, not their absolute value, that is of interest in determining the child's profile of strengths and weaknesses.

In discussing patterns of strengths and weaknesses, Sattler (1992) suggests that significant strengths and weaknesses be examined in combination with the other scores that are relatively high or low for the individual. This may be easily accomplished with the WISC-III by comparing the scores a child achieves in each of the four factors (Kaufman, 1994). For example, the two new factors, the child's Processing Speed and Freedom from distractibility, may be examined directly by comparing these standard scores with those from the Verbal Comprehension and Perceptual Organization factors. As a general guideline, information available in Table 5–2 can be useful for interpretation. It is important to understand that the Processing Speed and Freedom from Distractibility factors should not be interpreted as independent estimates of intelligence (Sattler, 1992, p. 1048). Sattler and others emphasize that the patterns thus identified simply provide hypotheses for understanding the child's actual strengths and weaknesses. The examiner uses the identified patterns in conjunction with other information known about the child (e.g., from observation during testing, interviews with parents and teachers, and other testing results). It is recommended that the psychologist responsible for interpreting the WISC-III data familiarize himself or herself with Kaufman's (1979; 1994) and Sattler's (1992) approach for identifying patterns of strengths and weaknesses.

As noted earlier, several patterns appear frequently in the subtest profiles of students with learning disabilities. Again, it must be stressed that these patterns are not to be used to determine whether or not learning disabilities exist, but simply to help the examiner better understand the nature of any learning disabilities once they have been properly identified. The patterns described in the following paragraphs are ones we have seen frequently in children with learning disabilities. These patterns are by no means unique, however, to the child with learning disabilities.

EXCESSIVE DISTRACTIBILITY. The WISC-III subtests contributing to a pattern that suggests excessive distractibility are Arithmetic and Digit Span. The K-ABC subtests that are useful in diagnosing distractibility or short attention span are Magic Window, Face Recognition, Hand Movements, Number Recall, Word Order, and Spatial Memory. The KAIT subtests that may be affected by excessive distractibility include Auditory Comprehension, Rebus Learning, Logical Steps, Mystery Codes, and Memory for Block Designs. When patterns of weaknesses in these areas are observed, the examiner should make certain to question parents and teachers about possible evidence of attention-deficit/hyperactivity disorder at home and in the classroom. The examiner should also take special care to report any observation of distractibility or short attention span noted within the testing situation. It is not unusual, however, for students who appear to be attentive in the testing situation to have serious attention problems in the classroom. These children often demonstrate weaknesses on the subtest profiles for excessive distractibility, even when they do not exhibit attention problems in the one-on-one testing situation.

PLANNING ABILITY. A pattern of weakness on the WISC-III Picture Arrangement and Mazes subtests suggests that the student works somewhat impulsively, not taking time to plan before approaching a task. Especially on the Mazes subtest, a child who approaches a task impulsively will make many errors that, on this task, cannot be corrected after the student recognizes them. Although Kaufman does not list planning ability as one of the subtest patterns to be observed on the K-ABC, the examiner might observe signs of poor planning ability in the child's approach to the Photo Series subtest.

VERBAL EXPRESSION, VERBAL CONCEPT FORMATION, ABSTRACT THINKING. Many children with learning disabilities, especially those from upper socioeconomic groups, have relatively good verbal skills, as measured by the WISC-III Similarities, Vocabulary, and Comprehension subtests. Skills measured by these tests can be practiced in the context of every-day experiences (e.g., listening to adult conversations, asking and answering questions, discussing), and do not rely heavily on "school learning," especially in the younger grades. As the child with learning disabilities gets older, however, a drop in Vocabulary skills is sometimes observed, because more of one's vocabulary is derived from reading as one gets older. (Similarly, a drop in the Information subtest score is often seen as the child with learning disabilities grows older.)

On the K-ABC, verbal expression patterns are measured in a limited manner involving the Magic Window and Gestalt Closure subtests of the Mental Processing Scale, plus the Expressive Vocabulary, Faces & Places, Riddles, and Reading/Decoding subtests of the Achievement Scale. Verbal expression is also measured in a limited manner by all of the Crystallized subtests from the KAIT.

PERCEPTUAL ORGANIZATION. A pattern of relative strengths on those subtests that measure visual-spatial perception and organization (WISC-III Picture Completion, Picture Arrangement, Block Design, Object Assembly, and Mazes; or K-ABC Hand Movements, Gestalt Closure, Triangles, Matrix Analogies, Spatial Memory, and Photo Series; or KAIT Famous Faces and Mystery Codes) is often seen in children with learning disabilities. It should be noted, however, that this pattern is also often observed on the WISC-III for children without learning disabilities, but from culturally different environments. As discussed previously, many of the skills measured on the WISC-III Verbal subtests are those which are encouraged by discussion with adults, listening to adult conversation, asking and answering questions, and so forth. In environments where the amount and quality of language stimulation is limited, Verbal subtest scores may be artificially deflated, thus causing many of the Performance subtest scores (which are less influenced by environmental stimulation) to appear as relative strengths.

VISUAL PERCEPTION OF ABSTRACT STIMULI. A pattern of weakness on the WISC-III Block Design and Coding subtests or on the K-ABC Triangles and Matrix Analogies is often seen in children with learning disabilities, especially those whose disability appears to be due to weaknesses in spatial perception, not auditory processing. It is speculated that these are the children who often continue to reverse letters and words long after their peers have stopped, and have difficulty recognizing visual configurations of words that cannot be "sounded out" (e.g., often confusing *though, tough, through*, and *thorough*).

ABILITY TO REPRODUCE A MODEL. A pattern of weakness on the WISC-III Block Design and Coding subtests can also indicate an inability to reproduce a model. This can be due to poor fine- motor skills rather than to poor ability to correctly process visual perception of stimuli. The K-ABC "Reproduction of a Model" pattern includes the Hand Movements, Number Recall, Triangles, and Spatial Memory subtests. These subtests measure ability to reproduce a model in a variety of modalities—orally, motorically, by pointing, and with manipulative materials. Fine-motor skills are less important in the K-ABC pattern than in the WISC-III pattern. Attention and memory factors are, however, somewhat more heavily tapped by the K-ABC pattern, as several of the subtests require the child to reproduce a model *from memory*.

Individual students with learning disabilities will, of course, exhibit many other patterns of strength and weakness, depending on their individual abilities, backgrounds, and educational experiences. The patterns listed are presented merely to remind examiners of some of the most common patterns observed in students with learning disabilities so that they can be "on the lookout" for them.

Social and Cultural Aspects of Test Interpretation

In sampling the child's behavior with psychological tests, the examiner has an opportunity to obtain a behavioral sample under a variety of different circumstances. It is the psychologist's role to integrate findings across these dimensions of cognitive and psychosocial functioning to arrive at a composite picture of the individual child. Important in understanding these dimensions of the individual is the qualitative analysis of the child's emotional and cognitive functioning. This process begins from the psychologist's first contact with the parent and child. We have previously noted how it is an important clinical practice to interview the parent and child at the onset of the evaluation process. It is equally important to remember that the interviewing of the child continues throughout the formal testing experience. For example, the examiner has an opportunity to observe how the child expresses frustration regarding his or her performance on the intelligence subtests. Frustrations and the content of particular test items often provoke emotional responses that could not be elicited in the initial clinical interview, allowing for subsequent inquiry with the child about cultural and life experiences.

Results from the evaluation of emotional status can and are quantifiable with systems such as Exner and Weiner's (1994) Comprehensive System for the Rorschach (1994) and Roberts' system for the Roberts Apperception Test for Children (1994). Unfortunately, the systems for examining social and emotional functioning do not as readily lend themselves to the quantitative systems such as those currently in place for measures of cognitive functioning. Thus, clinical interpretation of these measures occurs as a result of the training and experience of the psychologist and cannot be undertaken in an actuarial manner.

It is important that all sources of social and emotional functioning be carefully examined. These sources include not only the clinical interviews, behavioral observations, and personality tests, but the quantitative information available in behavioral questionnaires completed by parents and teachers. While these provide a valuable source of information, they too should be interpreted with caution, as attributional biases of the person completing the questionnaire cannot be directly examined. Yet, much as with results from intelligence tests, all of these sources of information help the psychologist generate hypotheses about behavior that can be compared with and complemented by the hypotheses generated in intelligence testing. For example, a hypothesis about attentional difficulties based on findings from test observation and the WISC-III Freedom from Distractibility score should be examined with results from the CBCL factors associated with attentional deficits. A hypothesis about anxiety should be examined in light of the child's failures on power tests such as the K-ABC and themes related to anxiety in his or her performance on personality tests.

Perhaps most difficult to interpret is the effect that the child's sociocultural experience may be having on test performance. Knowledge of the child's culture and observations by the examiner can lead to further questions for the family regarding the role of culture on test performance of an individual child. Cultural differences may also impact on interpretation of questions, such as those in the CBCL, or personality measures. Simply asking parents to complete behavioral questionnaires may present a cultural barrier, owing to language differences and the ideas underlying such a behavioral questionnaire. Likewise, requiring the child to sit at a table and work on activities may be culturally discrepant from the child's previous learning experiences. Interpreting responses from the child and family depends on the psychologist gaining an understanding of these facets of the sociocultural context. Research findings have not been forthcoming, owing to the myriad of difficulties in operationalizing sociocultural variables.

CONCLUSION

The psychologist provides a valuable contribution to the interdisciplinary diagnostic process by obtaining a history of the child's difficulties (from the parents' perspective), an accurate measurement of intelligence, social and emotional functioning, as well as supplemental information that will assist in understanding the nature of any learning disabilities that might be identified. The assessment instruments used by the psychologist must be reliable and valid and meet other specific criteria outlined in this chapter. The approach to test administration is also a critical issue, as many children with learning disabilities will exhibit behaviors that typically interfere with testing. Test interpretation for children with learning disabilities should be founded on research-based principles, not on misconceived views of the "typical" child's cognitive profile.

The interdisciplinary team must, of course, rely on test data in diagnosing learning disabilities. It is important, though, that team members understand that tests are merely instruments to assist in the process of diagnosis. The data should be used cautiously and only in conjunction with information about the student that has been obtained through the other sources available.

CHAPTER 6

Educational Evaluation

Judith Margolis
Barbara K. Keogh

Assessment has become a major enterprise in American schools. There are many purposes for assessment and many approaches or techniques which may be used. The effectiveness and the usefulness of assessment information depends, in part, on how well the purposes and the methods are matched. For example, it would be inappropriate to use a simple screening test to diagnose learning disabilities. Similarly, it would be inappropriate to assess a learning disabled child's vocabulary with a test of visual-motor skills.

DIFFERENCES BETWEEN PSYCHOLOGICAL AND EDUCATIONAL ASSESSMENTS

Within schools are two major assessment approaches: psychological and educational. They differ in several important ways and both contribute to our understanding of learning disabilities. In the preceding chapter Annett and Aylward discussed how the psychologist provides information regarding a child's cognitive functioning as well as information that helps rule out other conditions and explain the nature of the disabilities. In this chapter we will look at some of the approaches and utility of educational testing and its relation to psychological testing.

A major purpose of psychological assessment is to describe the psychological processes which are thought to underlie the achievement problems of children with learning disabilities, particularly the level of cognitive functioning. A major purpose of educational evaluation is to provide a differentiated and detailed picture of a child with learning disabilities in selected subject matter areas. Thus, psychological assessments are designed to describe basic, underlying processes such as memory, verbal reasoning, and attention. Educational assessments are subject-matter based, are focused on specific achievement areas such as reading, arithmetic, and spelling, and their subskills or components (e.g., arithmetic computation, word recognition). Both psychological and educational assessments are essential in establishing a discrepancy between ability and achievement.

Educational and psychological assessments typically differ in administrative conditions and procedures. Psychological tests usually are individually administered out of the classroom; educational testing is usually conducted in classrooms to individuals or groups, although individual testing is necessary when making decisions about children with learning disabilities. Psychological testing is restricted to administration and interpretation by psychologists; educational tests generally are administered by classroom teachers. Psychological evaluation is often limited to a few sessions; educational evaluation tends to be on-going and cumulative over time. Psychological tests, particularly tests of intelligence, are standardized and norm-referenced; educational tests may be norm-referenced but are often criterion-referenced and nonstandardized, although many standardized tests are available for use in establishing an ability-achievement discrepancy or in establishing a level of achievement in comparison to a norm group.

Tests are only one type of assessment, however, and both psychologists and teachers regularly use a whole range of techniques, including classroom observations, interviews, rating scales, and informal measures. However, the differences in educational and psychological approaches and the kind of information gained from each underscore the importance of appropriate applications and interpretations. Effective identification and intervention planning for children with learning disabilities requires information from both. In this chapter we focus specifically on educational assessment.

EDUCATIONAL ASSESSMENT

Information gleaned from educational assessment may be used in several ways: for determining eligibility for special education services; for instructional planning and monitoring; and for providing summary information about individual children, groups of children, or school districts. Sound educational assessment should yield a comprehensive picture of children's performance in the major subject matter or content areas and should provide direction for program planning, including remedial efforts or other special instructional requirements. It can also yield information about children's behavior in learning situations and about individual differences in learning styles. A number of specific methods or techniques are used commonly in educational assessment. In this chapter we have somewhat arbitrarily selected illustrative examples of widely used tests and other assessment instruments.

Standardized Achievement and Diagnostic Tests

A number of educational tests have been developed within a psychometric tradition, and like other psychometrically based measures, many have good technical qualities. Such tests typically represent major test construction efforts, including standardization on large samples assumed to represent the average or modal achievements of children within given age or grade groups. In general, the characteristics of standardized tests include specified and controlled procedures for administration, including time limitations; standardized procedures for scoring; and quantitative, normative scores presented in standard scores, percentiles, and grade or age equivalents. The normative information allows scores for individual children or groups of children to be compared; the normative information also allows comparisons across schools, school districts, and over time. For the purpose of diagnosing a learning disability, normative data also allow comparison of children's cognitive ability with their actual educational achievement.

Standardized tests may be administered individually or to groups, and vary in the breadth of material covered. Some provide information across different subject matter areas, others are focused exclusively on a single subject, for example, mathematics or reading. The format of many of the comprehensive test batteries allows selection of subsections which may be administered separately. Most comprehensive tests yield profiles of scores, thus affording comparisons of a given child's relative achievement in different subjects. Frequently children with learning disabilities have discrepancies across achievement areas, so that math scores may be markedly higher than reading scores, or arithmetic computation may be discrepant from arithmetic reasoning. A sampling of achievement in different subjects allows preliminary examination of the pattern of strengths and weaknesses and thus provides useful information.

Well-known examples of standardized achievement tests which may be administered to groups of children include the California Achievement Tests (CAT-5, 1992), the Comprehensive Tests of Basic Skills (CTBS-4, 1990), the Iowa Tests of Basic Skills (ITBS, 1993), the Metropolitan Achievement Tests (MAT-7, 1992), and the SRA Achievement Series (SAT-7, 1978). These comprehensive batteries are from established publishers and have been developed with sound statistical procedures, including sampling and norming considerations. They are generally of good technical quality and provide a range of scores. They are useful in educational assessment when the purpose is to determine relative standing of children, groups of children, and school systems. They do not provide detailed information about how solutions are reached or what processes or steps are used in deriving the answers. It is difficult to use information from these tests for instructional purposes, nor do they provide the kind of in-depth information necessary for the diagnosis of learning disabilities.

A number of standardized tests are individually administered and yield diagnostic data in specific subject matter areas. Such tests apply primarily to the basic skill areas of reading, math, and language arts. Well-known examples of standardized diagnostic tests for reading include the Woodcock Reading Mastery Tests—Revised (1987), the Stanford Diagnostic Reading Test (SDRT-4, 1995), the Gates-McKillop-Horowitz Reading Diagnostic Test (1989), and the Gray Oral Reading Test (GORT-3, 1992). The Durrell Analysis of Reading Difficulty (1980), a test with a long history, taps 16 areas, which include oral reading, silent reading, listening comprehension, word recognition, word analysis, listening vocabulary, phonic spelling of words, and visual memory of words.

The two most widely used norm-referenced diagnostic instruments for math assessment are the KeyMath—Revised (KM-R, 1988), and the Stanford Diagnostic Mathematics Test-4 (1995). Both tests assess the same skill areas, are technically adequate, easy to administer, and provide a good measure of strengths and weakness in mathematic skill and concept areas. The primary difference between the two is that the Stanford is designed to be group administered while the KeyMath-R is individually administered. Since the KeyMath-R requires almost no reading or writing ability it may provide a more accurate measure of math ability for children with learning disabilities.

A number of well developed and technically adequate tests assess educational performance across subject matter domains. The comprehensive tests are widely used in the identification of children with learning disabilities. They are individually administered, have good psychometric properties, and in some cases at least, have been normed using samples from different ethnic and language groups. Detailed reviews of many currently used assessment instruments may be found in two recent monographs, *Assessment for the 1990s* (Reeve, 1989–1990) and *Handbook of Psychological and Educational Assessment of Children* (Reynolds & Kamphaus, 1992). Because they so often provide the educational component in the aptitude-achievement discrepancy formulae, three illustrative tests are described here.

Kaufman Test of Educational Achievement (K-TEA)

The K-TEA comes in two forms, the Comprehensive Form (CF) and the Brief Form (BF). Although the two forms have the same name, they are quite different in comprehensiveness and technical adequacy and therefore should not be used interchangeably. Whereas the Brief Form is acceptable for screening, the Comprehensive Form is suggested for deriving standardized scores (i.e., percentile ranks, stanines, and normal curve equivalents) and for assessing a child's strengths and weaknesses in reading, math, and spelling. The internal consistency of the subtests is adequate, although the test-retest findings as presented in the manual are likely spuriously high since they were arrived at by combining the test results of a relatively small number of subjects (172) into two broad groups; one group for grades 1 through 6 and the other for grades 7 through 12. Bands of error for different confidence intervals are presented for math, reading, spelling, and battery composite, and range from 2 (grade 2) to 5 (grades 8, 10, and 12) at the 68% confidence level. The norming procedures were exceptionally good, being stratified within each grade level by sex, geographic region, socioeconomic status, and racial and ethnic group representation. Importantly, the racial and ethnic composition of the sample closely approximates that of the U.S. population at all grades.

Peabody Individual Achievement Test—Revised (PIAT-R)

The 1989 revision of the popular PIAT retains much of the format, structure, and administrative procedures of the original tests but is considerably changed so that it is psychometrically a better test. In addition to increasing the number of items in each subtest (Knowledge, Reading, Math, and Spelling) a Written Expression subtest has been added, and scoring procedures have been revised. The inclusion of a Written Expression subtest is in line with current concern for assessment in this domain. The new scoring procedures provide a range of options for interpreting children's performance in terms of interindividual and intraindividual differences. All subtests, with the exception of Written Expression, are scored objectively and raw scores can be converted to developmental scores, standard scores, and percentiles. The new Written Expression subtest is scored subjectively following directions found in the manual.

The norming sample is adequate in numbers at each grade and age level and in stratification in accordance with socioeconomic and ethnic and racial proportion in the population. Interesting is that although the PIAT-R is recommended for program development and evaluation for children with disabilities, no effort was made to include children in special education classes in the norming sample. Test-retest reliability reported in the manual is high for subtests and for composite scores at all ages with the exception of age 12. Internal consistency coefficients are also high. An important new addition is the inclusion of standard error of measurement (SEM) tables for all subtest and composite scores, resulting in a more precise estimate of a child's performance than was possible with the old form of the PIAT.

Validity of the PIAT-R is less well documented. In a review of the PIAT-R, Lazarus, McKenna and Lynch (1989–1990) report that those being assessed are sometimes required to respond to questions posed in a manner quite different from that commonly used in classrooms; therefore, children may know the content but be unsure of what they are asked to do. Lazarus, McKenna, and Lynch also criticize the reading comprehension subtest on the ground that it is not constructed to take into account contemporary conceptualizations of the reading process. Although the PIAT-R is a well-standardized test and includes a broad range of academic tasks, the test author emphasizes that the PIAT-R was not designed as a diagnostic test or as a method to provide a precise measure of the content areas addressed. Rather, the PIAT-R may be viewed better as a screening test for identifying children's strengths and weaknesses relevant to educational and career goals.

Woodcock Johnson Psychoeducational Battery—Revised (WJ-R)

The 1989 revision represents a substantial modification of the original test. Although the WJ-R consists of two sections (Tests of Cognitive Ability and Tests of Achievement), for the purpose of this review only the achievement battery will be discussed. The authors of the WJ-R have added 4 new tests, making a total of 14 tests, 9 of which make up the standard battery. Alternate forms are available. The norming sample was based on the most recent U.S. census data according to region, community size, sex, race, and socioeconomic status. However, stratification is not reported by age or grade level and only the timed subtests were examined for stability (test-retest reliability). For the standard battery 46% of the age by subtests correlations reported are below the accepted level (r = .90). Sufficiently high reliabilities are reported, however, for the Broad Achievement Clusters, allowing the test to be used in determining an ability-achievement discrepancy. The less than adequate reliabilities for subtest scores suggest caution in using these scores for making educational decisions.

The content validity of the WJ-R, based on correlations with criterion measures (BASIS, KTEA), varies by subtest, the bulk of coefficients being in the .50s to .60s range. Similar findings are reported for the cluster scores, although the Reading Cluster correlations are, in general, more robust (r in the .80s) when compared to other reading measures. Comparison of test scores of children who are gifted, learning disabled, mentally retarded, and nondisabled yields expected differences, arguing for the validity of the test for identification purposes. It is important to note, however, that children with learning disabilities may score lower than expected on the cognitive battery of the WJ-R. This, of course, would affect the size of the discrepancy between aptitude and achievement as measured with the WJ-R.

A recent addition to the family of Woodcock tests is the Woodcock-McGrew-Werder Mini-Battery of Achievement (MBA, 1994). This brief test offers subtests in the basic skills of reading, writing, mathematics, and factual knowledge. Since 90% of the items in this screening measure are drawn directly from the WJ-R battery, it is not surprising that the Mini-Battery correlates highly with the complete WJ-R. The high correlations between the Mini-Battery and the WJ-R may suggest to some that this is a quick alternative to the long and rather tedious scoring required in the complete battery. Note, however, that brief tests present too few items in each skill area to be valid measures of what a child really knows. This is particularly true for children with learning disabilities, who are known to have uneven patterns of learning. The Mini-Battery of Achievement might well be used as a quick screen to identify those children who need further assessment. The short form, however, should not be used as a replacement for the complete WJ-R Tests of Achievement.

Choosing and Using Standardized Tests

Two important considerations when choosing a standardized achievement tests are the reliability of the test and its validity and objectivity. Anastasi (1961) defined reliability as the "consistency of scores obtained by the same persons when retested with the identical test or with an equivalent form of the test" (p. 28). Most commonly used achievement tests have reasonably high test-retest and internal consistency scores.

A second important aspect of test selection has to do with validity. Does the test measure what it purports to test? Does the content adequately represent the subject matter area being assessed? Are the norms appropriate for the cultural and language background of the pupils being tested? Selection of an educational test requires going beyond the name of the test to consider the scope and relevance of the content. Many tests have "face validity." They have the right names and the content appears appropriate, yet close examination may reveal that the items are limited in scope or may not accurately represent the subject matter presumably being assessed. A test of reading comprehension may in fact be made up of items tapping only word recognition, or a test of arithmetic reasoning may be heavily weighted with computational problems. Closely related, the validity of a test of achievement in one subject matter area may be confounded because of problems in another. For example, the accuracy or validity of an arithmetic test may be threatened because the items are presented as word problems; thus, measurement of a child's competence in arithmetic computation may be inaccurate because of his or her level of skill in reading.

A test is merely a sample of behavior, and to be a valid sample it must contain a sufficient number of items to allow a judgment about a child's level of performance. Abbreviated tests and short forms may save administration time but result in less than adequate assessment of achievement. An example is the Wide Range Achievement Test—Revision 3 (WRAT-3, 1993) which has only a limited number of items in each subject matter domain (reading, arithmetic, spelling). In addition, the reading section assesses only word recognition and the arithmetic section only simple computation. The limited content restricts interpretation, and has led to a number of challenges to the use of any edition of the WRAT as the achievement component in the computation of a discrepancy. Similarly, in a review Doll (1990) concluded that there are not enough items in the Kaufman Test of Educational Achievement (K-TEA) at the first grade level to reliably differentiate children with learning disabilities from children with other disabilities. This, of course, suggests caution in interpreting KTEA results in the early school years.

Measurement Problems in Establishing a Discrepancy

The use of standardized tests in the identification of learning disabilities is of particular interest. Recall that a major definitional requirement in learning disabilities is a discrepancy between ability and achievement. This is a defensible distinction in theory, but one which has many practical and operational problems. Problems are due, in part, to the technical limitations of the actual tests used, including errors of measurement inherent in standardized measures, and in part to the strong association between ability and achievement. Thus, it is sometimes difficult to determine if a particular test is really a measure of aptitude and ability or of learning and achievement.

Three important factors must be considered when choosing a standardized achievement test in order to establish a discrepancy between cognitive ability and academic performance. These are the reliability of the test, its validity, and the cognitive test to which it is being compared (see Chapters 4 and 5 for discussion of cognitive tests appropriately used for identification of children with learning disabilities). Another important consideration in identifying a discrepancy is measurement error. The estimated error (the standard error of measurement) is an important statistic for the test user to include in determining a discrepancy between measures. Since test scores always contain some error, the score obtained by a child on any test consists of his or her true score plus the error present in the test. Because the true score is unknown, the standard error of measurement (SEM) provides a range of scores within which the true score probably falls. Thus, if a child obtains a score of 72 and the SEM is 10, with a 68% confidence criterion, the true score likely falls between 62 and 82. The smaller the SEM for a particular test, the more confidence the examiner can have in the obtained score.

The good news in computing a discrepancy is that the SEM for most standardized tests is reported in the technical manuals. The bad news is that different SEMs may apply for different ages and grades, and for different subtest or cluster scores. A given test may have a small band of error for grades 4 through 6 but have a large error band in grades 1 through 3, making it a good test for use in the upper grades but a poor choice for use with primary level children. Similarly, a particular test may have a small SEM in reading and a large SEM in arithmetic, making it a reliable test in one subject area but not for another. These differences underscore the importance of careful examination of the technical aspects of a test when making decisions about individual pupils.

It is important to note, too, that discrepancy scores are usually less reliable than the scores from each of the two tests being compared. Said differently, the standard error of measurement of the discrepancy score will be larger than the SEM for either the cognitive or the achievement score. Why? Because the reliability between the scores on two tests is a function of the reliability of test A, the reliability of test B, the correlation between tests A and B, and differences in the norming groups for each test. Let us assume that we have carefully chosen the cognitive and the achievement tests so that each has good reliability ($r = .90$). Using one of several accepted formulae for calculating the standard error of measurement of a difference score (see Thorndike, 1963, or Stake & Wardrop, 1971), we will find that the discrepancy score has a larger SEM than either of the two tests. We may infer, then, that the discrep-

ancy score is more variable (has a broader band of scores) than either of
the tests separately. The reliability of the discrepancy score may be improved by using more reliable tests of intelligence and of achievement,
by using tests normed on the same population, or both.

Limitation of Standardized Assessment

Before going on to a discussion of other approaches to educational
assessment, we wish to emphasize that a number of factors may affect
an individual child's performance. Standardized administrations, especially group tests, may present particular problems for children with
learning disabilities, thus raising questions about the accuracy and the
interpretability of results. For example, poor motivation, lack of interest or of confidence, difficulties in understanding and following directions, and limited familiarity with test taking may lower performance
and lead to underestimation of children's knowledge and skills. Time
limitations may also depress the performance of children with learning
disabilities. Similarly, because curricula for children with learning disabilities may differ from the instructional content provided children in
regular education, the material covered in standardized tests may not
overlap the content of instruction. Although test developers attempt to
separate language and reading ability from measures of arithmetic,
these are not entirely independent. Thus, problems in reading may influence how a pupil performs on a standardized arithmetic test. These
influences may be particularly important when assessing children with
learning disabilities from nonmajority cultural or linguistic backgrounds. The language demands may be troublesome and the content
of the test may be unfamiliar, but also cultural differences in how children interact with adults, or even prior experience in test taking may
depress or distort performance.

Finally, the use of tests that are inconsistent with a child's cultural
and language background poses a threat to validity, as the norms for
most achievement tests assume similarity of opportunity. From an applied perspective, the normative sample used in test development is an
important consideration in test selection. Test results are only as good
as the tests from which they are derived. Educational tests are essential
in the identification and diagnosis of children with learning disabilities,
and a number of tests meet the requirement of technical adequacy and
provide a comprehensive picture of children's patterns of achievement.
Tests that yield inconsistent and variable scores, that do not tap appropriate and relevant subject matter domains, or that are based on incomplete or inadequate norming samples do not provide a solid basis
for identifying children with learning disabilities. Decisions about test

selection should not be made on the basis of availability and popularity, but rather on the soundness of the measure, on the reasons or purposes for testing, and on the appropriateness of the test for the individuals being tested. These decisions can be made only when the tester has a thorough understanding of the test, its psychometric properties, and its limitations.

ASSESSMENT FOR INSTRUCTION

To this point we have focused on the use of tests to determine eligibility for learning-disabilities services. Another major purpose of educational assessment is to provide information for instructional planning. Norm-referenced tests have limited utility for this purpose, and there have been a number of efforts to develop formal tests that provide closer links to school curricula. These are usually referred to as performance-based approaches and may be either commercially prepared or teacher-made. Assessments that include collection of instructionally relevant data other than norm-referenced scores are generally considered informal assessments.

Informal assessment is probably as old as teaching itself, and is accepted as an essential step in educational evaluation. Teachers use informal techniques to gather information useful in planning or modifying instruction on a day-by-day basis. Informal assessment procedures range from casual and unstructured to systematic and structured. Examples include weekly spelling or math quizzes, rating scales, skills inventories, checklists, or observations. Many techniques are teacher-developed and specific to particular classrooms. Most allow for flexibility of administration and interpretation.

The case for the use of informal procedures with children with learning disabilities is particularly strong, as these children are characterized by idiosyncratic patterns of performance. Not only are they different from their normally achieving peers, they are different from each other. Their unique patterns of learning often result in gaps in knowledge and in uneven problem-solving skills and strategies. These "peaks and valleys" are often lost in the summary information provided by formal testing. Sensitive and powerful remedial planning requires detailed pinpointing of the nature of the difficulties. This kind of assessment is carried out often informally by skilled teachers, but may be systemized with the use of commercially prepared inventories, checklists, and behavior rating scales, and through observation. Criterion-referenced approaches are designed to test commonly taught objectives and many good commercially prepared instruments are available.

Criterion-Referenced Tests

Criterion-referenced tests (CRTs) and procedures are aimed at assessing information that is closely tied to the content of instruction. Formal and commercially prepared CRTs assess skill areas generally taught in "typical" school curricula. Terminal skills are task analyzed to produce a hierarchy of subskills and arranged in sequential order so that a child can be assessed in relation to mastery of that skill. CRTs may be particularly useful in the assessment of children with learning disabilities, who often have uneven profiles of learning and achievement. CRTs direct teachers to where in the skill sequence to begin instruction and what components to emphasize. Like other assessment approaches, CRTs differ markedly in technical adequacy, scope, and in requirement of administration.

The Brigance Diagnostic Inventories is a well-known and widely used commercial CRT. There are four Brigance batteries ranging in level from prekindergarten to Grade 12: the Inventory of Early Development—Revised (1991), for children with developmental ages under 7 years; the Diagnostic Inventory of Basic Skills (1977), for children functioning from first through sixth grades; the Diagnostic Comprehensive Inventory of Basic Skills (1983), for kindergarten through grade 9; and The Diagnostic Inventory of Essential Skills (1981), for use with grades 4 through 12. Reviewers note that the Brigance scales are useful for assessing young children's mastery of specific educational objectives, but also note the lack of information regarding reliability and validity. The strength of the Brigance scales lies in their close links to the content of intervention and in their clinical applicability, rather than to the quantitative findings they yield.

Recently, some of the more widely used commercially prepared CRTs have included norms so that they can be used as full-service tests to identify children with learning disabilities. These include the Multilevel Academic Survey Test (MAST, 1985) and the Basic Achievement Skills Individual Screener (BASIS, 1982).

Critique of Criterion-Referenced Tests (CRTs)

Although formal CRTs are useful in providing information on mastery of skills within broad content areas, they do have limitations. First, schools have different curricula, and skills are not always taught in the same sequence as presented on the test; thus, it can be expected that some children will do poorly on the tests although achieve adequately in class. Second, the number of items selected is limited due to constraints of administration time; it is conceivable and likely that a child with learning disabilities might know the material in one example but not in another. When CRTs are used to examine achievement, the question of curriculum match, along with the reliability of the limited sample of items to assess skills areas, must be considered.

Curriculum-Based Assessment and Measurement

Curriculum-based assessment (CBA) is an example of a criterion-referenced approach, which is specific to a given curriculum or class-room instructional program. CBA procedures assess children's performance within the context of the actual curriculum being taught. The purpose of CBA is to identify specific instructional needs. Accordingly, CBAs may include a range of classroom-based assessment techniques, including weekly spelling or chapter review tests. Although some applications of CBA are relatively unstructured and informal, the trend is toward more precise, prescribed procedures. Blankenship and Lilly (1981), Howell and Moorehead (1987), and Salvia and Hughes (1990), as examples, have developed somewhat different approaches based on common principles underlying CBA. First, the procedures are administered in the classroom and test items are drawn directly from the curriculum, and, therefore, are context-specific. Second, the assessment is ongoing. Direct and frequent measures of a child's performance on a series of sequentially arranged objectives are charted; this information is the basis for instructional planning. Finally, the assessments are peer referenced so that data are interpreted in relation to the performance of classmates of similar age, sociocultural, and school experience.

A well known structured approach to CBA is the Curriculum-Based Measurement (CBM) system developed by Deno (Deno & Fuchs, 1987). CBM is not a test in the traditional sense, but rather is a set of evaluation procedures that allow monitoring progress toward a specified curricular goal. The prescribed procedures specify test duration, frequency of administration, procedures for scoring, and rules for summarizing and evaluating assessment information. Both the content and the pace of instruction are continuously modified in response to the identified relationships between daily performance and anticipated progress. The validity, reliability, and objectivity of measurement is stressed in this system as in many other CBA approaches.

Strengths and Limitations of CBA

Whether formal or informal, CBA approaches differ from standardized norm-referenced tests in several important ways that are relevant to learning disabilities. The procedures are administered in the classroom and are based on the curriculum in that classroom. Assessment is ongoing and continuous (rather than semester- or year-end assessment) and information is gathered on a day-by-day basis. The detailed, context-based assessment data allow examination of specific skills and processes used in problem solving. Finally, the assessment data can be interpreted in relation to the performance of classmates, allowing inferences that a given child's underachievement constitutes a deficit in learning, although the reason for this deficit may not be a specific learning disability. Detailed description of CBA may be found in the November, 1985, issue of *Exceptional Children*.

Adherents of CBA argue that the approach is effective with children with learning disabilities as it pinpoints specific problem areas and allows teachers to implement different instructional approaches while systematically monitoring effectiveness. CBA proponents also suggest that many learning problems are curriculum-based rather than child-based, and are due to ineffective and imprecise instructional goals and methods rather than to deficits in children's abilities. These are appealing points when applied to children with learning disabilities. CBA is not without critics, however, and serious questions about its utility and appropriateness have been raised (Heshusius, 1991). Major criticisms have to do with the limited scope of CBA curricula and, thus, with the content of assessment; with the almost total control of the content and sequence of material to be learned; with the quantitative, measurement-driven emphasis; and with the lack of attention to broader and more complex aspects of learning and learning processes.

Observation

Observation is a direct method of assessment as it involves documenting behavior in the context in which it occurs. This reduces the inferential leaps required in interpreting test scores and allows a close relationship between assessment and intervention decisions. Observation techniques are frequently used to assess learning disabled children's social and classroom behaviors, and to identify behaviors which may disrupt or interfere with learning. Observation may also be useful in describing learning styles and problem-solving skills, and in diagnosing specific problem areas. Observations may be categorized as systematic or nonsystematic.

Casual or nonsystematic observation occurs naturally in classrooms and yields anecdotal, subjective information that can provide teachers with important diagnostic information. An experienced teacher can pinpoint problems in word analysis by observing and recording during oral reading sessions, or can identify a carrying or borrowing problem in arithmetic by watching the child attempt a series of simple numerical problems. One advantage of informal observation is that it allows the teacher to reach a tentative conclusion quickly and to try out remedial techniques, thus reducing the chances that the errors will be practiced or the problems compounded. On the negative side, unsystematic observation may not provide a clear or complete picture of a child's problems, as the observer may be overly sensitive to certain behaviors and ignore or be unaware of others. The possible effect of bias is real when observations are unsystematic.

Observer bias is lessened when more systematic approaches are taken. An important aspect of systematic observation is that the procedures are preplanned, performed in an explicit, prescribed manner, and the data are analyzed objectively. A number of behavioral observation systems and recording forms are available and are appropriately used with children with learning disabilities. They range from relatively brief and global "snapshots" to continuous, detailed, and comprehensive recording of specific behaviors. Examples include the Critical Incidence Log (Sugai, 1985) and the Code for Instructional Structure and Student Academic Response (CISSAR, 1978).

One of the most common methods included in systematic observation systems is frequency recording—how many times a particular behavior occurs within a specified time frame. The number and breadth of the time frame and the specific behaviors to record vary according to the nature of the problems under study. Guerin and Maier (1983) have detailed three types of observational techniques in addition to frequency recording: chronologs, sequence samples, and trait samples. All may be used by teachers in classrooms. *Chronologs* involve objective observations recorded at different times of day and in a variety of settings. Data include details about time, activity, location, and who is present. The approach is useful when attempting to determine the situations or events that elicit maladaptive behavior. Sequence sampling is situation-based, and requires recording the conditions and behaviors that precede and follow problem behaviors. In *trait sampling* the observer identifies a global characteristic, or "trait," divides the characteristic into more specific and objective behaviors, and identifies specific exemplars of each category. A broad descriptor like aggression might be defined as physical or verbal, or as acts against persons or property. These categories in turn would be divided into specific behaviors which could be observed objectively, for example, hitting or kicking another child, swearing at the teacher, or tearing up work books.

Whatever the specific method or approach adopted, we underscore the utility of observational information in understanding and planning interventions for children with learning disabilities. Systematic observations can provide an objective and differentiated picture of strengths and weaknesses. Observations conducted in the classroom provide information that links the problems to the context in which the problems occur. This is especially important for children with learning disabilities, as the inconsistencies in their skills and achievements make them particularly vulnerable to the impact of instructional techniques and to classroom organization and demands.

Inventories, Rating Scales, and Checklists

In addition to detailed behavioral observations in children with learning disabilities, impressions of children's abilities and problems are often gathered using checklists, rating scales, and inventories. Very often the techniques may be used in conjunction with one another. For example, a checklist of types of errors common in oral reading might be used with an informal reading inventory, or a checklist might be used to identify problems to be targeted in classroom observation. Inventories and checklists are often subject-specific. Well-constructed reading inventories frequently include items that specify skills in word definition, recall of facts, main ideas, and the like. Long-time favorites with teachers, the newly revised Classroom Reading Inventory (1994) and the Analytic Reading Inventory (1995), provide guidance in documenting which reading skills have not yet been mastered and determining the independent, instructional, and frustration level in reading.

Subject-matter inventories may be teacher-developed or commercially prepared [e.g., Enright Diagnostic Inventory of Basic Arithmetic (1983), Spellmaster Assessment System (1987), or Let's Talk Inventory for Children (1987)]. They all provide a direct and relatively simple way of describing children's component skills or problem areas. One limitation is, of course, that the components identified are restricted to those contained in the particular inventory, and thus important aspects of a learning problem may be overlooked. In addition, the accuracy of the information may be affected by the level of the teacher's experience and knowledge of the subject matter.

Rating scales are commonly used to describe behavioral indicators of problems such as inattention, inability to follow directions, poor social skills, and other personal, even stylistic characteristics. Rating scales are sometimes used as a way of monitoring the effects of medical interventions (e.g., stimulant medications in children with attention-deficit/hyperactivity disorder) or of behavior modification programs. As with inventories and checklists, rating scales can be useful in educational evaluation, but they also are restricted by the range or scope of content covered and by potential inaccuracies related to rater bias or to limited knowledge of the child or situation. Examples of widely used and psychometrically well-founded scales are the Revised Behavior Problem Checklist (Revised, 1987), the Child Behavior Checklist (1991), and the School Situation Questionnaire (1987).

Portfolio Assessment

Portfolio assessment is an example of a recent performance-based approach resulting from the current movement away from norm-referenced assessment toward ongoing classroom-based measurement (Black, 1993). Similar in concept to an artist's or writer's portfolio, educational portfolios showcase a pupil's talents, accomplishments, and progress on an ongoing basis. Stated somewhat differently, portfolios are the qualitative counterpart of the quantitative data gleaned from criterion- and curriculum-based tests and other assessment procedures.

The purpose of portfolio assessment is to show how children's competencies develop. Portfolios can include such things as attitudes surveys, interest inventories, lists of books read, summaries of teacher observations, photographs of projects in various phases of completion, and tapes of oral reading and work samples that demonstrate emerging and learned skills.

At present there is strong support for using portfolio assessment with children with learning disabilities, as the content of the portfolio can be linked to the goals established in the child's Individual Educational Plan (IEP). The wide use of portfolios for reading assessment was recently endorsed in a position paper issued by the International Reading Association, and portfolios have been used successfully to document progress in behavior, with self-recording of on-task behavior linked to the number of correct responses on daily seat work.

Portfolio assessment is not a single defined approach to assessment since there are no set rules for how much and what kind of work samples to include or what constitutes meeting the specified goal. The key to a successful portfolio is student ownership. Pupils know the goal and work collaboratively with their teachers to provide evidence that they are making progress toward the goal. Everything included in the portfolio is documented with a reason for selection, since without such narration, nuances of the learner's progress may be overlooked. We see portfolio assessment as a valuable adjunct to curriculum-based measurement. Whereas curriculum-based assessment can demonstrate that a skill has been mastered or not mastered, the portfolio can show change from first draft to final copy; whereas CBA is curriculum- and teacher-controlled, decisions concerning the portfolio are primarily those of the pupil.

DYNAMIC/INTERACTIVE ASSESSMENT

A growing number of psychologists and educators agree that meaningful educational assessment must focus on children's potential for change, must tap children's ability to profit from instruction. This, of course, is a very different view of assessment from the approaches already described. Although the specifics of content and techniques differ, several major assessment approaches are aimed at describing children's potential for learning. These include Feurerstein's (1979) Learning Potential Assessment Device (LPAD), Brown and Campione's (1986) assisted learning and transfer program, Budoff's (1987) learning-potential assessment system, and Carlson and Weidl's (1979, 1992) testing the limits approach. These approaches are often referred to under the rubric of dynamic assessment or assisted assessment, and they have in common a focus on identifying the processes used in learning rather than on the products of learning.

The purpose in dynamic assessment is to discover and describe the approach a child uses in problem solving and to aid the learner in using more effective strategies. According to Lidz (1987), dynamic assessment provides a picture of the learner's potential for cognitive development, identifies processes used in problem solving, and yields information that can be used in instruction. The goal is not just to describe what or how much has been learned, but how, and with what kind of help, learning occurs.

Dynamic assessment may take a number of different forms and target different skills. Some dynamic-assessment procedures prescribe protocols for the examiner's role and specify the nature and amount of help to be given during the teaching phase of the assessment. Other approaches are less structured and allow the examiner administrative flexibility. In all systems the examiner interacts with the child in a teaching-learning interchange, asks questions, and provides prompts and manipulations which lead the learner through problem-solving procedures toward a successful solution.

Examples of more structured approaches include those of Budoff; Carlson and Weidl; and Brown and Campione. These are systems based on some form of a test-teach-test model, beginning with an initial evaluation of a child's competence, followed by a mini-teaching session, and then retesting with a series of progressively more difficult tasks. The content of assessment may be domain- or subject-matter specific, or may be more general and nonspecific. In each case, however, the goal is to find out whether and to what extent the child was able to profit from the instruction, and to determine what instructional adaptations and cues were effective.

In contrast to the test-teach-test approach, Feurerstein (1979) argued for a more global approach in which the focus is on broad cognitive processes thought to underlie learning, and in which the assessment is clinical and unstandardized, individualized, and interactive. He has developed training materials which are different from schoollike tasks, but it is assumed that the materials will transfer if there is change in the underlying processes. In Feuerstein's approach, assessment and instruction are inseparable. The clinical nature of the LPAD makes it an attractive alternative to traditional, psychometrically based approaches. However, the lack of structure and the melding of assessment and instruction make it difficult to evaluate, and the direct impact or transfer of the training to school subjects is also uncertain.

Taken as a group, the assisted assessment or dynamic-assessment models are promising ways to gather instructionally relevant information about learners. They have considerable clinical-educational utility and deserve consideration when assessing children with learning disabilities, as many such children have unique or specific processing problems. Further, by definition these children have a discrepancy between presumed aptitude and actual achievement. This discrepancy may be documented by psychometric techniques, but the functional or instructional implications are obscure. The dynamic assessment approaches, on the other hand, integrate assessment and instruction. Also important, they allow children the opportunity to demonstrate their responsiveness to instruction, and they provide some cues or hints as to the potential for further learning. The reader is referred to a comprehensive review by Campione (1989) for a detailed discussion of these approaches.

CONCLUSION

Educational assessment is an integral component in the aptitude-achievement model commonly used for identifying children with learning disabilities. Standardized, norm-referenced tests are appropriately used for this purpose, provided they have adequate psychometric and technical properties and that they are individually administered. Educational assessment has another major purpose and that is to provide information that leads to appropriate and effective intervention. In our view there are two aspects of "testing for intervention." One is the demonstration of a child's maximum performance, so that we learn what the child can do, not just document what he or she cannot or does not do. The second is to identify the context or conditions in which successful learning occurs. The first goal implies assessment with appropriate and technically adequate instruments and techniques, assurance that the methods and procedures of administration and data collection are adequate, and that the conditions of assessment are positive. The second implies the need to consider a broad range of possible influences on children's performance, including assessment of the physical, social, and educational characteristics of the classroom and of the in-structural program. Many different approaches to assessment are available, and there is a plethora of specific techniques. The challenge in assessment is to be sure that the purposes and the methods match.

CHAPTER 7

Language Evaluation

Margaret H. Briggs

Communication connects humans through dynamic social interactions. Communication is manifested in many different ways: through language, a symbolic system of verbal and written rules; through speech, audible symbols; and through gestures, body movements, and facial expressions. Communication occurs between partners in a variety of different settings.

The purpose of this chapter is to explore the richness and complexity of language, to discuss the relationship between language and learning, and to offer a framework for assessing children as they communicate in different settings with their different partners. The role of the speech-language pathologist, the professional on the interdisciplinary team charged with assessing and treating children with communication problems, will be briefly addressed. Alternative methods of assessment that do not depend solely on the use of standardized tests of children's language will be presented. The discussion in this chapter will focus on language disorders rather than on differences that reflect the diversity of the cultures and communication patterns throughout the world. Lynch and Hanson (1992) provide an excellent resource for those interested in understanding cultural differences and associated language patterns.

RELATIONSHIP BETWEEN LANGUAGE AND LEARNING DISABILITIES

Since the term was first introduced by Samuel Kirk in 1963, problems of language comprehension and expression have always been included as identifying characteristics of a learning disability. In fact, many argue that a language disorder is at the core of learning disabilities.

Children who are late in developing language were once seen as experiencing temporary delays that would resolve spontaneously over time. However, in 1980, Snyder predicted that the language-delayed preschooler of today may well become the learning-disabled student of tomorrow. A growing body of evidence supports her prediction and suggests that many of these children do not "outgrow" these problems and that "simple" delays in communication may, in fact, be stable predictors of later learning disabilities (Aram, Ekelman, & Nation, 1984; Norris & Hoffman, 1993; Thal, Tobias, & Morrison, 1991).

A particularly interesting line of research has been conducted by Paul and her colleagues (Paul, 1991; Paul, 1993; Paul, Sprangle-Looney, & Dahm, 1991). They followed a group of children from ages 2 to 6. The children were first identified at age 2 as "late talkers" on the basis of their lack of expressive vocabulary development. Paul and her colleagues regularly assessed them on a variety of measures of language development until after entry into kindergarten. Although the majority of the "late talkers" outgrew their language deficits by age 4, they demonstrated delays in academic readiness at ages 5 and 6. Moreover, these children persisted in demonstrating social skills deficits, even when the language delays had apparently resolved. This suggests that an underlying deficit exists in the organization of the rules of symbolic systems (Lockwood, 1994).

Scarborough and Dobrich (1990) similarly concluded that young children may outgrow the presenting problem, the language delay, but not the underlying disorder in the ability to process symbolic information. They found that the severity of the language disorders in the children they studied decreased over time, giving the impression of a "recovery" by age 5. However, the majority of the children evidenced reading disabilities by Grade 2. They argued that previous studies demonstrating a resolution of early language disorders had failed to investigate fully the relationship between language understanding and use and reading achievement.

The relationship between early language delays and later learning and social-behavioral disorders is clearly not linear, and additional prospective studies should help to clarify this issue. Retrospective studies that carefully review the early development of students who in the elementary school grades exhibit learning problems may identify communication markers that predict later learning patterns. Based on the literature to date, however, it can no longer be argued that delays in the language development of toddlers do not indicate possible future academic and behavioral problems. What appears to happen is that, although a language disorder may disappear, it tends to reappear in different forms as task and contexts change over time. The "wait and see" approach frequently advised as the treatment for toddlers and preschoolers with communication delays can no longer be supported.

COMMUNICATION ASSESSMENT

In any evaluation, one has to start with a clear identification of the criterion or standard against which the child is to be compared. This understanding, then, argues for the use of a developmental model. A solid foundation in communication development along with opportunities to observe normally developing children will allow the speech-language pathologist to compare each child assessed against a standard of typical development.

Communication assessment is a process that occurs over time. Assessments of a child's communicative abilities are typically scheduled as a series of events that occur at various points along a continuum of development. The first assessment in the series is initiated by someone's concern about the child's ability to communicate effectively. Subsequent assessments will be scheduled as a result of the initial findings. If a problem is identified, then assessment should become a continuous process as part of the intervention program. The purpose of a communication assessment is to understand the child's communicative competence in different settings and with different partners. Knowing how a particular child communicates in different environments can offer a view of a child's ability to function successfully in social interactions.

The communication assessment process is accomplished by gathering information from a variety of sources, observing the child in typical settings with different partners, describing in some detail the child's strengths, and attempting to understand the child's needs. The process further involves a description of the environments in which the child communicates and any unique challenges that the child may encounter. A communication assessment is not merely the administration and scoring of a battery of tests. All information obtained must be analyzed, interpreted, and explained. The results of the process should yield a description of both the child's strengths and areas of need at various time points and an analysis of the communicative environments in which the child functions.

One should begin the assessment process with an open mind and a sense of wonder, similar to that adopted by anthropologists visiting a new cultural group. The focus should be on attempting to understand and learn from the activities and behaviors of others, not necessarily attempting to force order onto naturally occurring behaviors. With normal developmental expectations as a guide, the clinician should observe and attempt to understand the child's and partners' behaviors without a set of presumptions or operating principles.

One dilemma in designing the components of a communication assessment is balancing the need for normative data against the desire to capture the richness of a detailed description of communicative social interactions. Although these two goals may appear to conflict, it is possible to gather a sufficient amount and variety of information that will serve both purposes.

A Systems Perspective

Historically, assessment and intervention for children with language and learning problems have been viewed from a deficit model. The child has a disability which is caused by some underlying deficiency. The goal of intervention is to treat the deficit, which will theoretically result in a change in the child's abilities. This linear cause and effect model has driven much of what has been done therapeutically and educationally for children with language disorders in the past (Nelson, 1993).

An alternative approach is to attempt an understanding of the child's communication within a variety of contexts rather than to search for some specific deficiency as the cause of a problem. One such approach is grounded in systems theory. This orientation requires the adoption of a holistic view of a child as part of a larger system. Changes in any part of the larger system will affect each part, including the child being discussed. Satir (1988) uses the metaphor of a mobile to elegantly describe the delicate balance among the components of a family system. Any change in one component affects the balance and naturally alters each individual component as well as the entire system.

A systems perspective to assessment requires that the focus of the assessment be not just child-oriented, but systems-oriented. This requires that the systems in which the child must function—the home, school, and community—also be assessed. Adoption of a systems theory approach means that the clinician can no longer depend on typical measures of child language. New methods for understanding communication within a larger system must be designed.

Goals of Assessment

The goals of a communication assessment based on a systems perspective reflect changes in philosophy and methods. (See Table 7–1 for a list of typical goals of the assessment process.) Many assessments are conducted with only one or a few goals in mind. Specific tests of some types of language abilities are administered to qualify children for inclusion in intervention or education programs. Although program mandates may be met, the clinician or teacher may have acquired little useful information about that child's language, communication, and learning abilities. Further, typical language tests and procedures do not offer descriptions of the complexity of language in different contexts. Assessments should be designed over a period of time and to include all of the goals described in Table 7–1.

ASSESSMENT METHODS

A number of different procedures and tools for assessing children's language and communication abilities are available. Both quantitative and qualitative methods are available. Quantitative methods are the ones typically used by speech-language pathologists to measure discrete behaviors and yield scores, frequency counts, percentages, and the like. Typical measures assess a variety of behaviors believed to compose language understanding and use. These measures include, among others, a computation of average sentence length based on samples of a child's language production, a count of the number of vocabu-

TABLE 7–1
Goals of the Assessment Process

- identify a need for services
- determine eligibility for specific programs
- distinguish the nature of a problem
- describe areas of strength and areas of need
- establish a baseline for later comparison
- identify system strengths and needs
- outline goals for treatment
- evaluate progress made in treatment at regular intervals

lary words a child can demonstrate understanding of based on pictured representations, and judgments of the intelligibility of a child's speech articulation relative to age-matched peers.

A recent, exciting addition to the assessment process has been the inclusion of qualitative methods. Qualitative methods are derived from ethnographic research. Borrowing from the field of anthropology, an ethnographic approach to language assessment involves in-depth open-ended interviews, direct observations, and an analysis of written documents. An ethnographic approach is recommended by a number of researchers (Lund & Duchan, 1993; Patton & Westby, 1992; Westby, 1994) as a method to better understand the language of a child within the context of the child's culture or system.

Advantages and Disadvantages of Different Methods

Quantitative methods allow the speech-language pathologist to select discrete language behaviors for careful analysis. They allow for a comparison of a child's performance against a set of standard expectations. Most clinicians have been thoroughly trained to select, administer, score, and interpret standardized tests of language performance. Tests administration, then, can be routinely performed and their results reliably reported. Changes in a child's performance over time can be easily charted and progress, or lack of it, readily demonstrated. Standard test scores are usually used by state and federally funded programs as eligibility criteria. Discussion within the interdisciplinary team can be aided by the use of standard test scores where differences are described in terms understood by all members (e.g., number of standard deviations from a mean, as percentage differences).

A problem with quantitative measures, however, is the clinician's inability to guarantee that the behaviors being measured are valid representations of a child's communicative competence. Even the most rigorously constructed tests of language comprehension and production do not sample all important behaviors that comprise communication. While comparative analyses can be made, typically depth and detail are lost. Communication occurs within dyadic interactions, with a partner. Traditional quantitative assessment is linear, unidirectional, and cannot capture the interactional nature of communication between partners. Typical tests are not designed to assess the resources or challenges of the contexts or systems within which a child communicates. A further limitation is that most standardized tests do not represent the communicative competence of children from different cultural groups and for whom English may not be their native language.

Qualitative methods allow the speech-language pathologist to evaluate and interpret behavior, linguistic and otherwise, obtained from observing a child with familiar people encountering typical challenges. Qualitative methods provide the richness and detail lost on standardized measures of language. These methods also can assess the system and the interactions which occur naturally. A challenge of this method, however, is that the clinician must collect the detailed information, organize it in some logical fashion, and then interpret it in a meaningful manner. This process can prove to be difficult and is time consuming. This method also requires that thoughtful consideration be given prior to the assessment to decide which situations, behaviors, and individuals are significant and therefore important to describe. A concern is that while the clinician is focusing on one set of behaviors judged to be critical, other interactional patterns or behaviors may be missed.

Neither method, a quantitative or qualitative one, is inherently better than the other; each is selected to serve different purposes and to meet different assessment goals. A combination of both quantitative and qualitative methods will usually yield the most valid information. Whatever methods are chosen, however, the best tools in the assessment process are always the clinician's keen observational skills and the ability to interpret and explain the data obtained.

Formal Assessment

The purpose of this chapter is not to discuss specific assessment instruments. For a detailed list, see Bernstein and Tiegerman (1994) and Roberts and Crais (1989). An especially valuable resource is Nelson (1993), who provides an annotated bibliography of screening and assessment tools for children with language and learning disabilities.

A number of cautions regarding the use of formal assessment tools should be considered. In discussing assessment for the birth to age 3 population, Linder (1993) cites a number of disadvantages to traditional test-dependent assessment, including unnatural environment, unfamiliar examiner, biased tests (especially in relation to biases in tests of cognitive development against children with language delays), lack of information related to the processes a child uses in acquiring a specific skill, and failure to take into account temperamental, motivational, or interactional differences. These same disadvantages could also apply in considering tests for older children.

Regardless of the formal instruments selected, it is important to carefully observe a child's behaviors during assessment. Formal test administration poses a significant stress for children, especially for those who are not skilled in comprehending and using language in its many forms. The behaviors observed should include, but not be limited to, the behaviors specifically targeted on the test. If all of the speech-language pathologist's attention is focused on the specific behaviors being measured on the test, important information about how the child copes with the task demands will be missed.

Some behaviors to observe are (a) the child's approach to the task; (b) changes in the child's behavior or affect as the difficulty level increases; (c) differences between the child's test behavior and nonstructured tasks or casual conversation; (d) differences between child-selected topics of conversation and specific test requirements; (e) changes in behavior as shifts in task demands occur; (f) the child's behaviors at the completion of a task and as transitions between tasks occur; and (g) the child's ability to comprehend test instructions, requests for repetitions, or demands for clarification of directions.

Typical Behaviors of Children with Language and Learning Disabilities

A number of specific behaviors are associated with children who have language and learning difficulties (Boyce & Larson, 1983; Damico & Oller, 1980; Nelson, 1993; Richard & Hanner, 1985). During the assessment process, special attention should be made to make note of these behaviors. In interviewing members of the child's system, in conducting observations in different contexts, and during formal and informal assessment procedures these behaviors might be exhibited. These typical behaviors (see Table 7–2) may be used to help others determine whether to refer a child for a communication assessment.

While most of us experience many of these difficulties in communicating, a critical differentiating factor between competent communicators and children with language disabilities seems to be the ability to self-monitor and self-correct. Word retrieval problems, reformulizations, and memory delays occur regularly between all partners during their communicative efforts. However, these difficulties are irregular occurrences and do not predominate. Most competent communicators are readily able to recognize their difficulties and correct them spontaneously. They typically comment in an amusing manner about these temporary errors (e.g., "Oh, that word's right on the tip of my tongue; I must be getting older; I can't remember anything anymore") and continue with the conversational interchange. In addition to watching for the behaviors listed in Table 7–2, then, it will also be important to notice a student's ability to self-monitor and self-correct errors or breakdowns in communication.

TABLE 7–2

Typical Behaviors of Children with Language Disorders

Auditory—these behaviors may be related to auditory processing difficulties.

1. **Delays in responding**—after a partner makes a request or asks a question, there are long pauses before a response.
2. **Inappropriate responses**—response does not relate to the question or comment just made.
3. **Poor short term memory**
   Cannot remember recently presented information
   Requires frequent repetitions of auditory messages
   Difficulty in following a series of oral commands
   Few strategies available to recall and use new information.
4. **Need for repetition**—multiple repetitions are requested with no apparent improvement in comprehension.
5. **Rehearsals**—audible or subvocal repetition of partner's comment or direction.
6. **Avoidance or lack of response**—failure to respond or almost immediate response of "I don't know."

Verbal—These behaviors contribute to an unclear message that is dysfluent, vague, and difficult to follow.

1. **Reformulizations**—begins a sentence, then stops midway to revise a thought, formulate a message, recall the desired vocabulary word, or construct correct syntactical forms.
2. **Inappropriate word usage**—difficulty recalling the desired, most appropriate word. Child may provide the function rather than the label for an object (e.g., "cutter" for "knife"). Child may talk excessively or "talk around" a subject, searching out loud for the desired words or may pause and hesitate for long periods of time, searching silently.
3. **Nonspecific vocabulary**—overuse of "this," "that thing," "you know," and "stuff" when more specific expressions are required.
4. **Perseveration**—inability to shift. Child continues on one thought or phrase and is unable to shift to a new topic.
5. **Poor topic maintenance**—rapid and inappropriate shifts in topic without transitional cues to the partner.
6. **Word retrieval difficulties**—uses a word spontaneously; however, cannot recall the same word later when requested.
7. **Dysfluencies**—pauses, repetitions, use of fillers or starters (e.g., "um," "well"), and hesitations without accompanying patterns typically associated with stuttering.
8. **Poor repair strategies**—when partner requests clarification or identifies an error, child is unable to spontaneously correct or repair the mistake.

In reporting the results of formal assessment, the clinician often ignores behaviors exhibited by the child during the assessment process. Either the behaviors are not described at all, generalizations are made, or they are merely interpreted as "off-task" or "impulsive." A critical part of the total assessment process is to notice, analyze, and interpret all of the behaviors exhibited by the child in all of the contexts analyzed. Making sense of these behaviors is as important as computing the standard score on a test. A caution is that these behaviors can be overinterpreted. In other words, behaviors observed during formal test administration may not be representative of a student's typical behavior. In fact, these behaviors may occur only within the context of a stressful situation—a test of abilities that are not a strength for that child.

Many of these behaviors may be compensatory strategies, employed by students in their efforts to maintain a communicative interaction with a partner. These behaviors may be exhibited in many forms, including written, oral, and gestural.

Communication serves a number of functions (e.g., to request information, to initiate a conversational exchange, to express a feeling). It is important, therefore, to look at the underlying intent that a child is attempting to communicate. A focus only on the outward form (e.g., the words used, the structure of the sentence, the gestures accompanying the words) may cause the observer to miss the functional purpose a communicative attempt serves for a child. The intent of a child's utterance can be determined by analyzing what preceded and followed and what the consequences were as a result of that utterance.

A useful source of information about a child's communicative abilities, the functions they serve, and the system within which the child interacts is other members of the interdisciplinary assessment team. Other team members can provide observations about the child's communicative interactions during their assessments and offer insight into the student's communication needs in different contexts and with different partners.

Informal Procedures

Assessment involves more than just administering a battery of tests and making note of the behaviors exhibited during testing. Informal procedures should be planned as part of the process to assess the child's ability in less structured tasks and in typical contexts.

One type of procedure that will yield useful information is to arrange structured or semistructured situations and observe the child. The situations should mirror typical activities and experiences and should include familiar partners. Some types of situations might include play between a child and caregiver at home, peer interactions on a school playground, the child engaged in typical activities at school, and conversations between a child and caregiver in a homelike setting at a school or clinic. An analysis of these situations will best be accomplished if the interactions are videotaped. The tapes may later be reviewed and different behaviors targeted for inspection. For instance, a ratio between adult talk and child talk may be computed, a description of the child's level of play development could be made, and a listing of the types of language requirements within a classroom might be yielded.

Assessing the System

By observing the child within a variety of contexts with different language partners, the system can be assessed as well. In order for the process to be complete, the home context and the school context must be described and understood. The school assessment will necessarily include an understanding of the curriculum, a description of the language of instruction, an analysis of the language used in the textbooks, and a review of the procedures used to measure a student's progress. Although instruction methods typically involve lecturing, many teachers are also including a richer variety of activities, such as participatory learning and cooperative learning. Children with language and learning disabilities perform optimally in environments where a multisensory approach is used. A teacher's dependence on the verbal-auditory channel alone for instruction places a child with a language disability at a serious disadvantage. An observation of the classroom and the instructional style of the teachers will provide useful information in understanding a specific child and the types of demands encountered during the school day.

Although conducting a home visit may not always be an option, an opportunity to visit a child within the family system will typically yield useful insights. When a home visit is an option, it should be arranged at a time convenient for all family members. A specific length of time should be scheduled and the purpose clearly described prior to the appointment. A home visit will allow the speech-language pathologist and other team members to observe the language used among family members, the routines of the family, and the physical environment. With the family's permission, an interaction between the child and family members may be videotaped for later review and analysis. When a home visit cannot be arranged, family members should be asked to describe their environment and routines, the communicative partners available to the child, and typical interactions they have with the child.

CONTENT OF THE ASSESSMENT PROCESS

In order to a have a complete assessment of a child's communication abilities, the speech-language pathologist must sample different aspects or components of language, including the structure (e.g., sounds and sentences), the meaning (e.g., words and concepts) attached, and the social aspects of use (e.g., conversations). The contexts within which communication occurs (e.g., home, playground, and classroom) must also be assessed. Finally, language as it occurs under a variety of task demands (e.g., child-directed conversational topic, clinician-directed request for specific information, formal test administration, interactions at home) must be included.

Age Considerations

One important factor to consider in designing an assessment is the age of the child. Particularly challenging is the assessment of the birth to age 3 population. Linder (1993) provides a detailed list of components of a language assessment for infants and toddlers conducted within a play environment. In discussing children with language and learning disabilities in the past, little attention was devoted to infants, toddlers, and preschoolers. Since it is now recognized that many of the learning problems diagnosed during elementary school grades may have their origin in earlier communication delays, attention by the speech-language pathologist to assessing and treating children before entry into formal schooling is justified. A list of suggested topics to assess in young children is provided in Table 7–3.

Interactions between young children and their caregivers in naturally occurring conversations will provide the most useful context within which a judgement can be made about the child's and the system's capabilities. During these interactions, the young child's communicative abilities can be compared against a standard of typical development. Further, an evaluation of the caregivers use of facilitative communication strategies may be made. For a list of strategies found to facilitate communication in young children, see Linder (1993) and Roberts and Crais (1989).

For children of school age, a different set of challenges faces the speech-language pathologist in designing an appropriate assessment. When children enter school, they are faced with new language demands. The oral language traditions at school are different from those at home. According to Westby (1994), classroom language involves both a "social text"—the information about expectations for participation (e.g., who can talk, when, where, in what ways, with whom, for what purposes) and an "academic text"—the content of the lesson and the structure of that content. Based on ethnographic studies within classrooms, Scott (1994) reported that teachers use two types of language: information-based or management-based. According to her, teachers are basically concerned with either imparting information or managing classroom behavior. The language teachers use reflects those two concerns.

Soon after entry into school, written language is introduced. Written language does not follow a structure that is similar to oral language

TABLE 7–3

Topics to Assess in Young Children

Understanding and use of meaningful words: Response to simple commands, to one's name, specific words, and measures of vocabulary size

Nonverbal communication behavior: Eye contact, smiling, facial expressions, general affect, gesture, touch, vocalization, laughter, and vocal inflection in both receptive and expressive modes

Syntax Word combinations of four or more words and use of grammatical morphemes

Phonological development Crying, babbling, producing jargon and specific phonemes, and degree of intelligibility of speech

Word combinations Ability to combine two or three words in an utterance

Conceptual information Knowledge of basic concepts, such as colors and size, and ability to categorize items

Cognitive abilities Imitation, attention to stimuli, evidence of object constancy, and intellectual functioning

Responses to auditory stimuli Reaction to speech or environmental sounds, including alerting, localization, and discrimination

Pragmatics Language functions, ability to initiate verbal interactions, and general discourse skills

Play behaviors Symbolic, functional, interactive, imaginative, explorative, and stereotyped play as well as the absence of play

Evidence of oral integrity Feeding, oral motor movement patterns, and overall muscle tone

Parent-child interaction Readability of child's signals, parental response to verbal and nonverbal communicative attempts

Verbal response to questions Ability to give accurate responses to questions

Auditory memory Memory of digits, words, sentences, etc.

Source. From *Family-centered early intervention for communication disorders* (pp. 171–172), by G. Donahue-Kilburg, 1992, Gaithersberg, MD: Aspen. Copyright 1992 by Aspen. Adapted with permission.

patterns. Students in the early grades may be able to decode individual words and short sentences, but written language requirements increase rapidly through the elementary school years. The written language encountered typically offers the student few supportive cues and forces students to gain meaning without important contextual information.

One aspect that has received increasing interest as an important language component to assess is narratives. Narrative structures follow a set of rules that includes characters, a plot, an ordering of events, and a problem which ultimately is resolved. In order for children to construct a narrative, a monologue with specific structural rules and produced without the support of others, they must be able to integrate their language skills into a coherent whole. According to Westby (1994), students with language learning disabilities produce narratives that are shorter, less complex, less coherent, and more disorganized. A child's ability to extract meaning from and to construct stories must also be evaluated as part of a thorough language assessment.

In order for a complete assessment to occur, then, the written and oral language used in the classroom must be understood. Scott (1994) suggested a portfolio approach in which a variety of records are accumulated over time. A portfolio record is much more extensive, according to Scott, and more representative of a student's oral and written language abilities than are the results of one test or informal procedure conducted only at one point in time. Items in a portfolio record might include a student's written work samples; an audio recording of the student conversing with a partner; a written review of appropriate medical, developmental, or educational records; a transcribed sample of the student telling a story; or written notes obtained from an interview with someone familiar with this student.

Students in secondary grades require a different set of skills in selecting and implementing assessment procedures. Boyce and Larson (1983), in discussing the specific needs of adolescents with language and learning disabilities, emphasized the importance of evaluating a student's "survival language," or the language needed to cope with daily living situations such as job applications, shopping, using the telephone, and interpreting signs. Nelson (1993) urged that an information-processing perspective be adopted in assessing the written and oral communication needs of older students. She specifically recommended that an assessment of a student's metacognitive or executive functions be included. She offered suggestions to the speech-language pathologist in designing procedures to evaluate a student's ability to attend, organize, and execute a complex system of thinking, listening, reading, understanding, and speaking. Abstract, figurative, nonliteral, and inferential language all emerge during adolescence and pose specific challenges for children with language and learning problems. Reed (1994) provided a list of the listening and speaking competencies necessary for success in secondary schools, (e.g., one must distinguish between informative and persuasive messages, organize messages so that others can understand them, give concise and accurate directions).

SEQUENCE OF ASSESSMENT

The following recommended sequence for the assessment process is offered as an example. This example is taken from work done in a speech-language pathology clinic setting which serves children primarily between ages 2 and 6. Although the process may seem ideal, it is possible, and may be adapted to meet the needs of clinicians in a variety of work settings. Many of the recommended steps can be used with older school-age children as well. However, detailed descriptions of the school context would need to be added in order for the sequence to be complete.

Beginning with the initial contact, an active partnership with the child's family should be established. Collaboration, a process of working together towards a common goal, implies a partnership among equals (Hanft & Von Rembow, 1992). Forming an equal, collaborative relationship will allow the speech-language pathologist access to the family system and each member's unique perspective of the child. Andrews & Andrews (1993) suggested a technique called "joining" in which professionals become accepted into the family system. This joining occurs out of a sense of mutual respect and equality of contribution. An important part of this process is the use of a positive, nonjudgmental approach by the clinician. When the assessment process is explained to families, their involvement requested, and the benefits of their participation outlined, most family members will be eager to collaborate.

Although there are many barriers to family-professional collaboration (for instance, economic and travel constraints, work and time schedules, language differences, other family demands, and emotional unavailability), the philosophical orientation of attempting to develop relationships built on respect and equality will best serve the needs of children with language and learning difficulties. Even families who appear on the surface to be incompetent, often will be found to have many skills that can be mobilized toward meeting the needs of the children. Even systems in which family-professional partnerships have not previously been encouraged can attempt new directions and methods once the benefits of collaboration have been experienced. A willing attitude to learn and experiment, not a specific set of strategies is all that is required to implement positive changes in family and service-delivery systems.

Pre-assessment Planning

Prior to a child being assessed, a process of pre-assessment planning should take place (Gallagher, 1991; Linder, 1993; Lund & Duchan, 1993). During this time, it is the speech-language pathologist's responsibility to find out as much as possible about the child and the system before the actual meeting for the assessment. The clinician should interview as many different people as possible to get a complete picture of the child and each person's perspective, observations, and feelings about the child's strengths and needs. Appropriate written records that are available should be reviewed and summarized. In most instances, the clinician will have to begin a process of prioritizing in deciding which individuals to invite to the assessment session, which records to review, and which individuals to interview for background information.

The results of the communication assessment are significantly enhanced by the presence of the child's family. While this may be difficult in some settings, the extra effort expended (e.g., scheduling the appointment at a time convenient for the family's work schedule) will be offset by the valuable information provided by having family members present. Family members can offer historical information, share their observations and needs, ask pertinent questions, and provide a familiar communication partner for the child.

In setting up the appointment for the initial meeting, the speech-language pathologist should invite the family members to become involved in the assessment and explain the importance of their participation. The process should be described in detail: what each member will be expected to do, what will happen step by step, what information they should be prepared to discuss (review developmental milestones at home, talk to other family members, caregivers, or teachers), what they will need to prepare before the appointment (complete a questionnaire that will be mailed out ahead of time to them, collect written work samples). Further, the family should be advised of the benefits they will gain as a result of this appointment. The speech-language pathologist should plan for active participation of all relevant family members and be prepared to discuss immediately the findings, their implications, and any recommendations.

Based on the results of the pre-assessment planning, the speech-language pathologist will be able to prepare a series of interview questions, design informal procedures, and select appropriate standardized tests. Rather than attempting to rely on a set battery of procedures and tests, a customized approach will better meet the goals of assessment outlined in Table 7–1 and the unique needs of each student and system.

Adequate preparation will also allow the speech-language pathologist to coordinate assessment activities with other team members to avoid duplication of efforts or the failure to include important components. Some components of the assessment process may be completed in partnership with other team members. For instance the family interview may be conducted by several team members so that a complete description of all aspects of development is gathered at one time. This will allow team members to learn from each other and prevent family members from being asked repeatedly similar questions by different professionals.

Designing a Context for Assessment

The way in which the setting is organized will be critical to the success of the assessment process. The room in which the assessment takes place should be arranged specifically for the family and child to be served. Bright, colorful, interesting toys should be available for young children, with seating that is appropriate for their size. Materials for older children should be selected with the goal of stimulating conversations and sampling both written and oral language. Again, room arrangement and furniture size should be a consideration. It is always preferable to have a room that includes adequate floor space, comfortable seating for adults (e.g., sofa and arm chairs), and soft lighting. Attempts to approximate the look of a comfortable family room will allow for increased participation.

Many children, especially young ones, are reluctant to talk with an unfamiliar person in a new setting. See Table 7–4 for a list of suggestions on how to maximize the performance of young children.

Interviewing

Once the family has been greeted, the interview often begins the appointment. Portions of the interview may take place simultaneously with the caregiver-child interaction (see the description which follows). Although the speech-language pathologist has already gathered some background information as part of pre-assessment planning, an open

---

TABLE 7–4
Steps to Optimize Young Children's Performance in the Interview

1. *Choose developmentally appropriate toys and materials.* Select materials that will allow sampling of a variety of aspects of communication. For instance, have toys that are broken or missing crucial parts. Use toys that require adult assistance in their operation or jars with tight-fitting lids that hold enticing treats.
2. *Begin with the child and a familiar partner* (parent, sibling, peer) interacting before attempting to intervene directly.
3. As you join the interaction, start with *parallel play*, mirroring the child's actions. Gradually comment on an object or action. Limit your own talking, especially questions.
4. Watch for and *encourage any mode of communication* demonstrated by child (eye gaze, point, shrug, word, etc.).
5. Have *some objects tantalizingly in sight* but out of reach. If necessary, point to or comment on the objects to encourage a comment or request by the child.
6. *Follow the child's lead* in the toys and materials used and the topics of conversation discussed.
7. *Begin with activities that require little or no talking*, and gradually move to more verbal and structured tasks.
8. *Make questions and comments authentic.* Demonstrate warmth and positive regard in all interactions with the child.

Source. From Assessing communication skills, by J. E. Roberts and E. R. Crais, *Assessing Infants and Preschoolers with Handicaps* (p. 351), 1989, Columbus, OH: Merrill. Copyright 1989 by Merrill. Adapted with permission. From *Communication and Symbolic Behavior Scales*, by A. M. Wetherby and B. Prizant, 1993, Chicago, IL: Riverside. Copyright 1993 by Riverside. Adapted with permission.

attitude is most useful. The family will share factual information and provide anecdotes or stories as long as these are encouraged as part of the interview process. Family members may choose to use photo albums, video recordings, or written records to aid in their ability to recall information. A timeline may be drawn to provide a memory aid. Family celebrations and significant events may serve as markers (e.g., "Think back to your child's first birthday party. What words was she saying then?").

An outline of possible topics to pursue and information to obtain is useful, but it is wise to use this as a guide only. Questions should be open-ended and preconceived notions avoided. A good opening question is, "How can I help you?" It is best to avoid interrupting stories or attempting to direct the conversation. It is wise to initially keep the conversation general. More specific answers to questions on a prepared form can follow. Rather than rushing to complete an interview form, allow the family's narration to unfold. When in doubt, follow the family's lead. Remember to focus on both the child's strengths and needs. As both professionals and family members have such a strong tendency to focus on needs, special attention will have to be devoted to emphasizing strengths.

A number of possible topics can be pursued. In order to obtain a general impression of each family member's view of the child, a beginning request in the interview phase might be "Please describe your child." Getting a summary of the events and sequence of a typical day provides a snapshot of the child's experiences and adaptations. A question like, "What do you like to do together as a family?" allows the clinician to gain insight into the family system. Each family member should be asked to list the child's strengths and particular concerns about communication. Open-ended questions about the child's abilities and difficulties with communication in a variety of settings logically follows. Rich, detailed information that captures family members' own unique descriptions of their view of the child will greatly enhance the quality of the assessment.

The child should be included in the interview whenever possible. Because some family members feel that it is not appropriate to "talk about" the child in front of her or him, an open conversation among all members typically yields the most useful information. A family's request to have a separate time to talk without their child present should be honored. However, the benefit of active participation and collaboration of everyone should be explained. Specific questions should be addressed directly to the child about his or her views on communication strengths and needs. A good opening question might be, "Why did you come in to see me today?" or "Did your parents tell you what we were going to do here?" Children's insight into the nature and extent of the their own problems is often surprising and typically quite revealing.

A number of communication techniques to assist the speech-language pathologist in the interview process have been suggested (Andrews & Andrews, 1990, 1993; Briggs, 1993; Lowenthal, 1993; Molyneaux & Lane, 1990). One of the most useful communication skills, according to Briggs, is empathic responding, which requires that the listener be with the other person emotionally and intellectually for a moment in time. "Empathic responding does not involve judging, agreeing, or feeling sympathy for someone else. Rather, the person's physical presence conveys true understanding of another's feelings, thoughts, values, or beliefs" (p. 38). Verbal strategies of clarifying, neutral questioning, and summarizing can be effectively used during the interview phase.

Observing Caregiver-Child Interactions

One of the challenges of assessing and treating language and communication needs is in designing a method that replicates the conversational interchanges between partners within a clinical environment. Observing interaction patterns between family members can offer important insights into communicative supports, contingencies, and barriers that occur at home. It is wise to also include observations of other care providers, such as day care staff, other family members, and babysitters.

The assessment session should begin by requesting that one or several of the family members interact with the child. It is preferable to avoid providing a great deal of structure or specific instructions to the family. Spontaneous, nonscripted interactions should be sought. As part of the pre-assessment planning, the family could be asked to bring familiar toys or books from home. It is wise to videotape this interaction for later analysis and as a baseline against which future comparisons may be made. Although many formal scales and observational tools are available, an informal description is sufficient.

One particularly interesting interactional pattern to note is the amount of supportive cuing family members provide for the child, especially during formal test administration. This cuing or prompting may take the form of directive questioning, providing answers to therapist-directed questions, or encouraging the child to "talk" or "tell her more." While this prompting may seem disruptive and may, in fact, interfere with test administration protocols, the amount of support family members feel they need to offer the child to ensure communicative success is extremely useful information for assessment and program planning.

Informal Procedures

A thorough assessment should include a mix of unstructured and highly structured tasks in order to represent the range of possible challenges a child might typically face at home and in school. A recommended strategy is to conduct qualitative assessments first to gain an overall perspective of the child's strengths and needs. Quantitative measures next may be selected to evaluate in more detail specific information that was gathered in the qualitative procedures.

One procedure that allows for an evaluation of oral motor structure and function is scheduling a snack. The scheduling of this procedure as a break allows for it to also serve as a social time. It may be arranged that necessary equipment (e.g., a cup, napkin, or utensil) is not available and the child will have to leave the room with the speech-language pathologist only. During this separation, the child's communication without the presence of family members should be noted.

Replication of a play environment is important. Toys to consider include a doll house with family members, vehicles that can be moved and manipulated on the floor, baby dolls and equipment (e.g., diapers, bottles, combs, washcloth), blocks for building and designing, paper with crayons and markers, and bubbles and wands. Some toys included should have parts missing or broken or be difficult to activate, thus providing the child an opportunity to seek adult assistance or comment on the toy's apparent problem. A box of wind-up toys can encourage even the most reluctant child's participation in the assessment process. Puppets and books may prove to be useful as well as toys that are popular and heavily advertised at the moment on television. Duplicate sets of toys (e.g., matching sunglasses, two different horns or whistles) allow for mirroring, imitation, and turn taking.

Formal Assessment

During formal test administration it is important to order tasks according to a hierarchy of levels of difficulty. Pre-assessment planning will allow the clinician to order the presentation of tests and subtests based on each student's abilities. In addition to administering the test items, the clinician must assess how well the child performs as task demands increase, as contextual support diminishes, and as the level of abstraction increases. Certain linguistic challenges will increase the likelihood that some of the behaviors listed in Table 7–2 will occur. The behaviors noted during formal test administration should be compared and contrasted to those observed during informal procedures and casual conversations. It is the speech-language pathologist's responsibility to keep careful notes about the student's behavior as the level of structure in different contexts shifts during the assessment process.

Portions of tests, rather than the whole instrument, may be administered to tap specific areas of concern that have been identified during the pre-assessment process. When using this type of sampling approach, standardized test procedures may be violated and it may not be possible to generate a standard score. A review of the test manual will reveal the requirements for generating a valid score. It will be important in any reporting of test data to indicate that only portions of a test were selected and administered. It is also possible to administer, report, and interpret results from standardized tests in nonstandardized ways. One example of a nonstandardized method is to request that a family member, with coaching from the speech-language pathologist, administer a test or subtest. Again any nonstandardized procedures must be clearly described in any verbal or written reports.

Review of Assessment Data

The results and interpretations of the assessment should be discussed immediately with all family members present. Although it may be necessary to compute some scores at a later time, general findings should be reported to the family and to the child. It is best to report results in terms of relative strengths and weaknesses. The observation and interpretation of behaviors exhibited should be included in this verbal reporting process. It is important to ask family members whether or not the behaviors observed were typical and whether, in their estimation, a representative sample of the student's behavior was obtained.

Family members should be encouraged to share their own observations of their child during the assessment. Many parents report gaining useful insight as a result of observing their child during the assessment process. Both strengths and needs are either identified or confirmed as a result of their observation of their child in different contexts.

Conclusion, Diagnosis, and Recommendations

After all assessment information is collected, the final phase in the process begins. The speech-language pathologist should allow sufficient time for a thorough discussion. Family preferences for the amount of information they can absorb in one meeting should be honored. Subsequent telephone or face-to-face discussions can be scheduled. While the diagnosis of a language and learning disability may be suspected, the verification of this diagnosis may be difficult for family members to hear and accept. It is important to always attempt to foster support and offer hope. The family members' assessment and their ideas about interventions must be sought at this time. Although specific recommendations for treatment may be offered, family preferences must be considered and openly discussed. Suggestions for other services or evaluations may be provided at this time. Some initial attempts toward program planning should be made. It is most helpful if this final phase of assessment occurs as part of the interdisciplinary team process. Professionals and families will benefit from the collective input of all members of the team. Conclusions, recommendations, and future planning will best occur when all members, including the family, can meet together.

CONCLUSION

The focus of this chapter has been on redefining communication and the assessment process for children for whom language and learning problems are suspected. Rather than looking at communication as the sum of separate components, communication must be assessed as part of social interactions in typical contexts with familiar partners. Adoption of a systems perspective was recommended as a philosophy which included a holistic view of children within their usual environments. A further suggestion offered was the observation of a variety of behaviors that may be more revealing of a child's abilities or disabilities than simple standardized test scores. A number of alternative methods were provided in an effort to view children within a broader context. Finally, a sequence of assessment for young children was detailed in an effort to detect early possible learning difficulties. As a result of adopting a systems perspective, viewing communication in broad terms, utilizing alternative assessment methods, and observing behaviors rather than scoring tests, the speech-language pathologist and other members of the interdisciplinary team can design meaningful and appropriate intervention programs and strategies. These intervention strategies will be derived directly from the assessment process and can be implemented by a number of individuals, including family members, teachers, and other professionals.

CHAPTER 8

Occupational Therapy Evaluation

Winnie Dunn

Occupational therapists address activities of daily living, work, (including school work for children) and play and leisure as the necessary and desired outcomes for an individual's performance. The occupational therapist analyzes these areas by considering the contribution or barrier created by specific sensorimotor, cognitive, and psychosocial aspects of performance. Table 8–1 contains a list of common referral complaints addressed by occupational therapists.

OCCUPATIONAL THERAPY IN THE SCHOOLS

Occupational therapists work in schools to support educational outcomes. They accomplish this by identifying performance and environmental characteristics and by creating opportunities that facilitate successful educational outcomes. The interdisciplinary team structure supports these activities.

When occupational therapists work in schools, they have an obligation to provide services within an educational framework. P.L. 94-142 designates occupational therapy as a related service within educational settings. This means that occupational therapy is provided as it is needed to facilitate educational outcomes; other valid occupational therapy concerns that do not affect educationally relevant outcomes are dealt with in other settings.

TABLE 8–1

Common Referral Complaints Addressed by Occupational Therapists When Serving Students with Learning Disabilities

Gross Motor
Weaker than others
Unable to hop, skip, jump, run as others do
Movements are stiff and awkward
Confuses right and left
Bumps into furniture when walking around
Difficulty with dressing (e.g., donning jacket)

Postural Control
Slumps in desk
Holds head in hands
Hangs on furniture, other people for support
Fidgets in seat

Fine Motor/Visual Motor
Unable to cut
Difficulty manipulating objects (e.g., blocks)
Immature, unusual pencil grasp
Very tense pencil grasp
Weak pencil grasp, drops pencil frequently
Poor writing, coloring—light or too dark, poorly controlled
Cannot stay on the lines when writing
Cannot complete work in a timely manner
Cannot tie shoes, button shirt
Clumsy with personal hygiene items
Difficulty with mealtime utensils
Drops objects

Sensory Processing
Withdraws from touch, sounds, movements, bright light
Touches or grabs everything
Hates being hugged
Fearful about movement
Avoids heights (e.g., climbing)
Craves movement (e.g., swinging)
Lethargic

Perceptual, Cognitive, and Psychosocial Abilities
Difficulty matching, discriminating colors, shapes
Reversals in writing
Loses place on page
Poor copying ability
Cannot follow directions
Poor attention, distractible
Does not generalize skills
Low self-esteem
Difficulty with organization, time management
Emotional outbursts

Occupational therapists employ both screening and more comprehensive assessment procedures to evaluate children who are suspected of having learning disabilities. Screening procedures frequently are employed to identify developmental problems in preschoolers that may place them "at risk" for subsequent learning difficulties. Screening procedures may also be employed when a student has been identified as having difficulty with some aspect of the school experience. Team members, including occupational therapists, review records, speak to the classroom teacher, and observe during routine activities to determine whether further assessment is necessary. When problems can be resolved with simple adaptations, there is no need to conduct comprehensive assessments; they are costly and can be an arduous experience for the student.

If screening procedures suggest that more comprehensive assessment is warranted, the occupational therapist assesses performance in the areas of school work and learning, socialization, functional communication, work, play and leisure, and other life tasks. The occupational therapist assesses the child's performance in these areas as well as the underlying factors that enable or impede the student in carrying out the tasks. These underlying factors include sensorimotor functions, such as sensory and perceptual skills, modulation of responses to sensory input, motor planning, postural control, clumsiness/incoordination, and fine motor/visual-motor integration, as well as cognitive and psychosocial skills.

In addition to assessing the skills of the individual, occupational therapists consider the variables within the environment that support or impede task performance. The environment includes the persons and objects within the environment, the time and space needs for particular tasks, and the actual demands of the required tasks. Table 8–2 outlines the major assessment strategies used by occupational therapists to test students with learning disabilities. The formal tests available emphasize the sensorimotor systems; other areas are evaluated by skilled observation, interview, records review, and informal testing.

PERFORMANCE AREAS ADDRESSED IN THE OCCUPATIONAL THERAPY EVALUATION

Because the child's school performance depends on success in several different areas, the comprehensive occupational therapy evaluation will address performance in a variety of spheres, as discussed in the following sections (Dunn & Campbell, 1991).

Problems with School Work and Learning

There are many reasons for difficulty in learning and school work; the occupational therapist attempts to identify underlying factors that

TABLE 8-2A
Formal Tests Frequently Used by Occupational Therapists When Assessing Individuals with Learning Disabilities

Test Name	Age Range	Major Areas Tested						
		Gross Motor	Praxis	Fine Motor	Visual-Motor Integration	Visual Perception	Tactile	Vestibular
Motor-Free Visual Perceptual Test (MVPT)	4 – 8 years					X		
Sensory Integration and Praxis Test (SIPT)	4 years – 8 years 11 months	X	X	X	X	X	X	X
Test of Visual Motor Skills (TVMS)	2 – 12 years				X			
Beery Developmental Test of Visual-Motor Integration (VMI)	2 – 15 years				X			
Bruininks-Oseretsky Test of Motor Proficiency	4½ – 14 years	X	X	X	X			
Test of Visual Perceptual Skills (Non-motor) (TVPS)	4 – 12 years					X		

TABLE 8-2B
Other Strategies Employed by the Occupational Therapist When Assessing Individuals with Learning Disabilities

Assessment Strategy	Description
Skilled observations	The therapist observes the individual while the individual is performing functional tasks; records the features of task performance that promote or interfere with outcomes
Ecological assessment	The therapist records the features of typical performance of life routines, and then analyzes the differences between this pattern and the performance of the target individual
Interview	The therapist interviews a key person to obtain detailed information about the individual's performance abilities and difficulties; can be structured or unstructured
History taking	The therapist obtains information from checklists and interviews about the individual's development and past record of performance
Record review	The therapist systematically reviews materials which have been documented about the individual to determine salient features which might guide further assessment and intervention choices

support or interfere with learning. For example, the occupational therapist might evaluate a student who has the requisite knowledge and skills, but is unable to complete written assignments. The occupational therapist may identify problems in fine motor control for writing or perceptual deficits that make it difficult for the student to keep the place on the page while working. These underlying factors become the focus of intervention recommendations.

Problems with Socialization

Many students with learning disabilities have difficulty with some aspects of socialization. The occupational therapist analyzes the student's interactions and the settings in which they typically occur. Factors that facilitate and impede socialization are identified so that interventions can be developed. For example, a student approaches peers easily but often cannot sustain the interaction. Upon analysis of the situation, the occupational therapist determines that difficulty generally occurs in noisy environments, suggesting that the child is unable to maintain attention with the other noises. This observation provides the basis for intervention.

Problems with Functional Communication

Sometimes students with learning disabilities have difficulty with language and communication. Functional communication refers to the actions that support communication rather than the actual content of the messages. The occupational therapist addresses functional communication issues in collaboration with speech-language pathologists and educators. For example, successful communication requires the ability to recognize and use nonverbal cues (e.g., body posture, eye contact); this is a relevant aspect of communication to be assessed by the occupational therapist.

Problems with Play and Leisure

Students need to be able to make choices about the desired leisure activities and have the skills to engage in these activities. The occupational therapist assesses both skill development to support play and leisure and the cognitive and psychosocial development to support appropriate decision making. Assessment leads to recommendations regarding activities that might best suit the student, as well as accommodations that might be necessary to facilitate success in these activities.

Problems with Work

Adolescents with moderate to severe learning disabilities some-times have difficulties in work that are similar to those they encounter in school. Occupational therapists address both work preparation and work performance by examining the student's strengths and deficits and the match of these strengths and deficits to work requirements. Data obtained from this type of assessment are used to adapt the work site and provide support to students once they are placed. Home man-agement is also a relevant priority for some students; similar strategies are used to address these work tasks.

Problems with Life Tasks

It is less common for interdisciplinary teams to select personal ac-tivities of daily living as educationally relevant outcomes for students with learning disabilities. Although tasks pertaining to personal hy-giene, bathing, dressing, and eating can be difficult for students with moderate to severe learning disabilities, these tasks are more fre-quently carried out at home. When parents raise concerns and the be-haviors are not interfering with educational outcomes, it is appropriate to refer the family to an occupational therapist in the community.

UNDERLYING FACTORS THAT INTERFERE WITH PERFORMANCE

Although the ultimate goal of the occupational therapist is to in-crease the student's ability to perform functional tasks, it is the knowl-edge of the integrity of the underlying systems that guides individual-ized intervention planning. Occupational therapists use their expertise to determine the contribution or barrier produced by sensorimotor, cognitive, and psychosocial components of performance to overall suc-cess at the desired task. Interventions make use of this information by structuring situations to support students in their endeavors to learn and grow. Certain performance component problems are common for students with learning disabilities, and they will be discussed below.

Problems with the Sensorimotor Systems

The sensorimotor systems provide the mechanism by which indi-viduals learn about and act on the environment. Visual, auditory, touch, motion and body position information enable the individual to create maps about the body and the environment. When these maps are disrupted due to inaccurate or unreliable information from the sen-sory systems, behavior and performance are also affected. Table 8–2a contains a list of the formal tests that are used by occupational therapists to assess sensorimotor integrity. One of the most comprehensive tests is the Sensory Integration and Praxis Test (SIPT, Ayres, 1989), which consists of 18 subtests that evaluate skills in touch, movement, and body position, visual perception, praxis, and motor performance. Tests that contribute to the evaluation of each area are discussed in the following section.

Poor Sensory and Perceptual Skills

Some students with learning disabilities have difficulty receiving and processing sensory and perceptual information. Formal tests for assessing sensory and perceptual skills are listed in Table 8–2a. Deficits in visual perceptual skills may be observed informally in tasks such as copying from the chalkboard, writing answers in the place on the worksheet, or keeping one's place on the page. Perceptual problems may be reflected in the student's inability to follow directions, remember what has been said, and screen out environmental sounds while working.

The more basic sensory systems respond to touch, body position, and motion. These systems provide information that forms the individual's body scheme, or map of the body and how it works. Some students with learning disabilities have difficulty processing this basic sensory information, disrupting their body scheme. When the body scheme is unreliable or inaccurate, the student has difficulty using body parts to create effective responses to environmental demands. The SIPT contains specific subtests to assess the integrity of these basic sensory systems. Scores reveal a pattern of performance that is combined with other data to create a complete picture of sensory processing. The occupational therapist also assesses these areas by skilled observation of performance and through interviews and checklists from teachers and parents. The child with a poor body scheme has difficulty holding his or her body in the chair, or may "hang" on the back and hook his legs around the chair legs. Information from assessment of sensory and perceptual skills will be used to design interventions that include adaption of material and tasks as well as specific remedial activities.

Poorly Modulated Responses to Sensory Input

Most individuals have the ability to accommodate to environmental changes that occur during activities. Some students with learning disabilities have a poor ability to modulate the effects of sensory input on their performance. When a student is unable to accommodate to added sensory experiences, we describe them as hyperresponsive or hypersensitive to stimuli; when students require additional stimuli to notice or respond to the world around them, we use the term hyporesponsive or hyposensitive. Any sensory channel can be affected. The occupational therapist observes behavior, talks with the student, and obtains a thorough history about responsiveness to sensation to determine the pattern of this problem. Table 8–3 contains a list of common problems that students encounter when they are either hypersensitive or hyposensitive to sensory information.

TABLE 8–3
Common Observations When Sensory Systems are Poorly Modulated

Sensory System	Over-Reactive	Under-Reactive
Somatosensory (touch)	Defensive about others touching body Reacts emotionally or aggressively to touch Avoids selected textures Narrow range of clothing choices Rigid rituals in personal hygiene Extremely negative about dental work Picky eater, especially regarding textures Avoids haircuts, hairwashing	Slow to respond Does not notice others Uses poor judgment regarding personal space
Vestibular (movement)	Insecure about movement experiences Avoids or fears movement Holds head upright, even when bending over or leaning Avoids new positions, especially of head Holds onto walls or bannisters Very clumsy on changeable surfaces, such as a field	Clumsy, lethargic Slow to respond to movement demands Poor endurance, tires easily
Proprioceptive (body position)	Tense muscles Rigidity, diminished fluidity of movement	Weak grasp Poor endurance, locks joints Tires easily, collapses Hangs on objects for support
Visual	Avoids bright lights, sunlight Covers eyes in lighted room Watches everyone when they move around the room	Does not notice when people come into the room Difficulty in finding objects in drawer, on desk, on paper
Auditory	Overreacts to unexpected sounds Easily distracted in classroom Holds hands over ears	Does not respond to name being called Seems oblivious within an active environment

Poor Motor Planning (Dyspraxia)

Students with learning disabilities may also exhibit developmental dyspraxia (Cermak, 1985; Ayers, 1980). Students who have developmental dyspraxia have difficulty conceiving, organizing, and planning motor acts. Dyspraxia seems to be related to poor sensory processing, poor body scheme, and the resulting lack of adequate and reliable information upon which to build effective movements. The SIPT contains a set of praxis tests; the occupational therapist can gain understanding of the types of motor planning problems that exist and can verify test findings with observations and reports. As with other sensorimotor problems, the occupational therapist uses skilled observation of performance, interviews, and the child's developmental history to complete the picture of the motor difficulties.

Poor Postural Control

When students with learning disabilities hang on their chairs, lean on objects or persons when standing, and use external forces to keep them upright against gravity, problems with postural control are suspected. Poor postural control can have a sensory, experiential, or developmental base. When a student cannot hold his or her own body up against the forces of gravity, he or she is ill-equipped to engage in learning tasks. Classroom performance presumes the individual's ability to hold the body in place; when a student cannot even do this, little energy is left for learning. Occupational therapists perform clinical test of postural control, observe performance in school, and interview teachers and parents to determine the role of postural control in performance.

Clumsiness/Incoordination

Students with learning disabilities can display general difficulty with gross motor coordination. This is a common referral complaint received by occupational therapists in the schools. Clumsiness and incoordination can interfere with the student's own learning as well as disrupt the learning of classmates. Informally, the occupational therapist will observe that these students are clumsy; they drop their materials and trip on the furniture in the room, even when the furniture is in predictable locations. Motor tests are listed in Table 8–2a.

Poor Fine Motor/Visual-Motor Integration

It is very common for students with learning disabilities to have problems with fine motor (use of hands to manipulate objects) and visual motor (coordination of eyes and hands for manipulation) control. These skills are necessary for many school activities and tasks of daily life. When fine motor and visual motor skills are disrupted, the student has difficulty producing work efficiently; sometimes professionals misinterpret the poor work product as indicative of poor knowledge in content areas (e.g., the student is a poor speller) or of poor motivation.

Occupational therapists analyze the student's performance, task demands, the work product, and the results of formal tests to determine the exact type of visual motor integration problems that exist. Formal tests are listed in Table 8–2a. Intervention recommendations focus on adapting school work to decrease the demands for visual-motor output and providing specific activities to improve visual-motor skills.

Problems with Cognitive and Psychosocial Skills

In addition to the areas outlined above, the occupational therapy evaluation provides other information relevant to understanding the child's learning difficulties (e.g., difficulties in attention, motivation, behavior, organization, self-image, and generalization of learning). The occupational therapist provides support to the psychologist and special educator to identify cognitive and psychosocial ability and potential. While conducting a skilled observation in the classroom, the occupational therapist might identify behaviors that interfere with attention to seatwork, interaction skills with peers or authority figures, or coping and time management. During an individual session, the occupational therapist would record the student's ability to generalize skills to a new, but similar play situation. Several specific areas are addressed frequently by occupational therapists.

Attentional, Motivational and Behavioral Problems

The occupational therapist analyzes the contexts within which the student fails to exhibit adequate attention and motivation. When sensorimotor factors are barriers to increased attention and motivation, the occupational therapist addresses these concerns. When the problem lies in environmental areas, such as the need to establish an effective reinforcement method, the occupational therapist collaborates with other team members to identify an appropriate strategy.

The occupational therapist also considers the role of sensorimotor skills in behavioral problems such as frustration, aggression, and withdrawal. Many environmental and task adaptations are evaluated to decrease the impact of the student's problems on performance, and thus reduce frustration and inappropriate behaviors. Behavior management is also a viable team alternative.

Organizational Problems

The occupational therapist addresses organizational problems by evaluating the student's perceptual and sensorimotor difficulties, by observing learning environments (e.g., disorderly desk or locker), and interviewing the student regarding management strategies that work.

Poor Self-Image

The occupational therapist uses observation and interviews to clarify self-image status. The occupational therapist contributes to interdisciplinary, collaborative decisions in this area. Sometimes adaptations are successful because they enable the student to experience a positive outcome.

Problems with Generalizations of Learning

The entire team addresses systematically problems with generalization of learning, pointing out the similarities from one situation to another so the student can learn to tap already developed skills to solve current problems. The occupational therapist creates new situations that provide opportunities to practice these generalizations and collaborates with teaching staff to identify ways to make these opportunities available throughout the day.

CONCLUSION

Individuals with learning disabilities display a complex configuration of perceptual, cognitive, and sensorimotor difficulties. The occupational therapist evaluates the performance in many settings and assesses factors that may underlie observed deficits. These factors include sensorimotor function, sensory and perceptual skills, modulation of responses to sensory input, motor planning (dyspraxia), postural control, clumsiness/incoordination, and fine motor/visual-motor integration, as well as cognitive and psychosocial skills. By understanding the individual strengths and weaknesses of the child as well as the environmental barriers and facilitators, the occupational therapist assists in the development of appropriate adaptations and interventions.

CHAPTER 9

Interdisciplinary Diagnosis

Frank R. Brown, III
Elizabeth H. Aylward
Robert G. Voigt

The previous chapters described the methods for obtaining accurate assessments of intelligence and academic achievement, as well as other information relevant to understanding the child's learning difficulties. As stated previously, the diagnosis of learning disabilities for the school-age child is based on a significant discrepancy between a child's intellectual abilities and academic achievement. There is, however, a fair amount of controversy regarding appropriate methods for determining whether or not significant discrepancy exists. As discussed in Chapter 2, even more difficulty is encountered when we attempt to apply a discrepancy definition to identify learning disabilities in children who have not yet reached school age. This chapter will examine methods for integrating information from the various assessments to establish a diagnosis of learning disability.

IDENTIFYING SIGNIFICANT DISCREPANCY BETWEEN ACADEMIC ACHIEVEMENT AND INTELLECTUAL ABILITIES

Neither Public Law 94-142 nor other federal guidelines provide precise diagnostic criteria for establishing a significant discrepancy between academic achievement and cognitive expectation. Although many states and local school districts have convened committees to study this issue and have outlined procedures for identifying a significant discrepancy, there is, as yet, no universally accepted method for doing this. Cone and Wilson (1981) suggested that techniques for computing a discrepancy fall into four major groups: grade level deviations, expectancy formulae, standard score comparisons, and regression analyses. These methods or models vary in statistical rigor and yield somewhat different results.

Grade Level Deviations

Although widely used, possibly because of ease of computation, the grade level deviation approach is the most seriously flawed. In this method a child's score on an achievement test is compared to his or her actual grade placement. If achievement is markedly below grade level, a significant discrepancy is inferred. This is not an appropriate method for identifying children with learning disabilities. Grade level equivalents lack mathematical power, are imprecise, and are inconsistent across grade levels. The approach overidentifies slow learners and children in upper grades, while at the same time underidentifies more able and younger children. It will bar from services the bright child who is at or near grade level in academic skills but performs significantly below cognitive expectation. Similarly, children who are slow both cognitively and academically may be mislabeled as learning disabled. This method is also inappropriate because it generally delays the identification of learning disabilities until at least second grade. If a child does not qualify for special education services until he or she is two years below grade level, the child must experience at least two years in an inappropriate learning environment before receiving any special services, which results in undue frustration and wastes valuable time. Finally, the method is inappropriate because a child who is two years below grade level in the early elementary grades clearly is impaired more seriously than the child who is two years below grade level in secondary school. Many school systems fail to make this distinction when using this method to identify learning disabilities. In our view this is an inappropriate method for determining a discrepancy.

Simple Expectancy Formulae

Expectancy formulae provide a frequently used method for determining a discrepancy. They have considerable appeal as they also are relatively easy to compute and appear to be a straightforward way of combining cognitive and achievement data. In essence, a given child's expected achievement is predicted directly from his or her age or from

his or her score on an ability test. If the achievement is lower than expected, a learning disability is considered. Despite its appeal, the simple prediction method has limitations. Expectancy formulae which do
not take into account regression effects lead to identification of larger
proportions of brighter than duller children, and sometimes lead to
misinterpretations of formal fluctuations in ability-achievement. As
will be discussed in more detail in this chapter, unless regression effects
are considered, expectancy formulae based directly on IQ, like grade
level discrepancy methods, are inappropriate for identifying children
with learning disabilities.

Standard Scores

Standard scores provide still another approach to determining a discrepancy. Standard scores provide a common metric or common scale
for comparing the results of different tests. Test scores for a school district or classroom are statistically transformed to yield a score that represents the relative deviation from the average or mean. The mean in
standard score distributions is zero and the variance is expressed in units
of 1.00. Thus, a child who is achieving above the average for the group
might have a standard score of +1 or +2; a pupil whose achievement is
below the average would have a standard score of –1 or –2. These scores
then may be directly compared to scores on ability tests or on other
achievement tests. Applied to the discrepancy question, standard scores
allow a direct comparison of scores on aptitude and achievement tests,
even if the two tests have different ranges of actual scores and different
standard deviations. Standard scores also provide a common scale for
comparing performance levels across age or grade levels. Similar levels
of ability and of achievement, as is the case with average learners or
with slow learners, yield similar standard scores. Differences in standard
scores suggest differences between aptitude and achievement, thus indicating a possible learning disability. The method is technically sound
and yields relatively precise results. However, it also requires considerable statistical work and large samples and thus may not be feasible for
many school districts or diagnostic clinics.

A related method for computing a discrepancy involves comparing
scores on ability and achievement tests using deviations from average
as measured in standard deviations. Fortunately, most test developers
provide information about ability and achievement tests in standard
deviation units, based on the norming samples for the tests. This approach, like the statistical procedure described above, makes it possible
to compare test scores in terms of deviations from the mean or average.
Rather than transforming scores into units of 1.00, the variance from

the mean is shown as standard deviations. For example, the WISC-III or the K-ABC, described in Chapter 5, have means of 100 and standard deviations of 15. (The Stanford-Binet 4th Edition has a mean of 100 and a standard deviation of 16.). When used with achievement tests that have similar means and standard deviations, it is possible to define a significant discrepancy as 1, 1.5, or 2 standard deviation differences in scores (15, 22.5, and 30 points, respectively). A child with an IQ of 100 would have to obtain a score of 85 or below on the achievement test to be considered to have a learning disability, assuming that a cut-off of one standard deviation were being used; a child with an IQ of 115 would have to have a score of 100 or below on the achievement test to be eligible for learning disabilities services. It should be noted that the use of standard deviations for comparative purposes assumes that the norming samples from which the standard deviations were derived are appropriate for the children actually being assessed. Standard score methods are certainly superior to grade level comparisons when identifying a discrepancy between ability and achievement. Like those other methods, however, they do not account for regression effects.

The Concept of Regression Toward the Mean

Regardless of the trait being measured or the measurement instrument being used, there is always going to be some amount of error. A test with good reliability will have less "error of measurement" than a test that is less reliable. The WISC-III, which is considered to be one of the most reliable of all psychological instruments, has a standard error of measurement of 3 points on all verbal subtests and 4 points on all performance subtests (except block design, which is 3 points). This means that a child's "true IQ" (the average IQ that would be obtained if the test could be given an infinite number of times without any retest effects) will be no more than 3 points (verbal) or 4 points (performance, excepting block design where it will be no more than 3 points) higher or lower than the measured IQ approximately 68% of the time (the percentage of cases falling between +1 and −1 standard deviations on a normal curve). One can assume that the more deviant a score is, the larger the error of measurement it probably contains (Campbell & Stanley, 1963). Thus, the child with an extremely high score can be considered to have had unusually good "luck" (large positive error) and the extremely low scorer bad "luck" (large negative error). Because luck is capricious, one would expect students with extremely high scores on one test to score somewhat less well on a subsequent test. Similarly, the child unfortunate enough to receive a very low score on an initial test can be expected to score somewhat higher on a subsequent test. This phenomenon is known as *regression toward the mean*. That is, when a particular child has a score on one test that is above or below the mean, one can expect the score on a subsequent test to be nearer to, or to regress toward, the test mean. This is especially true when scores are farther from the mean or when the test is less reliable.

When one is comparing scores on two tests (e.g., an intelligence test and an academic achievement test), the problem of regression becomes even more serious than when one is comparing scores on the same test given on two occasions. The lower the correlation between the two tests, the greater the amount of regression that can be expected. Although regression toward the mean cannot be eliminated, it can be minimized by selecting tests that have good reliability. Based on the strengths and limitations of the various approaches, many diagnosticians and statisticians recommend a regression-discrepancy approach (Reynolds, 1984). For example, when using standard scores, regression effects are taken into account when the 10–15% of children with the largest discrepancies at each IQ level are identified. This ensures similar decision rules or "equal opportunity" across the IQ continuum. Estimating regression effects adds complexity but allows more accurate decisions about discrepancies, and also guards against over- or underrepresentation at any IQ level. This is well illustrated when predicting Educational Quotients (EQs).

Predicting Educational Quotients

School systems have begun to take the phenomenon of regression toward the mean into account by charting predicted Educational Quotients for children with various IQ scores. By looking at Table 9–1, it becomes clear that a child whose IQ is above average can be expected to have a lower EQ than IQ. Similarly, the child whose IQ is below average can be expected to have a higher EQ than IQ. For example, a girl with an IQ of 130, which is considerably above average, can be expected to perform very well on an achievement test, but not quite as high as the 130 score. Table 9–1 indicates that she should be expected to have an achievement test standard score of approximately 118, assuming that academic achievement has progressed at a level commensurate with her IQ. If the achievement test score is significantly below 118 (not 130), one can make a diagnosis of a learning disability (assuming that other causative factors, such as emotional disturbance or lack of educational opportunity, have been ruled out).

Regardless of the method used to measure cognitive ability and academic achievement, decisions must be made as to what will be considered a "significant discrepancy." Differences in the size of the dis-

TABLE 9–1
Predicted Educational Quotients (EQs) for Given VIQs, PIQs, and Full Scale IQs

VIQ or Full Scale IQ	Predicted EQ	PIQ	Predicted EQ
130	118	130	115
125	115	125	113
120	112	120	110
115	109	115	108
110	106	110	105
105	103	105	103
100	100	100	100
95	97	95	98
90	94	90	95
85	91	85	93
80	88	80	90
75	85	75	88
70	82	70	85

(Predicted EQs are somewhat different for PIQs than for VIQs or Full Scale IQs because the correlation between academic achievement and nonverbal intelligence is lower than that between academic achievement and verbal intelligence. See McLeod, 1979, for a more in-depth discussion of this issue.)

crepancy obviously lead to different numbers of children identified as learning disabled. McLeod (1979) suggests a cut-off of 1.5 standard deviations. Thus, if a child's score on a test of academic achievement is 22.5[1] points lower than the predicted EQ, a significant discrepancy has been identified, and the diagnosis of learning disability can be made. In the case described in the previous paragraph, the student's standard score on the test of academic achievement would have to be 95.5 (118 –22.5) in order for her to be diagnosed as having a learning disability. Some school systems may choose a cutoff of 1 or 2 standard deviations in defining significant discrepancy. The cutoff level chosen will depend upon the system's philosophy regarding learning disabilities, as well as on its ability to provide services for children identified as learning disabled.

Further Considerations in Identifying Discrepancy

Choosing the Measure of Intelligence for the Cognitive-Achievement Comparison

Even after determining which tests of intelligence and academic achievement will be administered and the degree of discrepancy

---

[1]This number is derived by multiplying 1.5×15 (which is the standard deviation of most intelligence tests and academic achievement tests).

needed to constitute significance, the interdisciplinary team must decide which individual scores will be compared in making the diagnosis of learning disabilities. For children whose Verbal IQ-Performance IQ (VIQ-PIQ), or Simultaneous-Sequential discrepancy is small, it is not unreasonable to compare the WISC-III Full Scale IQ or K-ABC Mental Processing Composite standard score with the standard scores from the test(s) of academic achievement. However, when there is a large VIQ-PIQ discrepancy, several different approaches to the discrepancy issue can be justified. Take, for example, a child with a WISC-III VIQ of 85, PIQ of 115, and Full Scale IQ of 99, and a standard score in "reading achievement" of 85. Because of the child's significant VIQ-PIQ discrepancy, it would not be appropriate to consider the child's Full Scale IQ of 99 as an accurate representation of intellectual functioning. Therefore, it would not be justifiable to use the Full Scale IQ in determining the presence of significant discrepancy between intellectual and academic abilities.

Because reading ability is more highly correlated with verbal abilities than with visual-spatial abilities, it could be argued that the child should not be expected to be reading at a level higher than the level of the child's verbal abilities. Thus, using the VIQ of 85 alone as the measure of cognitive functioning, Table 9–1 indicates that the predicted EQ would be 91. The difference between the predicted EQ of 91 and the actual reading achievement score would be 6 points. Because this does not meet the cutoff of 1.5 standard deviation discrepancy (22.5 points), no learning disability would be identified.

It could, however, be argued just as reasonably that the mechanism that is preventing verbal skills from developing at the same rate as nonverbal (visual-spatial) skills is the same mechanism that is preventing better development of reading skills. Using this reasoning, the "reading achievement" standard score of 85 could be justifiably compared with the PIQ of 115. Table 9–1 indicates that an EQ of 108 would be predicted for an IQ of 115. The discrepancy between the EQ and the actual reading achievement score in this case is 23 points, which would be significant if a cut-off of 1.5 standard deviations (22.5 points) is used. Thus, a learning disability would be identified. We believe that this approach is more attuned to the definition of learning disabilities outlined in Public Law 94-142, which includes disorders in "the understanding of language" as learning disabilities. Similarly, it would be justifiable to compare the score of academic achievement with the VIQ alone, if the VIQ were significantly higher than the PIQ, as the Public Law 94-142 definition includes such conditions as "perceptual handicaps."

The procedure for determining predicted EQs is not necessary if one uses the K-ABC for both measures of intellectual functioning and academic achievement, as the cutoffs for significant discrepancy between tests are provided in the manual. The K-ABC routinely requires the examiner to compare the standard scores for each of the Mental Processing Scales (Sequential, Simultaneous, and Composite) with the standard score for the Achievement Scale. Thus, a significant difference between achievement and any of the scores of Mental Processing could be an indication of a learning disability.

The K-ABC does not, however, encourage routine comparison of each of the Mental Processing scores (Sequential, Simultaneous, and Composite) with individual Achievement subtest scores, but rather with the overall Achievement composite score. Thus, the routine comparison of Mental Processing scores with the overall Achievement scale may not detect the child who is seriously delayed in only one area of academic achievement. Kaufman and Kaufman (1983) caution that the Mental Processing scores can be compared with individual Achievement subtest scores, if the number of comparisons is limited by selecting wisely the most appropriate comparisons to make, based on background information about the child. Of course, the interdisciplinary team will often want to compare the child's K-ABC Mental Processing scores with scores from achievement tests other than the K-ABC. In this case, the procedure for predicting EQs outlined earlier should be followed.

If the Stanford-Binet has been used as the measure of intelligence, it seems reasonable that either the Verbal Reasoning standard area score (SAS), the Abstract/Visual Reasoning SAS, or the Composite IQ be used as the measure of cognitive ability. SASs from the Short-Term Memory or Quantitative Reasoning Scales do not, however, reflect broad enough abilities to justify their use as the measure of cognitive ability for the diagnosis of learning disability.

Considering Individual Subtest Scores in the Cognitive-Achievement Comparison

It is important to point out that the interdisciplinary team, in making the diagnosis of learning disability, may sometimes need to consider the individual subtest scores that go into making up the overall scores of intellectual functioning (WISC-III VIQ, PIQ; K-ABC Sequential Processing standard score, Simultaneous Processing standard score; Stanford-Binet SASs or Test Composite) and overall scores of academic functioning (e.g., WJR-ACH Reading Cluster, Mathematics Cluster, and Written Language Cluster scores). For example, on the WISC-III, several of the subtests (Similarities, Comprehension, Vocabulary) are often considered to measure more "important intelligences" than other subtests (Information, Arithmetic, Digit Span). As described in Chapter 5, the Arithmetic and Digit Span scores can often be depressed in a child who has attention-deficit/hyperactivity disorder, and the Information subtest is greatly influenced by environmental stimulation (including reading). Thus, when a child's scaled scores on Similarities, Comprehension, and Vocabulary are significantly higher than his or her scaled scores on Information, Arithmetic, and Digit Span, his or her VIQ may not be an accurate reflection of the "more important" verbal skills-abstract thinking, verbal concept formation, and verbal expression, but may be depressed by verbal skills often considered less important—auditory attention, fund of general knowledge, short-term memory. The team may want to take this pattern of scores into account when making the diagnosis. If, for example, the child with the pattern just described did not have quite enough discrepancy between the VIQ and scores of academic achievement to meet the cutoff for the diagnosis of learning disabilities, the team may want to take into consideration other data to determine if the VIQ was not artificially depressed by factors not generally considered indicators of intelligence (e.g., distractibility) and adjust the criteria for diagnosis.

Similarly, the team should take into account variability within the subtest scores that comprise the measures of overall academic achievement. For example, a child may be reading on grade level, according to the overall reading cluster score. However, the child might perform three years above grade level in word recognition and application of phonics skills, but be functioning five years below grade level in passage comprehension. In this case the child's overall reading cluster score does not adequately summarize his or her reading abilities. The interdisciplinary team should again not abide by the strict criteria established for making the diagnosis of learning disability, but should consider other data that might explain the discrepancy within reading skills.

Need for Flexibility in Diagnosis

It is imperative that professionals use the formula for identifying learning disabilities as a guideline, and not as an absolute authority. For many children, it will be just as important to take into account reports from teachers and parents, observations during testing, and other data sources before arriving at a diagnosis. In some cases, it will not be possible to find a reliable and valid test to measure the child's skill in a particular area. For example, many children perform quite well on measures of written language ability, although teachers and parents insist that the child has a great deal of difficulty when required to organize his or her thoughts in writing. Because most of the tests available for obtaining a score in written language focus on the mechanics of writing (e.g., spelling, punctuation, usage, capitalization), it may not be possible to diagnose a learning disability in written language by using test scores alone. It would be necessary in such a case for the team to

take into consideration teacher and parent reports, to observe the child
in a situation that requires him or her to write a paragraph, and to evaluate subjectively the child's written work in terms of content, organization, neatness, and time taken to complete it, as well as correct use of
spelling, punctuation, grammar, capitalization, and so forth. Only then
can an accurate diagnosis be made, regardless of the presence or absence of significant discrepancy between test scores.

It is especially important that the interdisciplinary team consider
factors other than the EQ-IQ discrepancy when making the diagnosis
of learning disabilities in younger children. Because academic testing in
the early grades (kindergarten and first grade) is based primarily on
material that can be learned by rote (e.g., letter and number identification, sight words, addition facts), it may be difficult to identify the child
who will have problems with more complex processes (e.g., application
of phonics rules, reading for comprehension, understanding math concepts). For these young children, it is very important that the interdisciplinary team rely heavily on teacher and parent reports.

IDENTIFYING PRESCHOOL-AGE CHILDREN
AT RISK FOR LEARNING DISABILITIES

In Chapter 2 we pointed up the difficulties that arise when we attempt to use discrepancy definitions, that is, discrepancies between academic achievement and cognitive expectation, to identify preschool-
age children at risk for subsequent learning disabilities. At least two
approaches to early identification, each based on a discrepancy model,
can be envisaged to identify preschoolers with learning disabilities. The
first approach, delineated by McCarthy (1989a) and the National Joint
Committee on Learning Disabilities (Leigh, 1986), suggests that
preschoolers at risk for subsequent learning disabilities will manifest
abilities and behaviors that deviate from normative expectancies. Discrepancies between anticipated and realized developmental milestones
(i.e., developmental delays), especially in the areas of language and visual perceptual development, attention span, impulse control, and behavior, are used to identify preschoolers at risk for subsequent learning
disabilities. It is our contention that this neurodevelopmental approach
will identify preschoolers at risk for ongoing neurodevelopmental delays and slow academic achievement commensurate with cognitive expectation. We do not anticipate that this approach would specifically
identify that subgroup of preschoolers who will progress to have academic achievement that is discrepant from the slow achievement projected from the neurodevelopmental delay.

A second approach to early identification might be based on identifying significant discrepancies between cognitive expectation (as mea-

sured by appropriate preschool-age cognitive measures) and what might be termed "preacademics", that is, antecedents of subsequent academic achievement. While McCarthy (1989a) and others include the assessment of "preacademic skills" in their discrepancy definitions for preschoolers, it appears that they are referring to underlying cognitive skills that form the basis for learning (e.g., verbal comprehension and concept formation, auditory and visual attention, verbal and visual memory). We are using the term preacademic skills to refer to specific skills that can be considered the first actual demonstration of academic achievement in reading (e.g., letter identification, alphabet recitation, sound-symbol correspondence, rhyming, identification of words with the same initial sound), math (rote counting, number recognition, making a one-to-one correspondence, understanding concepts such as less than, more than, same as, most), and writing (e.g., copying geometric forms and letters, writing one's own name). In this discrepancy approach, preschoolers with learning disabilities would be identified through an extrapolation of the "significant discrepancy" definition used with school-age children, with "preacademics" substituted for academic achievement in the discrepancy definition. The difficulty with this approach is that, to date, very few instruments have been developed that measure preacademic skills, as we define them (e.g., the Basic Concept Scale, Bracken, 1990). Furthermore, this approach requires documentation that the child has had some exposure to preacademic skills, either through formal preschool, parental instruction, or, at the very least, regular viewing of Sesame Street and other preschool television programs. While this approach would probably result in a fair number of misidentifications, we feel confident that early signs of learning disabilities could be demonstrated in at least some subgroups of preschoolers (e.g., bright children who have had several years of academic preschool exposure and who are still unable to identify their own name in writing).

To our knowledge, no longitudinal studies have been conducted to investigate the predictive value of either the neurodevelopmental or preacademic/cognitive discrepancy formulations in identifying preschoolers at risk for subsequent specific learning disabilities. Pending such studies, we must conclude, as indicated earlier in Chapter 2, that identification of preschoolers at risk for subsequent learning disabilities is, at best, tentative at present.

IDENTIFYING STRENGTHS AND WEAKNESSES IN THE LEARNING STYLE

Many investigators have attempted to classify children with learning disabilities (particularly reading disabilities) according to their specific difficulties. Children with reading disabilities are often thought to fall into one of two categories. Children in the first group (sometimes called *dysphonetic* dyslexics) have difficulty with auditory processing and are unable to make accurate phoneme-grapheme correspondences, are unable to break words into their phonetic components and blend the sounds together to form the correct word, and have difficulty sequencing phonemes correctly. These children make bizarre spelling errors unrelated to the sound of the word. Children in the second group (sometimes called *dyseidetic* dyslexics) have difficulty with visual-spatial perception and may be unable to recognize individual letters, are slow to recognize simple sight words (visual gestalts), have poor visual discrimination of words closely similar in configuration, and have trouble recognizing nonphonetically spelled words. These children read very slowly, as they must decode each word as they go along. They spell words the way they sound, ignoring irregular patterns usually learned through a sight approach (e.g., *tough* may be spelled *tuff*).

Some investigators have divided children with reading disabilities into these or similar groupings based on the direction of the VIQ-PIQ or Sequential-Simultaneous discrepancy, subtest profiles from the intelligence tests, or by an analysis of reading and spelling errors. In some schools, attempts have been made to tailor the curriculum to address the strengths and weaknesses presumed to be exhibited by the different groups. Sadly, there is not much evidence for success in this type of approach. Learning disabilities must certainly be considered a heterogeneous disorder. The differences among students with learning disabilities are, however, probably too complex to allow us to base treatment on the child's membership in one of a limited number of broadly defined subgroups.

This is not to imply, however, that the team cannot learn much about the nature of the child's learning disabilities by examining test results and other data for specific patterns. After one has identified whether or not a learning disability exists, it may be helpful for those who are going to be working with the child to identify strengths and weaknesses in the child's learning style. In identifying strengths and weaknesses, the team should consider subtest patterns on the intelligence test as well as scores from some of the tests that were suggested as possible additions to the psychologist's battery. For example, it may be helpful for the child's teacher to know that he or she has excellent ability to perceive visual-spatial stimuli (as indicated by a high Performance IQ and good performance on a test of visual perception), but poor fine motor skills (as evidenced by slowness on the Coding subtest, sloppiness on the Mazes subtest, and poor performance on the Developmental Test of Visual-Motor Integration). The teacher would then know that he or she should not waste time on activities to strengthen visual-per-

ceptual skills, but should instead work on strategies to remedy or circumvent the poor fine-motor skills. Kaufman and Kaufman (1983) provide many suggestions for approaching children with various profiles on
the K-ABC (difficulties with Simultaneous Processing, Sequential Processing, or both). Although strategies based on the test pattern profiles
have reasonable face validity, there is little evidence that they are the
most effective approaches to remediating the learning disabilities.

IDENTIFYING ASSOCIATED PROBLEMS

In addition to diagnosing learning disabilities and identifying areas
of strength and weakness in the cognitive and achievement profiles, the
team should attempt to identify associated problems that may be interfering with learning. Many of the problems that teachers consider most
disruptive to the learning process are sometimes thought of as "behavior problems." By better understanding the basis of these problems, the
teacher can better help the child overcome them. The interdisciplinary
team has available several sources of data for identifying these problems that interfere with learning: teacher reports, parents reports, child
interview, classroom observation, neurodevelopmental evaluation, test
results, observation during testing, and subtest profiles. Various combinations of these data will be needed to identify the problems that exacerbate, or are exacerbated by, the learning disabilities.

Attention-Deficit/Hyperactivity Disorder

A disorder commonly seen in conjunction with learning disabilities
is attention-deficit/hyperactivity disorder (AD/HD). AD/HD is a primary neurologically based disabling condition manifest by levels of
inattention, poor impulse control, and excessive motor activity which
are inappropriate for a child's level of development, and which interfere with appropriate social, academic, or occupational functioning. In
analogy to our "significant discrepancy" model for the diagnosis of specific learning disabilities, AD/HD should only be diagnosed when there
exists a significant discrepancy between a child's attention span and his
or her underlying level of developmental (particularly cognitive) function. Most investigators estimate the prevalence of AD/HD to be between 3 and 10% of children younger than 18 years of age (Szatmari,
Offord, & Boyle, 1989). Studies of medication treatment for children
with AD/HD reveal a consistent doubling of the rate of medication
treatment every four to seven years, such that by 1987, approximately
6% of all public elementary students in Baltimore were receiving stim-

ulant medication (Safer & Krager, 1988). However, other investigators claim that the prevalence rate of AD/HD may well be over 20% (Shaywitz & Shaywitz, 1988). Some question whether these higher estimates of AD/HD prevalence may actually represent a cultural phenomenon unique to this country, rather than representing a true prevalence rate of a neurodevelopmental disability (Golden, 1992).

Diagnosis of AD/HD—Checklist Approaches

Before 1980, the majority of thinking about deficits of attention span, impulse control, and hyperactivity focused on neurodevelopmental perspectives. One such formulation was the concept of minimal brain dysfunction (MBD; Wender, 1971), which presented deficits of attention span, impulse control, and hyperactivity as part of a broader spectrum of subtle neurological dysfunction. While the MBD construct was in line with current neurodevelopmental thinking, the term MBD was unpopular—not surprisingly because of the combination of the words brain dysfunction—even if preceded by the word minimal. In part as a result, a trend has evolved to split the spectrum of minor motor and central processing dysfunction to define component disorders, including AD/HD. Since 1980 then, thinking about AD/HD has shifted from a neurodevelopmental to a behavioral focus, with a multitude of behavioral checklists currently available to describe behaviors often seen in children with AD/HD.

Probably the most widely recognized of these behavioral checklists used to describe the symptoms of AD/HD are those that have been devised by the American Psychiatric Association (APA) in the *Diagnostic and Statistical Manuals of Mental Disorders*—DSM-III (APA, 1980), DSM-III-R (APA, 1987), and the recently released DSM-IV (APA, 1994). Under current DSM-IV behavioral parlance, to meet APA criteria for AD/HD, the child must evidence at least six symptoms from a checklist of items describing either inattention and/or hyperactivity-impulsivity. Checklist items include (APA, 1994):

> INATTENTION
> (a) often fails to give attention to details or makes careless mistakes in school work, work, or other activities
> (b) often has difficulty sustaining attention in tasks or play activities
> (c) often does not seem to listen when spoken to directly
> (d) often does not follow through on instructions and fails to finish school work, chores, or duties in the work place (not due to oppositional behavior or failure to understand instructions)

(e) often has difficulty organizing tasks and activities

(f) often avoids, dislikes, or is reluctant to engage in tasks that require sustained mental effort (such as school work or homework)

(g) often loses things necessary for tasks or activities (e.g., toys, school assignments, pencils, books, or tools)

(h) is often easily distracted by extraneous stimuli

(i) is often forgetful in daily activities

HYPERACTIVITY

(a) often fidgets with hands or feet, or squirms in seat

(b) often leaves seat in classroom or in other situations in which remaining seated is expected

(c) often runs about or climbs excessively in situations in which it is inappropriate (in adolescents or adults, may be limited to subjective feelings of restlessness)

(d) often has difficulty playing or engaging in leisure activities quietly

(e) is often "on the go" or often acts as if "driven by a motor"

(f) often talks excessively

IMPULSIVITY

(g) often blurts out answers before questions have been completed

(h) often has difficulty awaiting turn

(i) often interrupts or intrudes on others (e.g., butts into conversations or games)

Compared with earlier DSM checklist approaches to AD/HD diagnosis, DSM-IV diagnostic criteria incorporate several important modifications that are much more in line with current neurodevelopmental thinking:

1. First is the subtle incorporation of a slash ("/") in the term attention-deficit/hyperactivity disorder. This slash indicates that deficits of attention span, hyperactivity, and impulsivity may occur separately or concurrently. This acknowledgment is consistent with the neurodevelopmental principle of associated deficits (delays in one developmental domain are most typically accompanied by delays in other domains, which may be more subtle and difficult to observe).

2. DSM-IV criteria for AD/HD diagnosis demand that symptoms of inattentiveness and/or impulsiveness be "maladaptive and inconsistent with developmental level" (p. 83). This acknowledgment that deficits of attention span and impulse control can only be interpreted within the

context of a child's level of developmental function is obviously consistent with neurodevelopmental principles we will discuss shortly.

3. DSM-IV criteria for AD/HD diagnosis require that symptoms of inattentiveness and/or impulsiveness be present across settings (e.g., at school and at home). This requirement is consistent with the neurodevelopmental perspective that AD/HD is a primary neurologically based disabling condition. As such, the clinician should expect that symptoms of inattentiveness and/or impulsiveness would be present across settings, and would not be as situationally restricted as in more behaviorally based disorders, such as conduct disorder or oppositional defiant disorder.

4. Finally, DSM-IV criteria acknowledge that AD/HD should not be diagnosed if the checklist symptoms are better accounted for by other conditions, including anxiety disorders, mood disorders, psychotic disorders, pervasive developmental disorders, or side effects of medications.

A major shortcoming of checklist approaches to the diagnosis of AD/HD is that checklists fail to recognize that inattentiveness and impulsiveness may be secondary, rather than primary phenomenon. Table 9–2 lists the more frequent causes of perceived "inattention," "poor impulse control," or "hyperactivity." Any entry in this table can theoretically present as meeting checklist criteria for AD/HD. Primary neurologically based AD/HD should not be diagnosed until all other secondary causes of perceived inattention and/or impulsiveness have been identified and appropriately addressed. Additionally, a diagnosis of AD/HD should not be made unless the symptoms are present across settings (home and school), appear chronic in nature, and interfere significantly with the child's ability to function effectively.

AD/HD—Neurodevelopmental Perspectives and Interdisciplinary Diagnosis

Appreciating some of the limitations of behavioral checklist approaches to diagnosis of AD/HD, we will look at an alternative diagnostic approach based on neurodevelopmental principles and an interdisciplinary process. This broader neurodevelopmental focus, looking both at the severity of attentional delay and for the presence of associated deficits, might help clarify many issues left unresolved by the current behavioral checklist approaches.

Research has shown that approximately one third of individuals with developmental disabilities will exhibit a limitation in one domain of development, another third, disabilities in two areas of development, and the remaining third, disabilities in three or more areas of develop-

TABLE 9–2
Causes of Inattention, Poor Impulse Control, or Hyperactivity

General Medical	Neurodevelopmental	Psychosocial-Psychiatric

Side effect of medication
  antihistamines
  anticonvulsants
  bronchodilators
	Hearing impairment
	Visual impairment
	Uncontrolled seizure disorder
		Chaotic social environment
		Inconsistent parenting, understructured family

Sleep apnea/other sleep disturbance	Neurodegenerative disorders	Child abuse/neglect
	AD/HD	Parental psychopathology
Malnutrition (skipping breakfast)	Learning disabilities	Conduct disorder
	Language disorders	Oppositional defiant disorder
Anemia	Perceptual disorders	Anxiety disorder
Hypo/hyperthyroidism	Slower learning	Post-traumatic stress disorder
	Mental retardation	Depression
Chronic medical illness necessitating frequent absences from school	Pervasive developmental disorder/autism	Manic-depressive illness
	"Average" child in a "high achieving" family	Schizophrenia/thought disorder
	Normal preschoolers	Personality disorder
	Increased intelligence (boredom in classroom)	Reactive emotional states
	Tourette syndrome	Adjustment disorder
		Drug abuse syndromes
		Mood disorder
		Dissociative disorder

ment (Conley, 1973). Neurodevelopmentalists bring focus on the issue of multiple disabilities through the concept of associated deficits. This term implies that although delays in one area of development appear most prominent, professionals examining children should be on the lookout for associated and perhaps more subtle areas of intercurrent developmental delay. In other words, individuals with an obvious disabling condition (e.g., short attention span) can be anticipated, until proven otherwise, to exhibit associated deficits in other areas of developmental function—multiple disabilities, as opposed to isolated singular deficits, will predominate (Brown & Elksnin, 1994).

Deficits of attention span or impulse control, like other primary neurologically based disabling conditions, rarely exist in isolation. Children with symptoms of short attention span and/or poor impulse control usually exhibit some degree of associated deficits in areas such as motor coordination (gross, fine, and/or oral motor), cognitive processing, and learning. If we reflect on the term minimal brain dysfunction, we will appreciate that the MBD construct included mild, diffuse neurological dysfunction in attention span and impulse control, but also included associated dysfunction in motor control (gross and fine motor dyscoordination, deficits of speech articulation), scatter or unevenness on psychological testing, learning disabilities, language disabilities, perceptual disabilities, and the like. The MBD construct is therefore broader than the AD/HD construct and makes allowance for the additional deficits frequently found in association with deficits of attention span and impulse control. All of this is not to advocate for a return to the older terminology of MBD, but rather to point up the need to carefully evaluate children for associated neurological deficits when they seem to manifest with predominant deficits of attention span and impulse control (i.e., AD/HD symptomatology).

As underscored in the current DSM-IV diagnostic criteria for AD/HD, when diagnosing AD/HD it is imperative that the clinician evaluate a child's attention span, impulse control, and motor activity level in light of the child's level of developmental function. In neurodevelopmental terms a definite relationship exists between a child's level of developmental (especially cognitive) function and his or her attention span. Thus, before diagnosing a child as having AD/HD, an assessment needs to be made as to what the child is inherently developmentally "able" to do (attend to). No conclusions about a child's attention span or level of impulse control can be made unless the child's underlying cognitive abilities are assessed. Such a cognitive assessment would serve to determine whether a child's perceived difficulties with inattention and/or hyperactivity are, in fact, inappropriate for his or her developmental level.

In addition to assessing a child's level of developmental function prior to diagnosing AD/HD, it is equally important to inquire into the level of developmental challenge in the home and school environment. A diagnosis of AD/HD cannot be made unless the clinician knows what a child is cognitively able to pay attention to, and once this is known, the diagnosis should not be made until environmental demands are made congruent with what the child is inherently able to attend to. Put simply, a child does not have AD/HD if he or she appears inattentive when required to pay attention to materials inappropriate for the child's cognitive abilities.

A final consideration in diagnosing AD/HD is the need to appreciate that neurologically driven deficits of attention span and/or impulse control are frequently accompanied by secondary behaviorally and emotionally based deficits. Put in other terms, deficits of attention span (neurologically based) are frequently accompanied by a surplus of attention-seeking behaviors. This creates much confusion in behavioral checklist approaches to AD/HD diagnosis, as many of these checklists include items which are behavioral in origin and tangential to the supposed components of AD/HD as reflected in DSM-IV diagnostic criteria. Thus, in many of these diversified checklists, it is difficult to assess whether we are identifying AD/HD or related and secondary behavioral expressions (Zelko, 1991).

From our discussion so far, it should be obvious that primary neurologically based AD/HD rarely exists in isolation. It is not uncommon for a child with primary neurologically based AD/HD to possess intercurrent difficulties that in and of themselves can be primary causes of perceived "inattention," "poor impulse control," or "hyperactivity" (Table 9–2). In such cases, it is often difficult to determine if both problems exist concurrently (co-morbid conditions) or if one condition is actually causing the other. For example, children with learning disabilities often have an intercurrent neurologically based AD/HD. It has been estimated that nearly three quarters of children with AD/HD also exhibit specific learning disabilities, and that approximately half of children with specific learning disabilities exhibit an intercurrent AD/HD (Accardo, Blondis, & Whitman, 1990).

Children with learning disabilities, however, even if they do not have AD/HD, are often misperceived by teachers and parents to be "inattentive" because of difficulties with school achievement. For example, in the case of a child with a reading disability, it is possible that a teacher may confuse difficulty with reading with "inattention" to reading assignments. In such cases, it is sometimes difficult to assess if the learning disability is causing the perceived inattention, if AD/HD is causing decreased achievement in reading due to inattention, or if in fact, the child is exhibiting learning disabilities and AD/HD concurrently. Also, children with unrecognized learning disabilities are often expected to achieve at a level for which they are not developmentally equipped (without accommodations and special help at school). In such cases, developmental abilities and environmental expectations are discrepant, and secondary social, emotional, and behavioral difficulties can develop. Again, the secondary behavioral and emotional difficulties might be misperceived as inattention, poor impulse control, or hyperactivity, and the child might well be misperceived as having AD/HD.

Given these and other complexities involved in diagnosing AD/HD, it can only be concluded that a comprehensive, interdisciplinary evaluation is required before reaching firm conclusions about the primary cause of inattention, poor impulse control, or hyperactivity in each child. Such an interdisciplinary team approach would consist minimally of the child's parents, the child's teachers, the child's primary care physician, and the school's educational diagnostician. In the process of making a diagnosis of AD/HD, the interdisciplinary team will want to consider data from several sources. Emphasis should be placed on data gathered from the environments in which the child typically functions (i.e., the classroom and the home), as the child may not display distractibility, impulsivity, and hyperactivity in the novel one-to-one situation of the physician's office or during educational diagnostic testing. The team will want to consider information gathered through the teacher'(s) interview, focusing especially on items regarding the child's activity level, ability to pay attention, follow directions, complete assignments, and control impulsivity. Similar information gathered through a classroom observation should also be considered. Data gathered from the parent interview will be of great importance in determining the existence of AD/HD symptomatology across time and across situations, thus guaranteeing that the symptoms result from a child's "wiring" rather than from being a response to a frustrating learning situation.

Some of the most important diagnostic clues from the individual assessments (medicine, psychology, and special education) include:

1. Inattentiveness may manifest in the physician's neurodevelopmental assessment in terms of variability in performance with tests of rote auditory memory, including variability in repeating digits and impulsive execution of the Gesell drawings. In addition, subtle associated neurologically based deficits in fine motor coordination, gross motor coordination, visual problem solving, language processing, and/or speech articulation will be noted during the neurodevelopmental assessment.

2. In the medical, psychological, and special education assessments, a child with AD/HD may evidence difficulty paying attention and staying on task. Examples would include frequent requests for repetition of oral questions and directions, easy distractibility to visual and auditory stimuli, irrelevant comments or attempts to relate personal experiences that are brought to mind by various test stimuli, and tendencies to lose track of the tasks presented. The impulsive components of AD/HD may manifest as tendencies to give the first answer that comes to mind, to begin tasks before instructions are completed, and to grab for materials before the examiner is ready to present them.

3. From the psychological assessment, a pattern of excessive distractibility can be hypothesized when relatively low scores are obtained on the WISC-III Arithmetic, Digit Span, and Coding subtests (i.e., the Freedom from Distractibility Factor) or on the K-ABC Magic Window, Face Recognition, Hand Movements, Number Recall, Word Order,

and Spatial Memory. (See Chapter 5 for a discussion of subtest patterns.) These subtests, which are affected by the child's ability to focus attention, are naturally also affected by many other unrelated factors, such as anxiety, during the testing situation. For this reason, a pattern of poor performance on these subtests should not be used as the primary determinant for making a diagnosis of AD/HD.

To repeat, in the diagnosis of AD/HD it is important to assess attention span within the settings in which the child is asked to function, namely the classroom and the home. Prior to making any conclusion about the existence of AD/HD, the child's cognitive abilities need to be assessed and environmental demands and expectations of the classroom need to be assessed in terms of the appropriateness of the classroom placement for the child. Only if a child's attentional difficulties are inappropriate for his or her developmental level, they are not resulting from inappropriate demands and expectations in the classroom, they are not attributable to other medical, neurodevelopmental, or psychosocial conditions, and they are significantly interfering with a child's performance across situations, can AD/HD be appropriately diagnosed. Figure 9–1 provides a flow sheet approach to the diagnosis and management of AD/HD.

Problems with Organizational Skills or Study Skills

Children with AD/HD often demonstrate difficulties with organizational and study skills. However, these problems can be observed in other children with learning problems as well and will, therefore, be discussed separately. As with the diagnosis of AD/HD, the primary sources of data for identifying problems in organizational and study skills are the teachers, parents, and, if appropriate, the student. Their responses to questions regarding completion of homework (amount of homework assigned, actual time taken to complete it, need for supervision), reasons for poor grades (lack of preparation for tests, failure to complete homework or classwork, lack of class participation), and the child's need for structure at home and school will be important for determining if there are problems with organizational and study skills. Relevant information may also be gathered from observation of the child during testing and from the results of certain intelligence subtests that require good planning ability. (See Chapter 5 for a discussion of these subtests.) It is important to note that problems with organizational and study skills are observed more frequently as the child gets older and is expected to take on more responsibility. Especially as children reach middle school, they are often expected for the first time to

(1) Are the symptoms of *inattention, poor impulse control, and/or hyperactivity* significantly interfering with the child's functioning across settings?

    YES→   └→NO →   No further intervention necessary

(2) Can the symptoms of *inattention, poor impulse control, and/or hyperactivity* be secondary to another underlying medical, neurodevelopmental, psychiatric, or psychosocial condition?

    NO→   └→YES →   Treat true etiology of symptoms

(3) Are the symptoms of *inattention, poor impulse control and/or hyperactivity* inappropriate for, or discrepant from, the child's overall level of developmental functioning?

    YES→   └→NO →   Special education services for mental retardation, slower learning, learning disabilities, communication disorder, etc.

(4) Are environmental demands and expectations (at school and at home) congruent with the child's developmental abilities?

    YES→   └→NO →   Adjust environmental demands and expectations (special education, classroom accommodations, counseling for parents)

(5) Are behavioral and educational interventions successful in remediating the symptoms?

    NO→   └→YES →   No further intervention necessary

(6) Is a trial of stimulant medication successful in resolving symptoms of inattention, poor impulse control, and hyperactivity?

    NO→   └→YES →   No further intervention necessary (continue behavioral and educational interventions)

(7) Are you sure that ADHD is the correct diagnosis and/or that the symptoms that persist are amenable to medication management?

    YES→   └→NO →   Re-evaluate patient [return to (1)]; Increase level of educational and/or behavioral intervention

(8) Trial of secondary medication (clonidine, imipramine)

FIGURE 9–1. *Pediatric Neurodevelopmental ADHD Flow Sheet.*

move from class to class on their own, and no longer have one primary teacher who will look out for them. Also, as children get older, long-term assignments are made that require more planning, more independent studying of texts is required, and parents often provide less supervision of homework.

Handwriting Slowness and Inefficiency

Although difficulties in written language are usually considered when making the diagnosis of learning disability, many of the tests that measure abilities in this area focus primarily on spelling and the mechanics of writing (e.g., punctuation, grammar, capitalization, word usage). Handwriting speed and efficiency, which are largely based on fine motor skill or visual-motor integration, are less often measured, but can play an important role in determining whether or not a child is able to perform in school at a level commensurate with his or her intellectual functioning. In order to determine if handwriting speed and efficiency are adequate, the interdisciplinary team should review data from the occupational therapy evaluation (if performed) and information from the teacher and parent interviews, focusing particularly on responses to questions regarding completion of assignments, time needed to complete assignments, and neatness of work. If possible, teachers should be questioned regarding the reasons for slow or inaccurate completion of assignments (e.g., daydreaming, slow but diligent work pace, failure to follow instructions, difficulty copying from the board).

Children with slow or inefficient handwriting often show difficulties with other fine motor skills, such as those presented during the occupational therapy evaluation or the neurodevelopmental evaluation. Scores on certain tests (e.g., tests of visual-motor integration) may be low. Observation during testing may also indicate reasons for the child's slow completion of assignments (e.g., perfectionistic approach, tendency to repeatedly lose his or her place during copying, off-task behaviors, awkward pencil grasp). Specific suggestions for circumventing handwriting difficulties can be made if the team can pinpoint the areas of weakness. (See Chapter 10 for a discussion of these strategies.)

Gross Motor Clumsiness

Some children with learning disabilities also demonstrate poor gross motor skills. These gross motor (play) skills represent one of the two major ways children relate to each other (the other being language). Although poor gross motor skills may not interfere with learning per se, they can certainly affect the learning disabled child's already vulnerable self-concept. Difficulties with gross motor skills are assessed through the occupational therapy evaluation and the neurodevelopmental examination. Teachers and parents will often comment on a child's clumsiness. Responses to questions about extracurricular activities (especially athletics) will provide data regarding the extent to which gross motor difficulties influence the child's selection of pastimes.

Language or Speech Problems

Children with learning disabilities often have a history of slow language development. Language problems may continue on into school age. Language problems may be first mentioned by parents or teachers, who might say that the child appears to have difficulty processing information, gives inappropriate responses to questions, has weak vocabulary skills, or is unable to relate common experiences or tell stories. Language difficulties might also be evidenced by a WISC-III profile where the PIQ is significantly and unusually higher than the VIQ. Observation during medical, psychological, and educational testing might also suggest language difficulties. (See Chapter 5 for a discussion of some of the signs examiners might observe in children with language difficulties.) A complete language evaluation should be obtained for children with suspected language difficulties. (See Chapter 7 for a discussion of the language evaluation.)

Speech problems will be more easily observed. The interdisciplinary team should attempt to determine whether speech difficulties are severe enough to interfere with learning. Consideration should also be given to the effects of speech difficulties on social and emotional adjustment. Evaluation by a speech pathologist will provide important information in determining the need for speech therapy.

Significant delays in speech or language warrant special education services, regardless of the existence of learning disabilities.

Emotional Problems

The child whose learning difficulties are assumed to be primarily the result of emotional problems is not diagnosed as learning disabled. However, the child with learning disabilities can and often does have concomitant secondary emotional difficulties. If learning disabilities are thought to be the primary disabling condition, special education services that lead to improved academic achievement may be sufficient to correct emotional problems. Conversely, if an emotional disorder is the primary disabling condition, psychotherapy may be sufficient to correct the learning problems. However, it is sometimes very difficult to determine the primary disabling condition—that is, to determine whether emotional problems are causing learning difficulties or vice versa. Regardless of the cause-effect relationship, the child with serious emotional and learning difficulties will benefit from help with both.

Data for determining the existence of emotional problems may come initially from the interview with the parents, teachers, and child. The team should focus especially on responses to questions regarding the child's self-concept, peer relations, eating or sleeping disorders, separation difficulties, level of motivation, unusual fears, mood swings, tendency to withdraw, and so forth. Observation during testing will also play an important role in identifying emotional disturbance. The child who shows excessive anxiety, anger, destructiveness, lack of confidence in his or her responses, avoidance behaviors, lack of eye-contact, inappropriate demonstrations of affection, low tolerance for frustration, or inappropriate affect should receive further evaluation. Results from projective psychological tests will be of value in making a determination regarding the presence of emotional disorders.

Family Problems

The presence of a child with learning disabilities, especially one who has associated AD/HD, can be very disruptive to family life. Parents (and teachers) may feel the child is lazy, not working up to his or her potential, deliberately failing to follow instructions, stubborn and willful, or simply "dumb." Some parents may blame their child for poor school performance, rather than being supportive and attempting to help the child overcome his or her difficulties. Other parents may blame themselves for the child's difficulties and try to overcompensate by making excuses, providing excessive help with assignments, or allowing the child to avoid school. Especially as children get older, parents expect them to take more responsibility for their schoolwork, but become frustrated as they observe their child fail to do so. Children become more resentful of parental interference with school work, although they need the additional structure.

Identification of family problems is based primarily on information gathered from interviews with the parent and the child. School personnel may also be aware of information pertinent to this topic. Projective tests can also provide valuable insights into family dynamics.

Specific Behavior Problems

Most behavior problems that will be mentioned by parents and teachers are, broadly speaking, manifestations of the child's reaction to his or her learning disability, AD/HD, or emotional problems. Therefore, the strategies used to deal with these disabilities and disorders (e.g., special education services, medication, psychotherapy) will generally be effective in improving the child's overall behavior and in reducing specific behavior problems. Many specific behavior problems will, however, respond well to behavior management techniques (described in Chapter 12). It is, therefore, advisable to identify the most salient problems at home (e.g., lying, failure to follow instructions, difficulty getting ready for school, temper tantrums, excessive fighting with siblings) and at school (e.g., failure to complete assignments, talking out of turn, wandering about the classroom, tardiness). Interviews conducted with the parents and teachers are generally the best sources for identifying these problems. When possible, attempts should be made to identify the nature of the problem, when and where the problem is most likely to occur, any specific occurrences that are likely to trigger the problem, strategies that have been used in an attempt to control the problem, and the success of these strategies. Specific behavior management strategies can be suggested by the interdisciplinary team if this information is carefully gathered and clearly presented.

CONCLUSION

As outlined in this chapter, the first task of the interdisciplinary team, when it meets to review the individual team members' data, is to determine whether a significant discrepancy exists between the child's level of cognitive functioning and level of academic achievement in one or more areas. Appropriate and inappropriate methods for determining whether this discrepancy is significant were discussed. Because learning disabilities cannot be defined strictly according to statistical formulae, the team is urged to consider factors in addition to test performance. The next task is to examine data from a variety of sources to determine factors that underlie the disability or help to clarify its nature. Finally, the team must determine the existence of problems often associated with learning disabilities. After completing this procedure, the team will have the information necessary to develop a comprehensive plan for treatment.

PART II

PLANNING FOR TREATMENT

CHAPTER 10

Planning For Treatment of Learning Disabilities and Associated Primary Disabling Conditions

Elizabeth H. Aylward
Frank R. Brown, III
Winnie Dunn
Linda K. Elksnin
Nick Elksnin

Chapter 9 included discussion of the diagnosis of learning disabilities, AD/HD, and associated problems. It is important for the team, once it begins to develop therapeutic recommendations, to appreciate that some of these conditions are neurologically based. The primary disabling conditions include (but are not limited to) learning disabilities, speech-language disabilities, gross and fine motor difficulties, and AD/HD. Because of these primary neurological disabling conditions, the child with learning disabilities (if provided with no special programming) falls progressively behind in achievement and may develop a variety of secondary disabling conditions, including behavioral and emotional problems. Treatment of learning disabilities is the subject of this chapter. Treatment of AD/HD will be discussed in Chapter 11. Treatment of secondary disabling conditions will be discussed in Chapter 12.

In planning for treatment of the learning disabilities, team members must keep in mind that special education services are mandated in the Education for All Handicapped Children Act (Public Law 94-142) and are currently amended by Public Law 101-476, The Individuals with Disabilities Act (IDEA). P.L. 94-142 requires the provision of a free, appropriate public education for all students identified with a learning disability. Furthermore, it defines learning disability as a handicapping condition and requires that services for students with learning disabilities be provided in the least restrictive environment, that is, in a setting that permits the student with learning disabilities to remain among nondisabled peers as much as possible. The Education for the Handicapped Amendments (P.L. 99-457) provides new incentives for the development of services to preschoolers who are disabled and their families.

As outlined in Chapter 1, the interdisciplinary team will diagnose primary and secondary disabling conditions and develop general therapeutic recommendations. For example, the team may recommend that a child with reading disability be provided with reading resource help and special accommodations to help circumvent reading difficulties in other subjects. The interdisciplinary team will not usually outline the specific goals and objectives to be accomplished as part of the child's curriculum for the school year or specify particular instructional methods. Individual team members will be given responsibility for ensuring that more specific guidelines are developed and implemented. The following sections discuss the development and implementation of a plan for providing the special education and related services legally mandated for the student with learning disabilities as well as the preschooler deemed to be at risk for subsequent learning difficulties.

INDIVIDUALIZED EDUCATIONAL PLAN AND INDIVIDUALIZED FAMILY SERVICE PLAN

The Individualized Educational Plan (IEP), required by P.L. 94-142, is a comprehensive plan of instructional activities to meet the needs of the school-age child. The IEP specifies "child-centered" goals and objectives as well as the strategies and timetables for reaching them. The Education of the Handicapped Amendments (Public Law 99-457) extends initiatives of P.L. 94-142 to infants, toddlers, preschoolers, and their families. P.L. 99-457 emphasizes a "family-centered" approach to intervention, as opposed to the more child-centered approach of the IEP. The Individualized Family Service Plan (IFSP) is the statement of these family-centered goals and objectives, as well as the strategies for reaching them.

IEP/IFSP Development Team

The IEP is developed by a committee, usually based in the child's school. This committee might be composed of the same members as the interdisciplinary team. In most cases, however, the IEP development committee will be composed primarily of school-based personnel, with selected input from outside professionals. The committee usually includes the child's current teacher, a special educator, a school psychologist, and an administrator. The committee will sometimes solicit the participation of other professionals, from either the school or community (e.g., physicians, speech-language therapists, behavioral psychologists, occupational and physical therapists). It is helpful if at least one member of the interdisciplinary team assists in developing the IEP or is at least readily available to the IEP development committee. In addition to professional staff, parents should be asked to contribute their understanding of their child's needs, as well as their desires for outcome.

The IFSP is developed from child and family assessments conducted by an interdisciplinary team, much as outlined above for the IEP. P.L. 99-457 emphasizes the importance of family participation in the design of programs for the child and family, and as such, this legislation stipulates that the IFSP must be developed with at least one of the child's parents or the child's guardian participating in the process. The goal in the development of both the IFSP and IEP is that parents be offered an opportunity to contribute their understanding of their child's needs, as well as their desires for outcome. In both the IFSP and IEP, parents are encouraged to present their perceptions of their child's developmental, learning strengths, and weaknesses and are encouraged to assist in the development of reasonable and realistic goals for remediation and instruction.

Components of the IEP

Although, by definition, each IEP is individualized to meet the particular student's needs, all IEPs have certain components in common, including:

1. *Current Levels of Achievement* must be stated from the most recent assessments. Scores or levels should be stated in understandable terms, so that members of the IEP development committee (including parents) can comprehend them.
2. Planning for the student with learning disabilities should reflect *goals*, that is, expectations for the student's accomplishments in a particular area during the period specified. The IEP must specify short

term *objectives* for attainment of the goal, that is, measurable or observable steps toward the achievement of the goal.

3. Appropriate objective *criteria* must be included to determine if and when an objective is achieved. Such criteria may be stated as a percentage or as a ratio. Criteria can change throughout the course of programming.

4. The IEP should indicate the extent of special education *(specific services)* and related services that will be needed to help the student meet the outlined goals and objectives. The amount of time the child will spend receiving special services is often defined according to levels. (These levels will be addressed later in the chapter.) Related services represent intervention provided by professionals other than educators and may include, for example, speech-language therapy, occupational therapy, physical therapy, or counseling. These services should be outlined, as well as the amount of time the child will need to spend with each specialist. In addition to specifying extent of specific services, the IEP may specify particular methods to be used with the student (specific remedial approaches will be elaborated later in this chapter). The IEP may outline modifications to be made in the instructional program, such as special seating, special management techniques, supplemental equipment or materials, computer assistance, or cassette recorders to supplement note taking. Special remedial or treatment methods, such as sensory integration therapy, pragmatic language therapy, articulation therapy, and supplementary vocational or prevocational training may also be specified.

5. An IEP should state when the program will take effect and when attainment of goals and objectives is expected *(duration)*. Usually, duration is either for a school year (9 months) or a calendar year. An IEP can be reviewed, revised, or rewritten at any time during implementation (with the parents' knowledge and consent), but all IEPs must be reviewed and updated at least annually.

Components of the IFSP

Part H of P.L. 99-457 specifies the content of the IFSP and certain requirements for participation and implementation. According to Section 677(d), the IFSP must be a written document that contains the following:

1. A statement of the child's present levels of physical development, cognitive development, language and speech development, psychosocial development, and self-help skills, based on acceptable objective *criteria*.
2. A statement of the *family's strengths and needs* relating to enhancing the development of the infant with disabilities.

3. A statement of major *outcomes* expected to be achieved for the child and family; the criteria, procedures, and timelines used to determine the degree to which progress toward the outcomes is being made, and whether or not revisions of the outcomes or services are necessary.
4. A statement of specific early intervention *services* necessary to meet the unique needs of the child and family, including the frequency, intensity, and method of delivering services.
5. Projected dates for initiation of services and the anticipated *duration* of the services.
6. The name of the care coordinator who will be responsible for implementing the plan and coordinating with other agencies and persons.
7. The steps to be taken to support the child's transition from early intervention into a preschool program.

IEPs and IFSPs should incorporate the components outlined above, but should be designed to allow flexibility in their implementation. For example, several methods can be suggested in the IEP or IFSP for instruction of specific skills, criteria for attainment of objectives can be adjusted, and provisions can be made for allowing the child to demonstrate attainment of skills in a variety of ways (e.g., orally, in writing, with manipulation of objects).

Implementation of the IEP/IFSP

The IEP must be developed before a student is placed in special education programming, and must be implemented no later than 30 days after its development. The IEP development team periodically updates the IEP, noting objectives met, success of methods, and whether or not the IEP still reflects realistic programming. If the IEP is inappropriate in any area, it is revised. Change in the nature or level of services provided cannot be made without the parents' consent. An addendum to the IEP or an entirely new document can be drafted by the committee. The student remains in the current program until the modifications are approved. The IFSP must be reviewed at least every six months.

Considerations for Developing and Implementing the IEP

In developing and implementing the educational plan, consideration should be given to the following assumptions regarding the student with learning disabilities and the learning process:

Students with learning disabilities are "normal" people with special needs. Students with learning disabilities have the same desire to learn and the same desire for acceptance in the process as their peers. They are entitled to enjoy the learning process, to have a good self-concept, and to be able to relate as normally as possible to other children, despite their learning disability. Without some accommodations in the learning process, they probably will not have these experiences.

Students with learning disabilities require more structure. Because children with learning disabilities often exhibit distractibility, poor impulse control, and poor organizational skills, they will usually benefit from increased structure and organization imposed from outside sources. Increased structure involves the clear presentation of expectations, clear delineation of consequences for meeting or failing to meet expectations, and consistency in feedback. Specific strategies for increasing structure and consistency are outlined in Chapter 11. Structure will also enhance the effectiveness of other treatment modalities (e.g., medication for AD/HD, behavior management strategies).

Many students with learning disabilities require more control of distractions. Distractions in the classroom should be minimized in order to maximize the child's ability to attend. Suggestions for decreasing distractions are discussed in Chapter 11.

Students learn best through direct experience. Abstract concepts and prolonged debate of esoteric issues do not work well as a foundation for teaching the student with learning disabilities. Instruction should be practical, and teachers should ask themselves "What can the student do with what he or she is learning?" Topics of interest are generated from daily experiences and, when possible, can be presented in conjunction with activities such as field trips, films, and special projects.

Skills taught in isolation have a transient effect. The curriculum for the child with learning disabilities should emphasize relationships among skills and repetition over time. Skills taught in one subject area should be reinforced in other subject areas. For example, application of language skills is not taught in the English or reading class alone, but must be reinforced by teachers in other content areas. Goals of today should relate to the goals of yesterday and tomorrow. The development of any curriculum for students with learning disabilities requires provision for repetition of concepts and procedures. Reinforcement and repetition will enhance internalization of concepts.

Learning is a multisensory experience. Internalization of concepts is believed to be enhanced though presentation in a variety of sensory modalities (e.g., visual, auditory, kinesthetic, and tactile). Multisensory strategies include audiovisual instruction, laboratory experiences, manipulation of materials, and so forth.

There is a point of diminishing return in remedial programming. In programming for the student with learning disabilities, planners sometimes automatically assume that more remediation is necessarily better.

The goals of special education should include instruction in content as well as remediation of skills. For example, the fifth grader, who for remediation of word-attack skills, is required to read first grade material, will not be provided with ideas, concepts, and information appropriate for his or her cognitive level. Therefore, remediation of skills and instruction in content must be appropriately balanced. Of course, instruction in content will have to be modified to circumvent areas of weakness. Suggestions for such modifications (e.g., *Talking Books*) will be discussed later in this chapter.

The most important issue for the child with learning disabilities is how he or she feels about himself or herself. Well-balanced programming affords the student with learning disabilities an opportunity to shine in his or her areas of strength. Successful experiences will serve as a reminder that he or she is normal and capable, despite his or her disability. This reassurance will, in turn, encourage the child to use and develop his or her inherent strengths, thus enhancing self-concept.

If these opportunities for developing strengths are not provided, the reverse may occur. The child with a poor self-concept may realize less than his or her inherent potential, and the prospect of disability becomes self-fulfilling.

LEVELS OF SERVICE

Once a child has been identified as meeting the eligibility criteria for special education, the IEP details the extent and types of special education deemed appropriate. In determining the extent of special education required, the IEP development committee should keep in mind that Public Law 94-142 mandates education in the least restrictive environment. Depending on the nature and severity of the disability, placement in special education settings will vary along a continuum, extending from mildly intrusive modifications in instructional programming to complete exclusion from the regular classroom. This continuum of special education services is portrayed in Figure 10–1 (Deno, 1973). As suggested by Figure 10–1, most children are placed in programs that offer integrated settings, such as regular classrooms, regular classes with ongoing consultation services, integrated special education services in the regular class, and special education resource rooms. There will be fewer children requiring less integrated settings, such as self-contained classrooms and out-of-school placements.

Although the descriptive terms applied to each level of service and the number of levels may vary from state to state or from district to district, the concept of a continuum of available services is generally applied. The levels of service portrayed in Figure 10–1 will be described as follows:

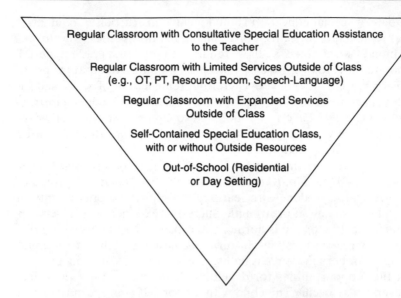

Regular Classroom with Consultative Special Education Assistance
to the Teacher

Regular Classroom with Limited Services Outside of Class
(e.g., OT, PT, Resource Room, Speech-Language)

Regular Classroom with Expanded Services
Outside of Class

Self-Contained Special Education Class,
with or without Outside Resources

Out-of-School (Residential
or Day Setting)

FIGURE 10–1.   *Levels of Special Education Service*

Regular Classroom with Consultative Special Education Assistance to the Teacher. The regular classroom teacher may receive consultative assistance from professionals in a variety of areas (e.g., special education, psychology, speech-language therapy, occupational and physical therapy). At this level, there is no direct contact between these professionals and the student.

Regular Classroom with Limited Services Outside of Class. At this level of resource placement, the student typically receives up to 1 hour per day of instruction outside of the regular classroom. Resource help is usually restricted to one subject area. A resource teacher usually schedules three to four children at a time to work on similar specific skill deficits.

One difficulty with a resource room placement is that a child who may already have problems with distractibility, impulsivity, and organizational skills must now relate to two teachers and complete two separate sets of assignments. For this reason, it is essential for resource teachers and regular classroom teachers to have good communication and to coordinate assignments. Because the child must typically leave the regular class to receive resource help, it is important that the child not be held accountable for the regular class instruction he or she misses.

At this level, the child is receiving his or her first direct exposure to any type of special education service. Careful monitoring at this level is important in order to determine whether the special education services should be continued at the same level, expanded, or discontinued. If the child's performance and behavior in the resource room is markedly better than his or her performance and behavior in the regular class, this may be a good indication that more resource help would be beneficial. In addition, the resource teacher is in a particularly good position to monitor the child's distractibility, impulsivity, and organizational skills, as the materials presented in the resource room are specifically designed to match the child's ability level and are presented in a less distracting environment.

Regular Classroom with Expanded Services Outside of Class. At this level of resource placement, the student typically spends up to one half of each day (3 hours) outside of the regular classroom. Resource help may be provided in more than one subject area. Considerations discussed in the previous paragraphs continue to apply at this level.

Self-Contained Special Education Class. If resource placement is still too distracting for the child, or if disabilities are too severe or too numerous, a self-contained classroom may be the best alternative. These classes usually contain 10 to 15 students with one special education teacher and perhaps an aide. Of course, a smaller pupil-teacher ratio is preferred. It is important that the student with learning disabilities be placed in a special education class designed specifically for students with similar learning disabilities.

In some schools, all children with learning difficulties are placed in noncategorical special education placements. Thus, slow learners, students with language deficits, and perhaps retarded students might be placed together with the students with learning disabilities. This is inappropriate and prevents the most efficient use of instructional time. Most school systems provide self-contained classrooms for a variety of disabling conditions, including mental retardation, orthopedic disabilities, communication disorders, emotional disturbances, and learning disabilities.

Out-of-School Placement. Out-of-school placements for children with learning disabilities are generally needed for only those students who have concomitant severe emotional or behavioral difficulties that prohibit their functioning in typical academic settings. Out-of-school placement also may be acquired in rural areas where there are too few students with learning disabilities to warrant special education classes within the school.

EDUCATIONAL APPROACHES TO REMEDIATE LEARNING DISABILITIES

In the section that follows, several instructional approaches that have been used effectively with students with learning disabilities will be reviewed. The first approach, Direct Instruction, is a model of instruction used to teach skills. The Strategies Intervention Model is an example of cognitive strategy instruction designed to teach students with learning disabilities *how* to learn rather than *what* to learn. Although academic instruction has received the bulk of attention of learning disabilities professionals, the need for social skills training has been recognized during the last decade, and this is the focus of the third model to be presented here.

Direct Instruction

Direct Instruction is an instructional model developed by Zigfried Engelmann and his colleagues at the University of Oregon. Successfully used with individuals with learning disabilities and other difficult-to-teach students, direct instruction has two major goals for students: skill mastery by every student and acquisition of skills at the fastest possible rate. This first goal is critical for students with learning disabilities. These students often become casualties of the general education curriculum as teachers move ahead even though students with learning disabilities failed to master critical grade-level objectives. It is equally important that students with learning disabilities be taught in the most efficient manner possible, as they generally lag behind their normally achieving peers in skill acquisition.

The Direct Instructional (DI) model has several distinctive features. Rather than use a loosely written lesson plan, the DI teacher presents a scripted teaching format, which is a series of steps carefully designed to effectively and efficiently teach a skill or concept. Although teachers may develop their own teaching formats, few teachers have the time for this activity and often rely on commercially available materials. *Reading Mastery* and *Corrective Reading* are examples of commercial DI instructional reading materials.

Direct Instruction usually occurs in small groups, depending on the nature of the material and the age and ability of the student. Restricting group size permits the learning disabilities specialist to continually monitor student performance during oral and written lesson activities. Lower performing students are seated nearest the teacher to permit even more careful monitoring of their performance.

In a traditional classroom, the teacher asks a question, several students raise their hands, and one or two students are called upon to respond. Students with specific learning disabilities may rarely volunteer to answer a question or may be ridiculed by peers if they volunteer an incorrect answer. Students may also get the message that they can be passive learners in the classroom and cruise on "automatic pilot" after they have been called upon by the instructor. In DI lessons, 80% of responses are group responses. *Unison oral responding* permits the teacher to monitor student performance, allows every student in the group to participate in the learning process, and demands the attention of each student in the group.

Unison oral responding is achieved through the use of signals or cues provided by the learning disabilities specialist. Teachers learn to use visual signals (e.g., pointing or touching to a stimulus) when students should be attending to the instructor or the instructor's material, and auditory signals (e.g., finger snaps, claps) when students' attention is directed toward their own materials.

The use of signals to elicit unison oral responding during small group instruction enables the teacher to monitor student performance and to correct incorrect responses. Errors are regarded as learning opportunities and each error is corrected in the group immediately and positively. Specific error correction procedures are used depending upon the type of error committed.

Direct Instruction lessons are presented at a rapid pace to sustain students' attention, minimize errors, and to reduce the amount of time wasted during instruction. The goal of a DI lesson is an average of nine student responses per minute. Results of studies designed to assess the efficacy of Direct Instruction are reported by Carnine (1979) and Gersten (1985), and the use of DI with students with disabilities in the regular classroom has been recommended by Larrivee (1989).

Cognitive Strategies Instruction

Students with learning disabilities often lack effective and efficient strategies for solving academic and social problems. For example, if you wanted to remember an unfamiliar phone number, you would begin by assessing your memory ability. You may decide that you need to write the number down on a piece of paper. If paper and pencil were unavailable, you would generate a strategy you could use to remember the information. You may rely on verbal rehearsal and repeat the number several times; you may cluster pieces of information and try to remember the first three numbers of the exchange (e.g., 792), and the next two numbers (52), and the last two numbers (19); you may remember a number by associating it with an important date (813-1492); or you may remember the number by visualizing the pattern the number makes on the touch-pad of the telephone. You would monitor and evaluate the use of your strategy and make modifications and adjustments if necessary. Many students with learning disabilities are unable to assess realistically their cognitive abilities; in addition they possess few effective strategies. Cognitive strategy instruction enables students with learning disabilities to become more efficient learners. Although several models of cognitive strategy instruction have been proposed (Pressley & Associates, 1990; Reid and Stone, 1991), the Strategies Intervention Model developed by Deshler and Schumaker and their colleagues at the University of Kansas Institute for Research in Learning Disabilities is implemented in many schools by learning disabilities professionals.

The Learning Strategies Curriculum of the Strategies Intervention Model is designed to teach students how to learn content material. In addition to giving the student with learning disabilities a series of steps that can be followed to take a test more efficiently, paraphrase, write a paragraph, and so forth, students learn *when* to use each strategy to promote generalization across settings and situations. Learning Strategies form three strands: acquisition, storage, and demonstration of competence. An example of an acquisition strand strategy is the Word Identification Strategy, which teaches students to decode unknown multisyllabic words. The First Letter Mnemonic Strategy helps students store information more efficiently through the generation of lists as memorization aids. Students with learning disabilities are able to demonstrate competence by learning the Error Monitoring Strategy which they use to detect and correct errors in their written work.

Each learning strategy is taught using the same eight-step instructional process (Schumaker, Deshler, Alley, & Warner, 1983):

Step 1: Pretest and Obtain a Commitment to Learn. The student's current level of performance is determined. Areas of weakness are discussed with the student and the student is asked to commit to learning the learning strategy.

Step 2: Describe. During this step the teacher describes strategy steps, along with giving students reasons for using the strategy.

Step 3: Model. The teacher models each step in the strategy by "thinking out loud."

Step 4: Verbal Rehearsal. The teacher leads the group in "rapid-fire verbal rehearsal," which requires each student to say a step in the strategy using a round-robin format.

Step 5: Controlled Practice and Feedback. Because the teacher primarily is interested in strategy mastery, students practice the strategy using "easy" materials. For example, if students are learning the paraphrasing strategy, which requires them to state the main idea and supporting details in a paragraph, they first practice using materials written at their reading levels rather than at their grade placement level.

Step 6: Grade-Appropriate Practice and Feedback. After students are proficient in using the strategy with less demanding materials, they learn to apply the strategy to materials used in their content area classes (e.g., English, history, social studies, health, and so forth).

Step 7: Posttest and Obtain Commitment to Generalize. Students are asked to generalize the use of a newly acquired strategy when posttest results indicate mastery of the strategy.

Step 8: Generalization. Three phases comprise the generalization step. During the *orientation phase*, the teacher and students discuss situations in which the strategy might be used, along with environmental cues which indicate when to use the strategy. Students also are encouraged to adapt the strategy to meet the demands of the situation. The student uses the strategy in a variety of situations during the *activation phase*. For example, the student might be asked to use the paraphrasing strategy in social studies class and to report back to the learning disabilities teacher. The teacher occasionally conducts a probe to ensure the student is proficient in strategy use during the *maintenance phase*.

Social Skills Training

Historically, the learning disabilities field was concerned with students' academic performance. More recently, learning disabilities professionals have recognized the importance of social skills and the fact that children with learning disabilities often lack social competence. Deficient social skills are associated with lack of peer acceptance, poor academic performance, and adult mental health difficulties. Deficient social skills may be due to a variety of factors, including lack of knowledge, lack of practice, lack of reinforcement, or problem behaviors (e.g., aggression, withdrawal) that may interfere with social skills acquisition or performance (Gresham, 1990).

Social skills are taught using modeling, role-play, performance feedback, and transfer of training. After a social skill is described by the teacher, the skill is modeled by a socially competent individual. Students are then given an opportunity to practice using a skill during role-play exercises. Performance feedback involves giving the student specific, informative feedback regarding the positive as well as the negative aspects of the role-play. Performance feedback may be provided by other participants in the training group as well as by the teacher. Students have been taught social skills using direct instruction and cognitive strategies instructional models.

There are several commercially available social skills curricula. These programs can be characterized as "skills specific" or as "problem-solving" approaches. A skills-specific program teaches discrete social skills: Each skill is defined and task-analyzed to determine the skill steps. Problem-solving approaches teach students to identify a social or academic problem, generate potential solution strategies, implement a strategy, and evaluate outcomes. The most powerful social skills training program may involve both approaches, with the skills-specific approach enabling the student to expand his or her social skills repertoire, making it easier for him or her to generate a wide array of solution strategies during problem-solving activities.

APPROACHES TO REMEDIATING PRIMARY DISABLING
CONDITIONS ASSOCIATED WITH LEARNING DISABILITIES

Speech-Language Therapy for
Children with Learning Disabilities

The majority of children with learning disabilities and intercurrent language disabilities display relatively mild language disorders. Their school placement and intervention needs will differ from the smaller percentage of children with learning disabilities diagnosed as having more severe "communication disorders."

For those children diagnosed as having a mild language disorder in conjunction with a learning disability, assignment to a regular classroom with resource services provided by a certified speech-language pathologist will be appropriate. The speech-language pathology services will be designed to meet the individual child's need (based on information obtained through the language assessment) and they may include diagnostic therapy (extension testing), comprehensive direct clinical intervention, or a specific program (e.g., occupational therapy) designed in association with and delivered in part by other members of the interdisciplinary team. Children assigned to such resource speech-language programs are not excluded from obtaining the benefits of consultation and support services provided to classroom teachers and families; rather, these benefits are recommended as additional services provided on an as-needed basis.

For the child with learning disabilities and more severe intercurrent language disability, it is the responsibility of the speech-language pathologist and the rest of the interdisciplinary team to determine whether the child's needs would best be met in a learning-disabled or a communication-disordered classroom. This decision will hinge in large part upon the team's perception of whether the child's major disabling condition is the learning disability with an associated language deficit or vice versa. Additional factors might include whether the team anticipates that the child will require specially designed curriculum of the speech-language pathologist, and whether language disabilities are of severe enough degree to cause a child to significantly lag behind other children socially. If, on balance, the language disability is felt to be the predominant cause of disability, a decision may be made to place the child in a self-contained program for children with primary communication disorder (and the associated learning disabilities will be addressed within this classroom setting). Specific speech-language intervention methods and strategies will not be addressed here; the interested reader may refer to texts by Wigg and Semel (1984).

Occupational Therapy Program Implementation

After gathering information about the student's abilities and needs and the supports and barriers in the environment, the occupational therapist creates interventions that make the best possible use of the individual's resources and the resources of the environment to optimize educational outcomes. Occupational therapists may address specific skills (e.g., attention or handwriting) or the basic foundational skills requisite for performing academic tasks (e.g., postural control).

Application of Theoretical Frameworks to the Needs of Students with Learning Disabilities

Occupational therapists apply several theoretical frameworks when addressing the needs of students with learning disabilities. The *functional-adaptation* framework enables the occupational therapist to consider the impact of specifically identified problems in performance of specific tasks. Adaptations evolve from attempts to match the individual's abilities and limitations with environmental features. For example, when a student with learning disabilities is having difficulty completing seatwork, the occupational therapist might employ an adaptive frame of reference when meeting with the teacher to identify alternatives to completing the assigned seatwork. They might agree that shorter assignments would be useful, or that providing larger spaces for writing makes it easier for the student to record the answers. The occupational therapist might also adapt the student's seat to make it easier for the student to work at the desk, or select a new writing surface to reduce paper slippage while the student is writing.

Developmental Frame of Reference

Using the *developmental* framework, the therapist considers the typical evolution of skills and milestones and selects strategies that will enhance skill development. For younger students, this might include selecting a variety of manipulatives for a math or art lesson to provide opportunities to develop visual motor integration. The occupational therapist might also work within a developmental frame of reference when consulting with the physical education teacher to design age-appropriate, but therapeutic tasks for a particular class that has a child who is clumsy. In high school programs, occupational therapists might work with extra curricular sponsors to identify opportunities for a student with socialization needs to participate with peers.

Cognitive and Behavioral Frames of Reference

When cognitive and psychosocial issues are present, the occupational therapist works collaboratively with other professionals, using a *behavioral* and *cognitive* theoretical framework. The occupational therapist considers the student's cognitive and behavioral repertoire and how these skills and difficulties might be affecting academic and social performance. When a student displays weak problem-solving skills, the occupational therapist might work with the student to design a set of options to consider during problem situations. For behavioral issues, the occupational therapist might work with parents and teachers to identify contingencies for desired performance.

Sensory Integration Frame of Reference

Another framework that is used frequently with students who have learning disabilities is the *Sensory Integrative* frame of reference. Sensory Integration (Ayres 1972, 1980) addresses the individual's sensory processing abilities and the subsequent ability to use that sensory input to create adaptive responses. Sensory integrative theory is based on several principles: (a) the individual must receive and understand sensory input to create adaptive responses; (b) intervention is directed at providing controlled sensory input to elicit adaptive responses; (c) adaptive responses increase organization through feedback, which can lead to more complex responses; and (d) child-selected activities are more likely to sustain performance and improve organization.

Controversy exists about the utility of Sensory Integrative (SI) theory for developing appropriate interventions for students with learning disabilities. Some researchers report that carefully designed sensory integrative procedures enable the child to establish functional patterns of responding to environmental demands (e.g., Ayres, 1977; Ayres & Mailloux, 1981; Horowitz, Oosterveld & Adrichem, 1993; Humphries, Snider, & McDougall, 1993; Ottenbacher, 1982; Polatajko, Law, Miller & Schaffer, 1991; Polatajko, Kaplan, & Wilson, 1992; Revelj, 1987; Tew, 1984; Van Benschoten, 1975; Wilson, Kaplan, Fellowes, & Gruchy, 1992). Other authors question the efficacy of sensory integrative procedures based on their findings or review of the literature (e.g., Arendt, MacLean & Baumeister, 1988; Ayres & Mailloux, 1983; Carte, Morrison, Sublett, Uemura, & Setrakian, 1984; Cummins, 1991; Densem, Nuthall, & Bushnell, 1989; Jenkins, Fewell & Harris, 1983; Kaplan, Polatajko, Wilson, & Faris, 1993; Morrison & Sublett, 1986; Werry, Scaletti & Mills, 1990). As with any evolving knowledge, it is important for those providing services to examine the features of successful and unsuccessful applications of the knowledge to gain insights about best practices.

Some researchers have demonstrated positive outcomes related to motor performance. Ayres (1977) showed that children with learning disabilities and choreoathetosis gained more on an eye-hand coordination test after receiving SI intervention than the control group children who did not have the intervention. Humphries et al. (1992) compared perceptual motor (PM), sensory integrative (SI) and no treatment control conditions with children who had learning disabilities and found variable results. The students who received PM showed the greatest gain in gross motor performance. The students who received SI showed gains in praxis. However, the treatment groups did not show differences from the students who did not receive treatment on longer term outcomes, such as academics, language, and attention. Horowitz et al. (1993) found they could improve smooth pursuit eye movements in children with SI dysfunction by providing at least 6 months of SI intervention. Case-Smith (1991) tested 50 preschool and elementary school children and found that children who cannot process information from their hands and who are overly sensitive to touch stimuli (i.e., tactile defensiveness) also have poor ability to manipulate objects in their hands.

Some studies have investigated the effects of SI intervention on academic and language performance. Wilson et al. (1992) compared tutoring for reading problems with SI intervention and found that the SI group improved as much as the tutoring group on reading measures, but that the tutoring group also improved on motor functions. These findings are equivocal, suggesting that both interventions were either equally effective or ineffective. Polatajko et al. (1991) found that both perceptual motor interventions and SI interventions led to improvements on academic and motor measures in their study of children with learning disabilities. However, only the SI intervention group showed significant improvements in self-esteem; perhaps the child-centered nature of the intervention contributes to this outcome. In a follow-up analysis the authors found that the groups contained a great deal of heterogeneity, and suggested that this might have contributed to the nonsignificant overall result (Law, Polatajko, Schaffer, Miller, & Macnab, 1991). Links have also been made with language development. Ayres and Mailloux (1981) demonstrated an increased rate of growth in language comprehension in children who had received SI intervention.

Other authors have questioned the effectiveness of SI intervention for children with learning disabilities. Earlier in the literature, Ottenbacher (1982) conducted a quantitative analysis of eight SI intervention studies and found that those that participated in SI intervention routinely performed significantly better than control group members. Arendt, MacLean, and Baumeister (1988) questioned the statistics and design choices in SI intervention studies. They argued that the weak design and statistical analyses make it difficult to derive any meaningful conclusions about the use of SI interventions. They offered alternative explanations for findings, including behaviorally based explanations. More recently, Polatajko et al. (1992) analyzed 7 studies that investigated SI interventions and concluded that the data do not support claims that SI intervention is an effective treatment for academic problems in children with learning disabilities. Kaplan et al. (1993) analyzed combined data for two studies with children who had learning problems and found that SI intervention was no more effective than more traditional interventions.

Other studies have revealed that there are no differences in children's performance after receiving SI interventions. Jenkins, Fewell, and Harris (1983) reported that after 17 weeks of intervention, there were no differences in gross motor or sensorimotor skills in groups of young children who had received either individual SI intervention twice a week or small group gross motor activities four times a week. After approximately 13 hours of intervention, 37 children with learning problems improved the same amount on reading, vocabulary, and perceptual motor function as a matched group of children who received no intervention (Werry, Scaletti & Mills, 1990).

Some of the SI literature suggests that children with depressed responses to rotary movement (i.e., poor vestibular processing) can be particularly responsive to SI interventions (e.g., Ayres, 1972; Ayres, 1978). However, Carte et al. (1984) found that 45 children with learning disabilities and depressed postrotary nystagmus (a measure of vestibular functions) did not improve in their developmental or academic performance with 9 months of individual SI intervention. In another study of 26 children with reading difficulties, more than 60 sessions of SI intervention did not affect vestibular or postural signs or visual motor integration (Morrison & Sublett, 1986).

The findings available in the literature on SI interventions remain unclear. It is likely that heterogeneity in the population of children identified with learning disabilities contributes to the equivocal findings. The studies that have been conducted have also had variable levels of control within the designs, which can also create questionable results. For example, the studies completed thus far have provided a wide time range and intensity of SI and alternate interventions; we do not know how much of any interventions are enough or how long it will take to show an effect. If SI indeed has an effect on the nervous system's organizational structure, then the significant effects might not be present in a shorter study. Another major factor is the choice of outcome measures selected by the researchers. Researchers selected motor milestones, academic performance, language, self-esteem, and abatement of abnormal neurological signs among others as outcome measures. We do not know from the results reported so far if any of these measures are appropriate to capture or refute an effect. The only clear outcome is that more study is needed to clarify the impact of SI interventions on children's performance and lives.

Service Provision Considerations When Serving Students with Learning Disabilities

Service Provision Approaches

Occupational therapists employ five primary approaches to service provision: establish/restore; adapt; alter; prevent; and create approaches (Dunn, Brown, & McGuigan, 1994). The *establish/restore approach* is also known as the remedial approach in educational environments. In this approach, the therapist identifies the problem areas and creates strategies that will "fix" them. Although many restorative strategies have been evaluated systematically through research, others appear to have clinical validity but need to be tested systematically through research.

An *adaptive (compensatory) approach* also acknowledges the individual's areas of difficulty but seeks to bypass the underlying deficit through knowledge of the student's capacities and modification of his or her environment. For example, if a student had incoordination, this might interfere with participation in recess activities. The teachers and therapist might adapt the recess games, so that the target student could be a referee or scorekeeper, thus keeping the student playing with peers and avoiding the difficulties related to incoordination.

Occupational therapists and school personnel employ an *alter approach* when they identify the student's optimal performance characteristics and select an environment that is the best match for the student. The alter approach does not require the student to develop new skills and does not require the environment to adapt to meet the student's needs; this approach takes advantage of naturally occurring opportunities for students to perform successfully without specifically targeted goals. Some classrooms are designed to accommodate more easily certain learners in the daily routine.

A *prevention approach* is used when the professionals recognize risk factors for the student and work to keep them from interfering with the student's ongoing development. This approach is most useful before the student has demonstrated a particular problem; the goal is to design environmental modifications that will prevent the development of behaviors that may interfere with future learning. For example, if a student is displaying frustration with reading assignments, this frustration could lead to a breakdown in peer relations in the future.

The therapist and teacher might collaborate to identify a positive inter-action this student could have with peers. Perhaps a new computer pro-gram is available for the class; the teacher might teach only the target student the program, so that other students see this student as compe-tent and helpful, thus "preventing" social isolation in the future.

A *creation approach*, frequently used in early intervention pro-grams, seeks to optimize the development of a student's skills and abili-ties through the design and provision of an optimal environment. A creation approach does not presume any particular disabilities but rather focuses on the ways that any student would profit from particu-lar situations or events. When the PTA works with professionals to de-sign an optimal playground, they are using a creation approach; the en-vironment is designed to capture optimal opportunities for the children who will play there.

Service Provision Models

Occupational therapists sometimes provide direct services to stu-dents with learning disabilities, but more frequently they provide moni-toring (i.e., supervised therapy) and consultation. The occupational therapist is most apt to be called upon to provide *direct services* when a student's sensorimotor systems are disrupted and this disruption is in-terfering with his or her ability to perform functional tasks. Whenever possible, the occupational therapist incorporates intervention strategies into the student's routine, so that the routine can begin to cue the stu-dent to perform more functionally. For example, the occupational ther-apist could work with the student on postural control in his or her desk (e.g., having the student reach to pick up a dropped pencil), so that when this occurs later in the day, the student can use those skills in an actual demand situation.

Sometimes physical therapists and adaptive physical educators col-laborate on sensorimotor issues. The physical therapist is more likely to focus on the motor control and capacity of the individual to perform the task (e.g., strength, trunk control); the adaptive physical educator is more likely to take a perceptual motor approach, which has a more established group activity program sequence, with drills and practice toward develop-ment of specific motor skills (Clark, Mailloux, & Parham, 1989).

Monitoring is a model of service provision in which the therapist supervises another person who carries out the activities on a regular basis. The occupational therapist identifies the problem areas, creates interventions, and instructs another person in how to carry out the in-terventions safely. The therapist also meets with the person carrying out the activities on a regular basis to ensure that the activities are being carried out correctly, to adapt the activities as the student improves, and to determine when the intervention can be discontinued or changed. This model provides ongoing support for the classroom routines and the teachers who see the students each day. Occupational therapists also use monitoring to assist parents when self-care and home skills are a problem.

In a *consultative model*, the occupational therapist addresses the needs identified by another individual in the student's environment (e.g., teacher, another therapist, physician, parent). A collaborative model of consultation is preferred because all parties contribute to problem identification and solutions (Idol, Paloucci-Whitcomb, & Nevin, 1986). A wide range of activities can occur within the collaborative consultation model, including adapting tasks, materials and environments, teaching adults new skills, and addressing postural and sensorimotor demands within natural environments.

Combining School-Based and Private Services

Some students with learning disabilities receive services from both a school-based therapist and an occupational therapist in private practice. This situation occurs when the student has needs that extend beyond the educationally relevant needs the student demonstrates at school. Many of the problems that students with learning disabilities have also affect life at home and in the community, so this is an appropriate pattern of service provision. For example, the perceptual problems that interfere with the student's ability to get his answer on the right place on the page can also interfere with his ability to tie his shoes or find clothes in the drawer. When both a school-based occupational therapist and a private practice therapist are serving a student, they collaborate to provide complementary services.

In all this service provision, it is important to recognize that individuals are best served when they are developing skills that are useful within naturally occurring activities throughout the day. Providing isolated services outside of the individual's routine does not address the need for those skills to be generalized into the individual's life. Occupational therapists are particularly well suited to address the needs of individuals within their natural environments.

ACCOMMODATIONS TO CIRCUMVENT LEARNING DISABILITIES

As discussed previously, the amount of time spent in attempting to remediate weaknesses and the amount of time spent in instruction of content must be balanced. The student who has a learning disability and whose intelligence is generally average or above must continue to be exposed to appropriate cognitive stimulation, despite the fact that academic skills are impaired. In order to provide this stimulation, teachers will have to make certain accommodations in their instructional methods, assignments, and methods of evaluation. The following paragraphs provide some suggestions on specific accommodations that may be necessary to ensure that the student with a learning disability can fully utilize his or her cognitive potential and to ensure that his or her mastery of material is acknowledged.

Accommodations for Reading Disabilities

For the student with reading disabilities, it will be necessary to select (or develop) text material that presents content at the appropriate cognitive level but that is written at the appropriate reading level. For students with less severe reading disabilities, the teacher may wish instead to read the regular text material together with the student, writing in appropriate substitutions for those words the student cannot decode alone.

Another approach, which allows the student to participate in regular classes and use regular text material, requires that the text material be dictated onto tape. This can be done by the teacher, parent, or another student. The student can then listen to the tapes as he or she follows along in the text. Although time consuming for both teacher and student, this approach reinforces reading skills, while at the same time circumvents reading disabilities.

Parents and teachers should be aware that the United States Library of Congress provides a service known as *Talking Books* to individuals who are blind, reading disabled, or otherwise unable to read regular materials. Students who have documented reading disabilities can borrow, free of charge, tape-recorded versions of books and magazines, as well as a cassette tape player. Librarians at the school or public library should have information regarding this service. If not, parents or teachers should contact the Chief, Network Division, National Library Service for the Blind and Physically Handicapped, Library of Congress, Washington, D.C., 20542.

Students with reading disability may also need special accommodation in evaluation. For example, students may need to have someone read test items and test instructions to them. Extra time might also be allowed for completing the tests.

Accommodations for Mathematics Disability

Accommodations for children with learning disabilities in mathematics will depend upon the areas of specific weakness. If, for example, the child has difficulty with computation, but not mathematical concepts, he or she might be allowed to use a calculator when working on applied problems. Alternatively, he or she might be evaluated separately on his or her ability to determine the correct procedure for solving the problem and his or her ability to complete the calculations correctly. Some students may have difficulty remembering the sequence of steps needed for certain mathematical operations (e.g., long division, finding lowest common denominators) or may be distracted easily before completing all the steps. These students should be allowed to refer to a written list of steps for each problem. Children with handwriting difficulties often have trouble copying math problems. Accommodations should be made to avoid unnecessary copying. Of course, children with learning disabilities in math should be given extra time for tests.

Accommodations for Written Language Disability

Students with written language disability often demonstrate extreme frustration because they are unable to express their thoughts in writing. Despite the fact that they can gather information with no difficulty and process the information intelligently, their efforts often fail to be acknowledged because they are unable to demonstrate what they know in writing. Teachers should allow these students to substitute oral presentations for written assignments and to substitute oral tests for written tests. Whenever possible, tests should use an objective format (e.g., true/false, multiple choice) rather than an essay format. When written work is required in content areas, it should be evaluated on the basis of content, not spelling, mechanics, or organization. Alternatively, teachers might give one grade for content and one grade for writing.

Students whose written language difficulties are limited to the area of spelling might be encouraged to keep a list of those words that regularly give them trouble and be allowed to consult the list whenever necessary. These students might also benefit from the use of a word processor or a hand-held spell-checker that will automatically check their work for spelling errors.

Accommodations for Handwriting Difficulties

Because handwriting difficulties, like attention deficits, are often neurologically based, attempts at remediation in this area often are futile. For this reason, accommodations for students with poor or inefficient handwriting must be made to prevent excessive frustration. The suggestions made for accommodating children with written language disability are equally appropriate for children with handwriting difficulties. In addition, the amount of written work required of these students should be decreased. Students with handwriting difficulties should be allowed to dictate assignments onto tape or to dictate them to a parent or to another student. They should be allowed to use a tape recorder in class to supplement note taking. If copying assignments from the blackboard presents problems, the student with handwriting difficulties should be allowed to dictate onto tape the material he or she does not have time to copy. Alternatively, another student might be asked to make a carbon copy when he or she is writing the assignment. Unnecessary copying should be avoided. For example, if an assignment requires students to copy sentences and underline the subject of each sentence, students with handwriting difficulties should be allowed to write only the subject of the sentence. These students may find it easier to use a typewriter or word processor than to write by hand (although poor fine motor skills often interfere with attempts to learn to type). If the student can learn to use a typewriter or word processor efficiently, he or she should be allowed to use it for both class assignments and homework.

CONCLUSION

After the interdisciplinary team has formulated diagnoses and outlined general recommendations for treating the disorders identified, a separate committee is usually convened to outline specific methods for remediating and circumventing learning disabilities. The Individualized Educational Plan (IEP) or Individualized Family Service Plan (IFSP) is written to outline the goals and objectives to be met during a specified period of time. The amount and type of special education services, related services, or family services that will be needed to help the child meet these goals are also outlined in the IEP or IFSP. In developing and implementing the IEP or IFSP, the development committee must keep in mind that the most important component in the process is the child and the family. By identifying weaknesses, potential strengths, and placing primary emphasis on the child's self-concept, the committee will be able to develop a plan to meet the goals and objectives they have outlined, as well as to minimize the stigma of the child's being labeled "learning disabled."

CHAPTER 11

Planning For Treatment Of Attention-Deficit/ Hyperactivity Disorder

**Robert G. Voigt
Elizabeth H. Aylward
Frank R. Brown, III**

In earlier chapters we introduced a distinction between primary and secondary disabling conditions for children with learning disabilities. As discussed, primary disabling conditions are neurologically based and include learning disabilities, speech-language disabilities, gross and fine motor dyscoordination, and attention-deficit/hyperactivity disorder (AD/HD). Chapter 10 discussed remediation of learning disabilities and any associated deficits in speech-language and gross or fine motor dyscoordination. This chapter addresses remediation of AD/HD.

PLANNING FOR REMEDIATION OF ATTENTION-DEFICIT/HYPERACTIVITY DISORDER

The most important factor to be considered in the management of children suspected of having AD/HD is to be sure that AD/HD is the appropriate diagnosis (cf. Figure 9–1). A child's attentional difficulties need to be compared to his or her developmental abilities, and there needs to be a congruency between environmental demands and a child's inherent cognitive capacity before a diagnosis of AD/HD can be

227

made. In addition, all other secondary causes of inattention should be identified and addressed (Table 9–2) before diagnosing the attentional difficulties as resulting from AD/HD.

Once the diagnosis of AD/HD has been established, the American Academy of Pediatrics (AAP, 1987) recommends educational and behavioral interventions before a trial of medication is attempted. However, in practice, medication is often used as an isolated treatment (Jensen, Xenakis, Shervette, Bain, & David, 1989; Wolraich, Lindgren, Stromquist, Millch, Davis, & Watson, 1990; Amaya-Jackson & Cantwell, 1991). These studies suggest that physicians and colleagues involved in the interdisciplinary management of children with AD/HD may not be following these AAP recommendations. Jensen et al. reported that while all children in their study diagnosed to have AD/HD were receiving stimulant medication, only 19% were receiving behavioral interventions. Wolraich et al. reported that while 88% of children with AD/HD were receiving stimulant medication, only 22% were receiving behavioral interventions. Finally, Amaya-Jackson and Cantwell reported that while 91% of children with AD/HD received stimulant medication, only 37% received special educational services. The 400% increase in stimulant medication use in the past four years (Wallis, 1994) may well be attributed, at least in part, to overreliance on stimulant medication in lieu of other therapies.

Research overwhelmingly has been convincing that stimulant medication is the best short-term treatment for improving the symptoms of AD/HD (Gittelman-Klein et al., 1976; Abikoff & Gittelman, 1984; Horn et al., 1991). However, few well-controlled studies have documented any long-term benefit of using stimulant medication (Hechtman, Weiss, & Perlman, 1984), and children who receive stimulant medication in isolation of other treatment modalities, in the long run, have no better prognosis than children who never receive medication (Satterfield, Satterfield, & Cantwell, 1981). Studies indicate that in the long run, a multimodal treatment approach, which includes educational, behavioral, and medical interventions, improves the outcome of children with AD/HD (Satterfield, Satterfield, & Schell, 1987).

We will now explore more specifically the management of AD/HD including both environmental (home and school based) accommodations and the use of psychotropic medication. Interdisciplinary treatment for AD/HD is summarized in Table 11–1.

MANAGEMENT OF ATTENTION-DEFICIT/HYPERACTIVITY DISORDER—ENVIRONMENTAL ACCOMMODATIONS

All children need structure and consistency. As children grow older, however, parents and teachers usually expect them to take more

TABLE 11–1

Interdisciplinary Treatment of AD/HD

Educational	Behavioral	Medical
Assignment modifications/ accommodations	Parenting classes	Stimulant medication Ritalin
Preferential seating	Behavior management counseling	Dexedrine Cylert
Consistent behavior management strategies	Family counseling	Antidepressants Imipramine
Special education services	Individual counseling	Prozac
	Social skills training	Clonidine
	Organizational skills training	

responsibility for their actions, require less structure and supervision, and be able to deal with less consistency in the daily routine. Children with primary neurologically based AD/HD (who are often thought of as "immature") need more structure and consistency for a longer time than most children their age.

It is not easy, for many reasons, to deal with children who have AD/HD. At times, they appear able to function at an age-appropriate level, making parents and teachers believe that the child's inappropriate behavior is completely volitional. At times (especially as they reach adolescence), children often resent interference from parents and teachers and want to be responsible for themselves, but do not have the organizational abilities that will allow them to do so successfully. Their impulsivity causes them to do "stupid" things that they know are inappropriate, causing frustration for both themselves and adults.

Parents and teachers need to understand that AD/HD is a primary neurologically based disability that prevents children from paying attention, following instructions, organizing themselves and their materials, completing work on their own, tuning out distractions, and controlling impulsivity. Just as parents and teachers of a physically impaired child would not insist on taking away the child's wheelchair or braces when he or she reaches a certain age, parents and teachers should not insist that the child with AD/HD function without the extra support, structure, and consistency he or she needs.

Parents and teachers will need to provide extra support, structure, and consistency of the type discussed in the remainder of this chapter to help the child with AD/HD to function. In some instances, these accommodations may be all that is required and they may obviate the need for stimulant medication. In most circumstances, however, one finds that environmental and behavioral accommodations combined with administration of stimulant medication are more effective than any of these modalities alone in minimizing the negative effects of AD/HD.

School-Based Accommodations to
Increase Structure and Consistency

Teachers of children with AD/HD will have to make special efforts to provide the extra support and structure these children need, as well as attempt as much as possible, to reduce the number of distractions in the classroom. The following suggestions might be shared with the teachers of children who are diagnosed as having AD/HD.

Children with AD/HD have difficulty making transitions from one activity to another. It is important, therefore, to keep the daily routine as consistent as possible. The child should be able to expect that various activities (e.g., reading, recess, lunch, physical education) will occur at approximately the same time each day. Changes from room to room and from teacher to teacher should be minimized, as the child often has difficulty making transitions and organizing himself or herself in new situations. If the child must be taken out of the room for special education services, the services should be provided at the same time every day. The child should not, of course, be expected to make up work he or she misses when taken out of the room for special education services. The special education services should be provided at the same time that the children in the regular class are being presented with material in the same subject area (e.g., special reading help should be provided at the same time the regular class is having the reading lesson). A child with AD/HD will have more difficulty paying attention to classroom instruction. In order to work around this difficulty, teachers should make certain they have the child's attention before beginning instruction. This can, of course, best be accomplished by working with the child one-on-one or in a small group. Because this is usually impossible, teachers can use other strategies, such as standing next to the child, placing a hand on the child's shoulder, maintaining eye contact, and frequently asking direct questions to make certain the student is following along. When giving directions for a particular assignment, it may be necessary sometimes to repeat instructions individually for the child or to ask him or her to repeat the instructions to make certain that he or she understands what is expected.

Directions for specific tasks or assignments should be stated precisely and simply. Young children should be given only one direction at a time. Older children may be able to remember two or three directions, but if the directions are at all complex, they should be put in writing. Teachers must specify clearly what they expect. For example, teachers should not ask the child with AD/HD, "Organize your materials to go home." Instead, the child should be told, "Check to make certain you have your math book, homework assignment, and notebook."

The child with AD/HD often becomes overwhelmed when faced with a large assignment. Teachers can help overcome this obstacle by breaking down tasks into small, manageable segments. For example, if the child has a page of 50 math problems to complete, the teacher should cover up 40 of them and tell the child to complete only the first 10. After the first 10 are completed, verbal praise should be provided, and the next 10 problems should be uncovered. This procedure should be continued until all 50 problems are complete. Gradually, the child can be taught to break assignments into segments on his or her own and to provide his or her own verbal reinforcement.

It also may be beneficial to set a reasonable time limit for completion of each task. A kitchen timer will be helpful, as the child may not have a good concept of how much time is passing. Using the previous example, the teacher might tell the child he has 10 minutes to complete the first 10 problems. The teacher should then set the timer and come back when it rings. The child should be reinforced positively for completing the segment, and the process repeated. The time limits can be adjusted as appropriate.

Teachers should attempt, as much as possible, to limit the number of distractions for the child with AD/HD. Whenever possible, instruction should be provided individually or in small group settings. When instruction is provided in large group settings, the child should be seated near the teacher. When independent work is required, the child might benefit from the use of a study carrel. Alternatively, the child might be allowed to go to the library or other quiet place that would be relatively free of distractions. These strategies should be used only if they are handled in such a way that the child does not feel he or she is being punished by the isolation (for the obvious reason of the child's self-concept).

The classroom environment also may need to be modified for the child with AD/HD. Too many posters, bulletin boards, and equipment will add unnecessary distraction. An open space environment is especially inappropriate because it prevents the teacher from controlling external auditory and visual distractions.

Teachers should attempt to provide plenty of reinforcement for successful completion of tasks. They should give verbal praise whenever the child improves in his or her ability to complete tasks, work independently, or pay attention. Teachers should not expect major changes to happen quickly. By reinforcing the small gains, teachers can motivate the child to work toward larger gains.

These suggestions are for increasing the structure and consistency for the child with AD/HD. If specific behaviors need improvement, teachers should be encouraged to establish a behavior management system, which will be described in Chapter 12.

Home-Based Accommodations to Increase Structure and Consistency

Some parents will need assistance from the professional team in providing the extra support, structure, and consistency their child needs. Depending on the parents' level of sophistication, willingness to cooperate, and own level of organization, they may or may not need assistance in implementing the following strategies. The interdisciplinary team should assume, however, that parents will need regular follow-up if they establish behavior management strategies on their own. (See Chapter 14 for a discussion of follow-up with the families of children with learning disabilities.) The interdisciplinary team may want to share with the child's parents the following suggestions for home management of children with AD/HD.

Parents should attempt to increase the structure of the daily routine. Children with AD/HD have difficulty making transitions from one activity to another. It is important, therefore, to keep the daily routine as consistent as possible. Parents should try, as much as possible, to have the child do daily tasks-such as getting up in the morning, getting ready for school, eating meals, starting homework, getting ready for bed, bedtime-at the same time every day. As much as possible, the child should be allowed to finish each task before being asked to start another. For example, parents should not set up the daily schedule so that breakfast comes in the middle of getting ready for school.

A child with AD/HD will have more difficulty in paying attention to directions. In order to work around this difficulty, parents should make certain they have the child's attention before giving instructions. For example, parents should not walk through the den and say "Pick up your shoes" while the child is watching television if they really expect the job to be done. Instead, the parent should first cut down on all distractions as much as possible (turn the television off for a moment or get the child away from his or her friends or toys for a moment). The child should be called by name, and the parent should wait for a verbal response and eye contact. Instructions should be stated clearly and simply. Younger children should be given only one instruction at a time. Older children may be able to remember two or more directions, but if the directions are at all complex, they will need to be put in writing. The child might be asked to repeat the instructions so the parent knows the child understands what is expected.

When giving instructions parents should specify clearly what they expect. For example, the child with AD/HD should not be told "Clean your room." Instead, parents should indicate specifically what they mean by clean your room. (The parent's idea of a clean room and the child's idea of a clean room are probably not the same.) Parents might, for example, say instead, "Pick up your clothes. Put the dirty ones in the hamper. Hang up the clean clothes. Put toys in the toy chest. Empty your waste basket. Make your bed." (Instructions, should not, however, be presented all at one time. Parents may need to give each instruction separately and check to see whether the child has carried it out before giving the next instruction, or they might put instructions in writing.)

The child with AD/HD often becomes overwhelmed when faced with a large assignment. Parents can help the child overcome this obstacle by breaking down tasks into small, manageable segments. For example, if the child has difficulty getting himself ready for school, the parent might divide the task into segments by first asking the child to wash his hands and face. After this is done, the parent should provide verbal praise and tell the child to get dressed. This procedure can be continued until all steps of the larger task have been completed. Gradually, the child can be taught to break tasks into segments without help and to provide his own verbal reinforcement.

It may also be beneficial to set a reasonable time limit for completing each segment of a task. A kitchen timer will be helpful for the child who does not have a good concept of how much time has passed. The timer can be set, and the parent can come back when the timer rings. The child should be reinforced positively for completing the segment, and the process repeated. Time limits should be adjusted as appropriate.

If the task requires any amount of concentration, parents should attempt to limit the number of distractions as much as possible. The child should not do homework in front of the television or in a room full of activity. Parents should not allow telephone calls during homework time. Some children complete homework best if sent to their room to work alone, but it is important to remember that even a quiet room may have lots of distractions, as from toys and books. (It is also important to remember that the child with AD/HD can create his or her own distractions!) It may be more convenient for parents to provide the supervision needed by having the child sit at the kitchen table or other centralized place, assuming that the area can be kept fairly quiet. Parents will need to experiment to see what works best for them and their child.

Parents should provide lots of reinforcement for successful completion of tasks. It is unreasonable to expect behaviors to change in one day. Parents must keep in mind how long it took the child to develop the habits they are attempting to correct and realize that the resolution of these problems may also entail a great deal of time. Praise should be provided whenever improvement is observed, no matter how slight that improvement is. Parents should be encouraged to be patient and not give up.

Although the previous suggestions are based on psychological principles that have been tested and proven over the years, there are always exceptions. Parents should remember that these suggestions are for helping their child work around attention problems and are not steadfast rules. The suggestions should be implemented consistently for a few weeks. If something is not working, parents should experiment on their own to see if they can find a better approach. Again, the goal of behavioral and educational interventions in the child with AD/HD is to help the child learn to work around his or her neurologically based difficulties with inattention and impulse control. Long-term studies of children with AD/HD show that long-term improvements result only through multimodal treatment strategies that include behavioral and educational accommodations. Because the child's primary neurological deficit is present across his or her life span, these multimodal therapies serve to teach children how to compensate for their neurologically based difficulties.

A final environmental accommodation for children with AD/HD would be to encourage children to engage in extracurricular activities which they feel they are good at, in order to serve as a source of self-esteem. Extracurricular activities also provide opportunities for appropriate peer interaction and socialization. These activities should include activities both within and outside school. The in-school activities, including sports, clubs, stage crew, and the like, can help prevent the school negativity often experienced by children with AD/HD; extracurricular activities serve to ensure that school remains a positive experience.

Children with AD/HD, as a result of their difficulties with inattention and poor impulse control, are often difficult to coach in team sports. Thus, many of these children may well excel in activities that focus more on individual skills than on teamwork. Karate, wrestling, swimming, fencing, track and field, and tennis are examples of individual sports where coaching tends to be more one-on-one. Karate may well be more beneficial to children with AD/HD, as the children are instructed in self-control and listening skills in addition to the athletic skills involved in the sport.

These suggestions are for the management of general behaviors. If specific behaviors need improvement, parents should be encouraged to establish a behavior management system, as described in Chapter 12.

MANAGEMENT OF ATTENTION-DEFICIT/HYPERACTIVITY DISORDER—USE OF PSYCHOTROPIC MEDICATION

Stimulant Medications

About 50 years ago, a chance observation was made that stimulant medications (amphetamines) improved school performance and behavior and had a paradoxical calming effect on hyperactivity (Bradley, 1937). Ever since, stimulant medications (including methylphenidate, Ritalin; dextroamphetamine, Dexedrine; and pemoline, Cylert) have remained as a bulwark in the treatment of children with AD/HD, although their use and popularity has waxed and waned significantly. In the period from 1990–1994, use of methylphenidate was up some 400%, at an all time high (Wallis, 1994). Some of the fluctuation in popularity of stimulant medication usage probably relates to the periodic misuse of stimulant medications as a first recourse in treatment, rather than as one component of a comprehensive remediation program that includes environmental accommodations and behavioral modifications. As the "easiest" step in an AD/HD treatment program, stimulant medication periodically becomes employed as a "cure all," delaying implementation of other appropriate and specific interventions. Additionally, frequently no monitoring systems are in place to assess the efficacy and need for continuance of the medication.

Institution of psychotropic medication can be considered for any child who exhibits symptomatology compatible with AD/HD, but only after an evaluation of cognitive potential, academic achievement level, and assessment of the appropriateness of the existing academic placement. It should always be remembered that medication is only one part of the management program for the child with AD/HD. All team members participating in the management of the child with learning disabilities and AD/HD will need to ensure that other important treatment modalities are not ignored.

If medication is to be implemented, the medications that have been most well studied, that have been found to be most effective, and that have been found to produce the fewest side effects, should be the first medications attempted. Because more research has been conducted on the effects of stimulant medication on the functioning of children with AD/HD than any other treatment modality for any childhood disorder (Barkley, 1990), stimulant medication would far and away be the first choice medication. Stimulant medication has resulted in well-documented short-term improvements (Rapoport, Zametkin, Donnelly, & Ismond, 1985), and the side effect profile for stimulant medication (decreased appetite, insomnia, stomach ache, and head ache) is favorable (Barkley, McMurray, Edelbrock, & Robbins, 1990). It is our opinion that methylphenidate is the stimulant medication of choice for children with AD/HD, and that related central nervous system stimulants (i.e., dextroamphetamine and pemoline) have no particular pharmacologic advantage over methylphenidate. We believe the physician should learn to use one of these medications effectively, and therefore in this discussion methylphenidate will be used as a prototype.

It is important to appreciate that, both diagnostically and therapeutically, disorders of attention and physical overactivity (hyperactivity) may exist separately or together. A number of studies point out that acute control of excessive motor activity (hyperactivity) with methylphenidate does not necessarily ensure academic improvement (Sprague & Sleator, 1977). In general, as the dosage of methylphenidate is raised, a child will become quieter. However, above a certain dosage (around 1.0 mg/kg/dose), the child's academic performance may start to decrease, even though he or she is physically less motorically active. A dosage of methylphenidate of approximately 0.3 to 0.6 mg/kg/dose is generally better for improving attention span, decreasing impulsivity, and maximizing reaction time, although it may not always reduce motor activity level (Sebrechts et al., 1986). Our recommendation is that a dosage of approximately 0.3 to 0.4 mg/kg/dose be used as a guideline for initiation of methylphenidate and that this dosage be adjusted subsequently (up to a maximum of approximately 0.6 mg/kg/dose) on an individual basis.

Parents should be alerted to anticipate initial mild side effects, consisting chiefly of appetite loss and sleep disturbance, as well as the more serious side effect of an increase in frequency of tics in a child with underlying complex tic disorder (Tourette's syndrome). Loss of appetite and sleep disturbance can be minimized by starting with a low dosage (perhaps one half of the anticipated optimal dosage) and increasing gradually for the first week or two to the optimal level (the smallest effective dosage).

The short-term benefits of stimulant medication are easily demonstrated and may include improvement in attention span and in relationships with peers, improvement on visual-motor tasks (handwriting), and decreased impulsiveness. Stimulant medication should be initiated on an empirical basis and should be continued based on feedback from the parents and school regarding its effects on attention span and impulse control. In this feedback process it is important to apprise parents and school personnel of what stimulant medication can and cannot do.

The desired effect is an improvement in attention span and impulse control, that is, the components of primary neurologically based AD/HD. Stimulant medication will not affect behavioral problems under the child's willful control, such as oppositionalism, noncompliance, and attention seeking. Because problems of AD/HD (not under willful control, but affected by stimulant medication) and attention-seeking behaviors (under willful control, and not affected by stimulant medication) often occur together in children with learning disabilities, parents and school personnel must be aware of what specifically to monitor when stimulant medication is employed. If they are not, they may conclude erroneously that medication has not helped (with willful behavior problems) and they may discontinue it prematurely.

The other responsibilities in monitoring stimulant medication usage are to know about its rate of metabolism, dosage adjustment, and when to discontinue it. Methylphenidate has a very short half-life in the blood stream, approximately 3 to 4 hours. This has several important ramifications for its administration:

1. Children will typically require two doses (approximately 8 a.m. and noontime) to cover the typical school day. If they are having attentional interference with homework activities, they may require a third dose in the day, typically around 4 p.m.

2. Because of the rapid rate of metabolism, one is not concerned with the total dose administered in 24 hours, but rather with what is the correct individual dosage at any one time. This means that if the correct dosage at any one time is, for example, 10.0 mg, then this same dosage should be used at other times of administration in the day. One does not reduce subsequent dosages out of concern for the cumulative amount taken in the day.

3. A dosage of 0.3 to 0.4 mg/kg/dose is only a rough guideline (which implies that the typical school-age child will be taking approximately 10.0 mg/dose) and the dosage will have to be adjusted to fit each child. One usually starts with a somewhat lower dosage (e.g., 5.0 mg) and slowly increases the dosage to obtain the desired improvement in attention span and impulse control.

4. It now appears that a significant number of young children with AD/HD will continue to exhibit symptoms, especially excessive fidgeting and restlessness (as opposed to gross motor overactivity), into adolescence and adulthood. The best way to monitor ongoing need for stimulant medication is to give the child a drug respite once or twice a year, monitoring attention span and impulse control before and after these drug interruptions. In order to remove day-to-day variations in performance, except in very obvious situations, these trials should be of approximately one to two weeks' duration. If needs for continuance are monitored in this fashion, legitimate objections about open-ended medication usage can be obviated.

Unfortunately, the response to stimulant medication is independent of the accuracy of the diagnosis of AD/HD (Wolraich et al., 1990). Multiple studies have established that stimulant medication increases one's ability to pay attention and concentrate and decreases impulsivity and excessive motor activity, whether one truly has AD/HD or not (Weiss & Laties, 1962; Rapoport et al., 1978; Peloquin & Klorman, 1986). Thus, children may well be diagnosed to have AD/HD, and if they are placed on stimulant medication, in the short run, their performance at home or at school may well improve, even if they do not have a primary neurologically based AD/HD. However, in many cases where a true primary neurologically based AD/HD is not the etiology of the symptomatic behaviors, this initial improvement in performance only serves to hide the true, underlying etiology of the child's difficulties. This results in delays in appropriate diagnosis and initiation of appropriate treatment strategies. Such delays in diagnosis and treatment might well lead to a handicapping degree of secondary social, emotional, and behavioral difficulties, which could have been prevented with appropriate diagnosis in the first place.

It is possible that the nonspecific "performance enhancing" effect of stimulant medication has contributed to its more liberal, and possibly inappropriate, use. Prescriptions for Ritalin have increased approximately 400% in the interval from 1990 to 1994 (Wallis, 1994). Charles Bradley, in one of the original papers advocating the use of stimulant medication for children with symptoms of inattention, poor impulse control, and excessive motor activity, provided a warning about the inappropriate use of stimulant medication that remains as true today as it was in 1937: "Any indiscriminate use of benzedrine (stimulant medication) to produce symptomatic relief might well mask reactions of etiological significance which should in every case receive adequate attention" (p. 584). By employing a neurodevelopmental perspective in the diagnosis of AD/HD, inappropriate diagnosis and use of stimulant medication for its "performance-enhancing effects," rather than to treat a neurodevelopmental disorder, can be avoided.

Stimulant medication, despite its documented short-term effectiveness and its favorable side effect profile, should not be considered a benign medication. It is a controlled substance and could be abused if decisions to use medication are not made judiciously, and if medication trials are not appropriately monitored. These medications should not be used if drug abuse is suspected in the child's family. In addition, given the nonspecific performance-enhancing effect of methylphenidate described earlier, there have been anecdotal reports that some students may be selling medication to others to improve school performance (*Pediatric News*, 1994). Further, adverse side effects of methylphenidate in mentally retarded children, including severe social withdrawal, have been described (Handen, Feldman, Gosling, Breaux, & McAuliffe, 1991). Stimulant medication can also exacerbate tics in a patient with an underlying tic disorder (Golden, 1988), and controversy remains whether stimulant medication can actually cause irreversible tic disorders. Finally, stimulant medication appears to be less effective, with more side effects, in preschoolers, and it can increase visual perseveration and sterotypic behavior in children with pervasive developmental disorders.

The potential side effects of chronic, long-term stimulant medication usage are currently unknown. Because stimulant medication mildly increases heart rate and blood pressure, there is some question whether these effects over time could result in an increased risk of cardiovascular problems in later adult life. There has been one report of an unexpected increase in diastolic blood pressure in black adolescents who were receiving methylphenidate (Brown & Sexson, 1989).

Stimulant medication is assumed to be effective in treating the symptoms of AD/HD by causing release of both dopamine and norepinephrine from synaptic terminals and inhibiting the re-uptake of these neurotransmitters into synaptic terminals. A theoretical long-term consequence of such chronic exogenous administration of stimulant medication may well be a "resetting" of receptors for dopamine and/or norepinephrine in the brain. Stimulants can aggravate movement disorders (motor tics) acutely. Lipkin, Goldstein, and Adesman (1994) found that approximately 9% of children with AD/HD treated with stimulant medication developed movement disorders (motor tics and dyskinesias). These movement disorders were predominantly transient in nature, with less than 1% of the children developing chronic tics. In this study a personal or family history of tics, the type of stimulant medication used, and the medication dosage were unrelated to the onset of movement disorders. Another study (Borcherding, Keysor, Rapoport, Elis, & Amass, 1990) reported an incidence as high as 60% of movement disorders in children with AD/HD treated with stimulant medication. Again, however, most of these movement disorders were transient in nature. In any event, given the frequency of movement disorders seen acutely in children treated with stimulant medication, it is important that patients on long-term chronic stimulant medication be monitored closely for any signs of a movement disorder.

In the past, potential long-term side effects of stimulant medication were not as much of an issue; previous thinking was that the medication should be used only for a short time to provide the patient with a "window of opportunity" to work around attentional difficulties. However, today, there is a greater trend toward treating adolescents as well as adults (Wender, 1987) with stimulant medication throughout their life span. Thus, these issues of potential long-term cardiovascular and neurologic side effects need to be considered. However, stimulant medication has been used safely for over 50 years, and so far, no permanent neurologic or cardiovascular sequelae have been documented.

A final issue to be resolved in continuing stimulant medication over the course of a lifetime is the belief of some investigators (Levine & Melmed, 1982) that children with AD/HD may demonstrate superior creativity. Whereas off-task and impulsive behaviors are detrimental to elementary school performance, it is quite possible that these behaviors, resulting in creative thinking and decisiveness, would be beneficial in an adult setting. Thus, it could be questioned whether stimulant medication can actually blunt creativity and thus be detrimental to adult occupational functioning. However, one study (Funk, Chessare, Weaver, & Exley, 1993) did not find boys with AD/HD to perform better on a task of creativity than boys without AD/HD. In addition, the boys with AD/HD did not show any differences in creativity whether they were taking stimulant medication or not.

Alternative Medications in AD/HD (Antidepressants/Antihypertensives)

For those children with AD/HD who show no therapeutic response to an adequate trial of methylphenidate, some alternative or adjunctive medications can be considered, especially the tricyclic antidepressants, imipramine (Tofranil) and desipramine (Norpramin), and the antihypertensive agent, clonidine hydrochloride (Catapres). Although stimulant medication has been well studied and documented to improve the symptoms of AD/HD in the short term, these secondary medications have not been as extensively studied. Most research on the secondary medications has involved small sample sizes and anecdotal reports. In addition, in many of these studies, whether the medication being employed is actually treating AD/HD, or whether it is actually treating another condition that may well be misperceived as being AD/HD is questionable.

Tricyclic antidepressant medications, including imipramine (Werry, Aman, & Diamond, 1980), desiprimine (Biederman, Baldessarini, Wright, Knee, & Harmatz, 1989a), nortriptyline (Wilens, Biederman, Geist, Steingard, & Spencer, 1993), clomipramine (Garfinkel, Wender, Sloman, & O'Neill, 1983), and doxepin, have been reported to improve symptoms of AD/HD. However, investigators of tricyclic medications have reported that a subgroup of children with AD/HD who respond better to tricyclic antidepressants are characterized by high levels of anxiety or depression (Pliszka, 1987). Thus, it is questionable whether the tricyclic antidepressant medication is treating AD/HD, or whether it is actually treating anxiety and/or depression masquerading as AD/HD. In addition, tricyclic antidepressant medications have as a side effect sedative and antihistaminic properties (Rao, Menon, Hilman, Sebastian, & Bairnsfather, 1988), and thus, it may well be that sedation caused by the tricyclic antidepressants is being misinterpreted as improving hyperactivity. Of the tricyclics, doxepin exhibits the most potent antihistaminelike properties, and desipramine the least potent of these properties. In the few studies of tricyclic antidepressant medications in children with AD/HD that have employed objective measures of attention, no improvement on object vigilance tests, such as the continuance performance test, have been documented (Levy, 1991).

Tricyclic antidepressant medications certainly should not be viewed as benign drugs. In addition to their sedative and antihistaminic effects, these medications can produce dry mouth, constipation, and urinary retention. More important, tricyclic antidepressants have been documented to affect the cardiac conduction system (Biederman et al., 1989b), and in 1990 three cases of sudden death were reported in children taking desipramine for AD/HD (The Medical Letter, 1990). As the cardiovascular side effects of tricyclic antidepressants are for the most part dose related, overdosage, either accidental or deliberate (suicide attempt) are real concerns. It appears that children may be more susceptible to the cardiac toxicity of these drugs than adults, and it may be preferable not to use these medications until after puberty, when the cardiac conduction system has matured. Whenever used, pretreatment EKGs should be obtained, and periodic EKGs and drug levels should be monitored throughout the duration of treatment. The recommended dosage for imipramine is 0.5 to 3.0 mg/kg/day in one to two divided doses, and for desipramine, 2.0 to 4.0 mg/kg/day as a single dose.

Other medications have been reported to be effective in small groups of children with AD/HD, including the antidepressants buproprion (Casat, Pleasants, Schroeder, & Parler, 1989) and fluoxetine (Prozac) (Barrickman, Woyes, Kuperman, Schumacher, & Verda, 1991). Again, only a limited number of patients were involved in these drug trials and no objective measures of improved attention were utilized. Thus, again, the question is raised whether these antidepressant medications are treating AD/HD or are treating depression which is being misperceived as AD/HD or co-occurring with AD/HD. The anticonvulsant medication, carbamazepine (Tegretol), has also been reported to benefit children with symptoms of AD/HD (Evans, Clay, & Gualtieri, 1987).

The antihypertensive medication, clonidine (Catapres), has also been suggested as an alternative medication for AD/HD (Hunt, Minderra, & Cohen, 1985). This medication has been particularly heralded as a treatment for children with AD/HD and comorbid tic disorders (Steingard, Biederman, Spencer, Wilers, & Gonzalez, 1993), cases where stimulant medication would be contraindicated. As clonidine does present with sedation as a side effect, it is again questionable whether clonidine is actually treating inattention, or whether its sedative effects appear to improve hyperactivity and conduct problems. Clonidine has been reported as a treatment for aggressive and conduct disordered children (Kemph, Devane, Levin, Jarecke, & Miller, 1993). Clonidine can be used as either a sole agent or in combination with methylphenidate. The recommended dosage is 4.0 to 5.0 µg/kg/day. Clonidine appears to work best when given in small dosages throughout the day. The primary side effects are sedation, hypotension, and dry mouth. It has to be taken 7 days a week in order to avoid problems with rebound hypertension. In addition, it can be life threatening if overdosed, either accidentally or deliberately.

CONCLUSION

Learning disabilities and AD/HD represent primary neurologically based disabling conditions, which are in large part beyond the child's control. Chapters 10 and 11 have addressed remediation of these primary disabling conditions. It can be argued that separation of problems into primary disabling conditions (e.g., learning disability and AD/HD) and secondary disabling conditions (e.g., attention-seeking behaviors and poor self-concept) is artificial, in the sense that a child with learning disabilities often has a mixture of these problems. Nevertheless, we feel that it is useful when thinking about remediation to separate initially the child's problems into those that are neurologically based (and beyond the child's control) and those that are more emotionally and behaviorally based.

The first step in addressing the needs of a child with learning disabilities will be to identify a remediation setting (as discussed in Chapter 10) that can provide an individualized educational course appropriate for the child's cognitive and academic strengths and weaknesses. The second step is to ensure that appropriate home-based and school-based accommodations are in place to help the child focus attention and control impulsivity. If the child continues to show attention deficits and poor impulse control, additional therapies, including stimulant medication (methylphenidate, Ritalin) can be instituted. Even when an individualized educational plan is established and primary AD/HD is addressed in this fashion, many children with learning disabilities will be left with some secondary disabilities (e.g., attention-seeking behaviors and poor self-concept). Suggestions for minimizing these problems will be discussed in the following chapter.

CHAPTER 12

Planning For Treatment Of Secondary Disabling Conditions

Elizabeth H. Aylward
Frank R. Brown, III

The primary disabling conditions of the child with learning disabilities (learning disabilities, speech-language disabilities, fine motor dyscoordination, and AD/HD) are, as discussed in Chapters 10 and 11, part of the child's "wiring" and are, as such, somewhat out of his or her control. The strategies discussed for dealing with these primary disabling conditions (e.g., individualized educational programs, accommodations at both home and school to increase structure and consistency, and stimulant medication), although appropriate given our present understanding of learning disabilities, are often inadequate to resolve the primary disabilities. As a result, the child with learning disabilities may not receive the usual "strokes" that go along with school success, and is very apt to resort to inappropriate attention-seeking behaviors to get the recognition that he or she would otherwise not receive. Additionally, children with learning disabilities are aware that their performance does not measure up to the standard of the group, resulting in poor self-concept. Inappropriate attention-seeking behaviors and poor self-concept are examples of secondary disabling conditions that parents and professionals must attempt to prevent or minimize. This chapter presents strategies for managing these secondary behavioral and emotional problems. It is our opinion that implementation of these strategies is most important for ensuring optimal outcome.

MANAGING BEHAVIOR PROBLEMS

Establishing a Behavior Management System

If there are specific behaviors upon which parents and teachers would like to see the child improve, or certain tasks that need to be completed with less supervision, it may be worthwhile to establish a behavior management system. Quite simply, a behavior management system requires that the desired behaviors be specified clearly, that the child's performance on these behaviors be carefully recorded, and that successful performance be systematically rewarded. The key is consistency, both in recording the child's performance and in administering rewards.

Steps are offered for establishing a behavior management system. They are equally appropriate for the home and the classroom. In some cases, parents and teachers may want to work together to create one behavior management system that covers both home and school behaviors. In order to do this, the teacher might be asked to send home a report each day that tells how many objectives the child accomplished at school. Parents can record on the home behavior management system the child's performance on school objectives. Parents can be responsible for providing a reward at the end of the week if the child has met both home and school objectives.

The behavior management system requires a commitment from the parent or teacher who chooses to establish one. A behavior management system should not be attempted by parents or teachers who do not have the motivation or time to carry through with it. This will only result in the child being taught that parents or teachers do not follow through with their own goals. On the other hand, teachers and parents should remind themselves that it may be easier to work hard to control some undesirable behaviors than to ignore them and have them escalate into more serious problems in the future.

The first step in establishing a behavior management system is to specify the behaviors or tasks upon which the child needs to improve. Objectives for improving the child's behavior and completing tasks should be outlined in writing. In order to do this, the parent or teacher should list the daily tasks that the child is expected to complete, being as specific as possible. For home behavior management, the list should include the child's assigned chores (e.g., clearing the dinner dishes, emptying waste baskets, feeding pets), as well as other tasks that the child may have difficulty completing independently (e.g., getting ready for school on time, completing homework assignments, taking baths). At school, various regular tasks should be listed (e.g., copying the homework assignment, completing daily assignments in reading, spelling, and arithmetic, participating in social studies discussion). Parents and teachers should be specific regarding their expectations. For example, instead of listing "Get ready for school on time," parents may need to specify "Get dressed, brush teeth, wash hands and face before 7:30 a.m." The list can also include behaviors parents and teachers would like to see the child improve. As much as possible, these should be stated in a positive way. For example, instead of listing "Don't wander around the classroom," the teacher might want to state "Ask permission before leaving your seat." It may be more difficult to specify the behaviors that need improvement than the tasks to be completed, but again teachers and parents should try to be as specific as possible. For example, "Be polite to parents," should not be included as an item. Instead, parents may want to specify "Say please and thank you when appropriate, wait your turn before speaking, and look at your parents when they are speaking to you."

The list of objectives should be discussed with the child. The child should have some input regarding which household chores he or she would prefer and when he or she might prefer doing them. Parents and teachers should discuss with the child the reasons they would like the child to take more responsibility for personal tasks and to improve certain behaviors. The child should not be allowed to dictate the list, but his or her cooperation should be elicited in setting objectives.

In selecting objectives on which to begin the behavior management system, the parent or teacher should choose four or five critical objectives on which to start, together with two or three easy objectives. All of the child's shortcomings cannot be expected to improve at once. Both adult and child will become frustrated if the behavior management system attempts to address too extensive a list of objectives. By initially targeting a few selected critical and easy behaviors and demonstrating some immediate success with these, parents and teachers will be more likely to maintain motivation for continuing the system and will generalize the system to deal with additional behaviors in their listings.

For each of the objectives selected, the parent or teacher should set reasonable time limits (if appropriate), criteria for success (if appropriate), and any other limitations or restrictions for successful completion. For example, if the objective is "Start your homework on your own," it may be desirable to set a time limit (e.g., "Before 7:30 p.m."). If the objective is "Complete 25 math problems," a criteria for success can be added (e.g., "with at least 90% accuracy"). If the objective is "empty the wastebaskets in all rooms every day," the restriction "without reminders" might be added. Clearly, it is inappropriate to set time limits and criteria for each objective. This should be done only when it helps to clarify the expectations for completion of the objective.

The next step is to set up a checklist where objectives are listed down the side of a sheet of paper, and days of the week are listed across the top of the page. (See Tables 12–1 and 12–2.) If some objectives are to be accomplished only on certain days, x's should be placed in the boxes corresponding to the days on which objectives are not to be completed. The child's successful completion of each objective will be recorded each day, with either a check or sticker in the corresponding box. It is important that the child's performance be recorded consistently every day. Parents and teachers should not wait until the end of the week and try to remember what objectives were achieved each day.

The behavior management system is based on reward for successful completion of objectives. First, parents or teachers need to decide how many of the objectives must be accomplished successfully within a week in order for the child to earn a specific reward. The behavior management system outlined in Table 12–1 has 26 spaces for recording successful behavior. It is a good idea to start with a fairly easy criteria (e.g., "18 of 26 objectives must be met in order to receive a reward at the end of the week"). The number of objectives selected for criteria will depend on the difficulty of the objectives and on the likelihood

TABLE 12–1
Sample Behavior Management System To Be Used at Home

OBJECTIVES	Mon	Tues	Wed	Thurs	Fri	Sat	Sun
Make bed every morning before 7 a.m. without reminder (10 a.m. on nonschool days).							
Get ready for school (wash face, get dressed, get books and papers together, eat breakfast, brush teeth) before 7:30 a.m. without reminders.						X	X
Take out trash cans on garbage pick-up days before school, with one reminder.	X		X	X		X	X
Keep your hands to yourself when playing with your sister.							
Start homework on your own before 7 p.m. without reminder.						X	X

Criteria for reward: Successful completion of 18 out of 26 objectives.
Reward: Going bowling on Saturday with Dad and a friend.

TABLE 12–2
Sample Behavior Management System To Be Used at School

OBJECTIVES	Mon	Tues	Wed	Thurs	Fri	Sat	Sun
Be seated and have materials on your desk by 8:30 a.m.							
Complete daily assignment in arithmetic without supervision, within a 20-minute time limit, with 90% accuracy.							
Ask permission before leaving your seat 90% of the time.							
Participate in social studies discussion by making at least two appropriate comments, without being asked by the teacher.							
Walk quietly in the halls.							

Criteria for reward: Successful completion of 20 out of the 25 objectives.

Reward: One-half hour of "free time" on Friday, to be spent on playground, in the classroom, or in the library.

that the child will be able to complete them. The number of objectives necessary for reward can be increased as the system continues and the child achieves more success.

The next step is to work with the child in deciding what would be an appropriate reward for successful completion of the prescribed number of objectives. It will be important to provide verbal praise for the completion of each objective every day. However, more tangible reinforcement will be necessary for rewarding the child for success at the end of the week. Parents should not get carried away with promises of expensive toys or activities. They should keep in mind that they may have to provide the reward every week. Some rewards that might be appropriate for the behavior management system at home include:

☐ Staying up until midnight on Saturday night to watch a special movie (one that already has been approved)

☐ Having a friend spend the night on a weekend

☐ Money for roller skating, movie, or bowling

☐ Purchase of a small toy, perhaps part of a collection the child has started

☐ Going to lunch or on an outing with mom or dad, without siblings

Rewards that might be appropriate for the behavior management system at school include:

☐ A half-hour of "free time" on Friday afternoon

☐ Being selected as the teacher's "special helper" to run errands or help younger students

☐ Being allowed to use special materials for an art project of the child's choice

☐ Being allowed to play with particular educational toys

☐ Participating on a particular class outing

The teacher might also be able to solicit cooperation from parents in providing a reward for appropriate school behavior.

In selecting a reward, parents and teachers should keep the following in mind:

☐ The reward should be obtainable at the end of the week. Parents should not tell the child, for example, that he or she can have a big reward, such as a bicycle, if he or she succeeds on the objectives for ten weeks in a row. Similarly, a teacher who promises the child an "A" at the end of the term may not be able to elicit much motivation for the system. Most children cannot delay gratification much longer than a week and will lose interest in the system.

☐ The reward should not be a continuation of privileges the child already has. That is, the child should not be threatened with the removal of existing privileges if he or she does not meet criteria.

☐ Money can be used as a reinforcer if parents desire. However, it is better to earmark the money for a particular purchase so that the child has something to work toward. It is better not to use this with younger children and probably should be used only if the parent and child cannot think of less mercenary reinforcers.

☐ If possible, reinforcers should be chosen that incorporate values parents and teachers would like to see developed (e.g., family togetherness, sharing with classmates, socializing with friends, physical fitness).

☐ If the child does not meet the criteria, parents and teachers must be consistent in not administering rewards, so they should not select as a reward something they intend for the child to have regardless of his or her behavior (e.g., summer camp, birthday party, class picnic).

It may be necessary with very young children (under 6 years) to provide reinforcement on a daily basis rather than on a weekly basis. If so, the parent or teacher should use the same procedure outlined, but make the reward smaller (e.g., playing a game of the child's choice with mom or dad for a half hour before going to bed, choosing the story that will be read to the class). The time between reinforcers can gradually be lengthened as the child gets older and begins to have consistent success with the system.

Parents and teachers should make certain the child understands the rules of the system from the outset and understands what the reward will be. If the child thinks something about the system is unfair, the problem should be worked out before starting the system, if possible. The child's success on each objective should be recorded every day. The child can be allowed to put stickers or checks in the boxes on the chart, with supervision.

At the end of the week the parent or teacher should review the child's progress with him or her. If the child does not meet criteria, the parent or teacher should not scold, but should stay calm and say, "We'll try it again next week." (If the system is begun with fairly easy criteria for reinforcement, failure can be avoided in the beginning. Parents and teachers should remember that the objective is to have the child succeed.) The parent or teacher may want to spend some time with the child discussing where he or she experienced the greatest difficulty in meeting the objectives and suggest some ways to help him or her do better next week. If the child has succeeded in reaching the criteria for reinforcement, parents or teachers should provide verbal praise, tell the child how proud they are of his or her accomplishments, and make arrangements for administering the reward as soon as possible. If the child has succeeded in reaching the criteria for reward several weeks in a row, the difficulty for reaching criteria can be increased, either by adding new objectives or by requiring that more of the existing objectives be met each week.

If the child does not reach criteria for reward, no matter how close he or she came, the reward must not be administered. If it is administered, the parent or teacher will be teaching the child to see how little he or she can get away with doing and still get the reward.

In summary, parents or teachers should clearly specify what is expected, the criteria for earning the reward, and what the reward will be. They must be consistent in recording daily performance and in administering the rewards. Plenty of verbal praise should be given along the way. Nagging and criticism should be avoided.

Psychotherapy for Behavior Problems

The two defining characteristics of AD/HD are inattention and impulsivity. The child with AD/HD often misbehaves because he or she impulsively acts before thinking about the consequences of his or her behavior. Therapists have attempted to modify impulsive behavior through many techniques, including imposed delay, modeling, identification of failures, establishing response-cost contingencies, and self-instructional training (Kendall and Finch, 1979). One type of therapy that appears to have good potential for success is cognitive behavior therapy. Using this approach, therapists teach children strategies for thinking before responding. In some cases, modeling, self-instruction, and response-cost contingencies are used as part of the training. Some programs (e.g., the "think aloud" program developed by Camp, Blom, Herbert, and Van Doornenck, 1977) emphasize social behaviors by teaching children to evaluate how their behavior affects others, to develop alternative strategies for addressing conflicts, and to think before acting. As with most therapies, the success of cognitive behavior therapy depends a great deal on the skill of the therapist. Furthermore, the strategies presented during therapy do not always generalize sufficiently to situations outside the therapy session. Despite these common drawbacks of psychotherapy, cognitive behavior therapy appears to be appropriate for many children with AD/HD, especially those with good verbal skills.

MANAGING SECONDARY EMOTIONAL DISTURBANCE

The most common emotional disturbance observed in children with learning disabilities or AD/HD is poor self-concept. After years of academic failure, social failure, and criticism from parents and teachers, this outcome is not at all surprising. Parents and teachers should make efforts to maintain a young child's self-concept before the effects of learning disability and AD/HD have a chance to damage it. For the older child whose learning disabilities and AD/HD are not diagnosed until after self-concept is damaged, special accommodations will be needed to help the child feel more positive about himself or herself. The following suggestions are appropriate for either maintaining or remediating poor self-concept:

☐ The child should be encouraged to participate in structured nonacademic group activities that will allow him or her to compete successfully with peers in areas where he or she is not so far behind. Because so much of the poor self-concept of the child with learning disabilities derives from academic problems at school, it is especially important to identify, if possible, school-related activities in which the child may be expected to succeed (e.g., participation in school athletics, clubs, and offices). All too often the child with learning disabilities is excluded from these activities because of poor grades. These extracurricular activities may be important in drawing the child back into what is inherently a difficult learning process.

☐ Parents and teachers should attempt to identify and encourage any special strengths or talents a child might have (e.g., music, art, leadership, creative writing). It is important for the child to be able to achieve success and earn praise for some special skill or talent, especially if academic achievement is not a source of positive reinforcement.

☐ Parents should make efforts to identify, encourage, and praise strengths that distinguish the child from siblings, especially if the child perceives siblings as more successful.

☐ Parents and teachers should make efforts to provide the child with special responsibilities that the child can handle with success. For example, the teacher might regularly ask the child to take messages to the school office, to assist in classroom chores (e.g., taking inventory of materials, organizing shelves, taking attendance), to assist younger students, or to act as a member of the safety patrol. If possible, the child should be given opportunities that will allow him or her to feel important in the eyes of peers. For example, he or she might be allowed to assist the teacher in directing the class play, teach a lesson on a subject in which he or she has particular expertise, or share a special experience with the class.

☐ The child should be praised for good attempts at new activities, regardless of the outcome of these efforts.

☐ Parents and teachers should solicit the child's input when planning activities. Whenever possible, the child's suggestions should be incorporated into the plans in order to make him or her feel that his or her input is valued.

In general, parents and teachers should attempt to make the child feel that he or she is special in a positive sense in order to overcome all of the negative attention he or she receives as a result of having learning disabilities and attention problems. Parents and teachers must become attuned to every opportunity that warrants praise and reinforcement. If strategies for maintaining self-concept are integrated into the educational process as soon as academic difficulties are identified, serious behavioral and emotional problems may be obviated. Sadly, the maintenance of self-concept is sometimes ignored until problems have gotten out of hand. When efforts by teachers and parents are insufficient or delayed, psychotherapy is often necessary. Although poor self-concept is the most common emotional disturbance observed in conjunction with learning disabilities and AD/HD, other concomitant disorders can include depression, school phobia, eating disorders, substance abuse, excessive tension, anger, or hostility. Most parents and school personnel are unequipped to deal with these more serious emotional disturbances. In these cases, professional counseling for the child must be sought. The physician may be able to help convince the parent of this need and to assist in selecting an appropriate therapist. Family therapy is often necessary when the child's learning disabilities or AD/HD have led to conflict within the family.

CONCLUSION

Strategies discussed in Chapters 10 and 11 for dealing with primary disabling conditions are often inadequate to fully resolve the problems. As a result, the child with learning disabilities often experiences secondary disabling conditions, including behavior problems and poor self-concept. Strategies for dealing with behavior problems include the establishment of behavior management systems, both at home and school, and, when necessary, psychotherapy. Poor self-concept is addressed through the consistent application of positive reinforcement. If these strategies for handling behavior problems and maintaining self-concept are consistently employed, many of the secondary disabling conditions can be minimized or avoided altogether.

CHAPTER 13

Making the Transition From High School to Work or to Postsecondary Training

Nick Elksnin
Linda K. Elksnin

Interest in the unique needs of adolescents with learning disabilities began in the late seventies as professionals realized that, although some manifestations of learning disabilities could be lessened through remedial and compensatory strategies, learning disabilities could not be "cured." Only recently have parents and professionals acknowledged the need to reconceptualize programs for children with learning disabilities and thus prepare these young persons to make the successful transition from high school to employment or postsecondary training (Trapani, 1990). Our ideal goal for individuals with learning disabilities for after high school is 100% integration in employment settings, nonbaccalaureate programs, or baccalaureate programs. However, only approximately 60% of students with learning disabilities graduate from high school, with about half of this number earning a high school diploma. The remaining graduates with learning disabilities exit high school after successfully meeting Individual Education Program objectives, but failing to meet graduation requirements. The National Transition Study (Wagner, 1989), which followed approximately 8,000 youth ages 13–23 with disabilities, showed that only 16% of students with learning disabilities entered postsecondary training programs, with

1.6% enrolled in four-year colleges and universities, 4.9% in two-year colleges, and 1.1% vocational schools. Sitlington and Frank (1990) surveyed individuals with learning disabilities the year after graduation and reported that only 54% made a successful transition to adult life. Individuals making successful transitions were employed or engaged in post-secondary training activities, were at least partially self-supporting, and were involved in more than one leisure activity. Employment outcome data are no more encouraging. Results of follow-up studies indicate that individuals with learning disabilities tend to be underemployed and unemployed more frequently than their nondisabled peers. This need not be the case, as a number of federal laws are designed to enable adolescents with learning disabilities to make an effective transition from school to work or postsecondary training (Elksnin & Elksnin, 1995a).

LEGISLATION AFFECTING SECONDARY AND POSTSECONDARY PROGRAMMING

Public Law 94-142, the Education for All Handicapped Children Act of 1975, requires that vocational education be made available to school-aged students with handicaps. The act defines vocational education as

> organized educational programs which are directly related to the preparation of individuals for paid or unpaid employment, or for the additional preparation for a career requiring other than a baccalaureate or advanced degree (Section {2}a.4(b)(3).

Subsequently in 1990, The Individuals with Disabilities Act or IDEA (Public Law 101-476), which amended P.L. 94-142 requires transition services defined as

> a coordinated set of activities for a student, designed within an outcome-oriented process, that promotes movement from school to postschool activities, including post secondary education, vocational training, integrated employment (including supported employment), continuing and adult education, adult services, independent living, or community preparation (SS 300.18).

School districts are required to include transition services in the IEP for children no later than age 16. Vocational rehabilitation services were added to the list of appropriate related services potentially necessary for an individual to benefit from learning disabilities services.

Three other pieces of legislation also are relevant to secondary and postsecondary training designed to enable students with learning disabilities to be successful adults: Section 504 of the Rehabilitation Act (P.L. 93-112; 1973), the Carl D. Perkins Vocational Education Act and

Amendments (P.L. 98-524; 1984), and the Americans with Disabilities Act (P.L. 101-36; 1990).

Enacted in 1973, Section 504 often is referred to as the civil rights law for persons with disabilities. The act prohibits an institution that receives federal funds from discriminating against otherwise qualified individuals with disabilities. Institutions include schools, colleges, universities, and places of employment. The courts have interpreted otherwise qualified to mean that the individual must be able to meet all essential requirements for the job or postsecondary training program in spite of the disability. Employers and educators, however, must make "reasonable accommodation" to allow the person with the disability to meet the requirements. Section 504 essentially mandates equal educational opportunities for individuals with learning disabilities in colleges and universities, since most institutions receive federal assistance in the form of financial aid to students. This legislation not only has implications for recruitment and admission of qualified students with learning disabilities to postsecondary institutions, but also impacts upon program and activity accessibility. There is no official federal interpretation of reasonable accommodations, but states, colleges, and universities have interpreted this requirement in ways that suggest that reasonable modifications of academic requirements may include (a) course substitutions, (b) modifying or waiving foreign language requirements, (c) additional time to complete degree programs, and (d) permitting part-time rather than full-time study.

The Carl D. Perkins Vocational Education Act, legislated in 1984, enables students who are disabled and disadvantaged to access the full range of vocational programs available to individuals who are not disabled. Students with learning disabilities who are enrolled in vocational programs are entitled under this Act to have their interests, abilities, and special needs assessed; instruction, equipment, and curricula modified to meet their special needs; counseling services needed to enable them to make a smooth transition from school to employment and career opportunities. In addition, students must receive appropriate guidance, counseling, and career development activities during their secondary careers. In 1990, the Perkins Act was amended and renamed the Carl D. Perkins Vocational and Applied Technology Act. This legislation takes a broader view of vocational education and regards it as a means of acquiring higher level thinking and academic skills in addition to learning occupational skills. The amendments also differ from the original legislation in that a clear distinction is made between secondary and postsecondary levels of vocational education, with separate funding mechanisms for each level.

The Americans with Disabilities Act of 1990 (Public Law 101-336) further expands and specifies the civil rights of all individuals with a disability. This is particularly important in the area of employment. Private industry with 15 or more employees, or state and local governments, irrespective of the number of employees, cannot refuse to hire an otherwise qualified individual with a disability. This places individuals with learning disabilities on an equal footing with other employment seekers, provided they have been trained appropriately and have marketable skills.

SECONDARY SPECIAL EDUCATION PROGRAM MODELS

In order for students with learning disabilities to make an effective transition to employment or postsecondary training, students must be placed in secondary learning disabilities programs which are compatible with transition goals. In the following sections we review prevalent secondary programs, including *remediation, tutorial, compensatory, strategies intervention*, and *work-study* models. The compatibility of each model with effective transition is considered.

The *Basic Skills Remediation Model* is an extension of the predominant elementary model. Basic skills in reading, mathematics, and written expression continue to be taught to adolescents with learning disabilities who failed to master these skills as elementary students. Although we do not discount the importance of being able to read and perform rudimentary mathematics calculations, we would argue that teaching academics for academics sake at the secondary level does little to promote use of these skills in real-life situations. Secondary students who are significantly deficient in basic math and reading skills are unlikely to respond dramatically to basic skills instruction, leaving them ill-equipped to read or solve rudimentary mathematics problems or to pursue postsecondary training or employment after high school.

In the *Tutorial Model*, the learning disability specialist tutors the student in regular education classes. For example, the student (or the student's regular education teacher) may request that the learning disability specialist help the student prepare for a unit test in U.S. history, learn a list of vocabulary words for the English quiz, or help the student learn to solve simple algebraic equations. Many leaders in the field of learning disabilities have referred to the tutorial model as a band-aid approach that results in students becoming dependent rather than independent learners. The student may pass a test but continues to lack skills required to be successful on future exams. The tutorial model does little to facilitate successful transition to postsecondary training or employment. Although tutorial services may supplement learning disability services for students requiring them, we question the use of a highly trained learning disability specialist for this purpose.

Peer tutoring or tutoring provided by school volunteers are reasonable alternatives, permitting the specialist to more appropriately assist the student with learning disabilities to become an independent learner.

The previous two models focus on improving the learner's skills or knowledge. The *Compensatory Model* relies on changing the student's instructional environment. Modifications and accommodations are made with regard to how content is presented and evaluated. Presentation modifications might include delivering content through films and demonstration in addition to lecture and reading assignments. Evaluation modifications include permitting the student with learning disabilities to demonstrate competence through demonstration or successful completion of an oral examination. This model may promote successful transition if students become aware of their learning characteristics and are able to request appropriate environmental modifications in postsecondary settings.

Don Deshler, Jean Schumaker, and their colleagues at the University of Kansas Institute for Research in Learning Disabilities developed an alternative model. The Strategies Intervention Model (SIM) is designed to enable students with learning disabilities to become more efficient and effective learners. The *Learning Strategies Curriculum* of SIM enables secondary-level students to learn *how* to learn rather than *what* to learn. Students are taught strategies that are applied across academic and vocational content areas. Strategies that enable students to decode multisyllabic words, find the main idea of a passage, take notes, write themes, and take tests more efficiently enable students to become independent learners. SIM promotes effective transition to postsecondary training or employment by teaching students with learning disabilities strategies that generalize across settings, foster student independence, and help students become their own advocates.

The *Work-Study Model* advocates direct teaching of job-related academic skills. For example, for the student with learning disabilities enrolled in a carpentry program, measuring actual objects to the sixteenth of an inch may be more appropriate than having the student measure lines on a ditto sheet to the nearest quarter inch. This model requires collaboration between the learning disability specialist and the vocational educator. An effective work-study model should also address job-related social skills as well as academic skills. Effective social skills have been found to be more desirable by employers than entry level technical skills (Elksnin & Elksnin, 1995b). The model can facilitate successful transition to the world of work or postsecondary vocational training programs.

In our discussion of transition of adolescents with learning disabilities, which follows, we consider transition needs of those students who obtain employment immediately following high school and of those students who desire postsecondary training.

MAKING THE TRANSITION FROM HIGH SCHOOL TO EMPLOYMENT

The goal for some students with learning disabilities is to get and keep a job immediately following high school. For this goal to be achieved, students must have access to effective vocational programs. Sitlington (1986) identified three vocational education program models that typically are used to serve students with learning disabilities. When students enter vocational programs designed for regular education students, professionals either have attempted to *change the system, assist the learner to fit the system*, or *ignore the system*. The first model is dependent on the special education teacher providing consultation to the vocational educator regarding the types of appropriate instructional modifications. Several approaches have been used to enable the student with learning disabilities to fit into the existing vocational program more effectively. The student may receive in-class assistance from support personnel such as the learning disabilities specialist. The specialist may provide instruction in the resource room which supplements the vocational teachers' instruction in much the same way the student is tutored in academic subject areas. The learner may also receive instruction in generalizable skills designed to complement the vocational program. Generalizable skills are academic and interpersonal skills, which appear to generalize across vocational programs. A third model bypasses the system by creating a separate vocational program for students with learning disabilities. This third option has become less popular, owing to the legal mandate to educate students with learning disabilities in the least restrictive environment (i.e., with their nondisabled peers). However, for some students with severe learning disabilities an intensive self-contained vocational training program that utilizes job coaches may be appropriate.

VOCATIONAL EDUCATION PROGRAMMING

In order to obtain employment, an individual must have entry-level marketable skills. These skills are usually acquired through vocational education. Vocational education is organized into seven occupational areas: agriculture; business and office; health occupations; home economics; industrial arts and technology; and trades and industry. A typical vocational program requires a half day of specific occupational instruction using both traditional classroom and laboratory experiences during the junior and senior year. Specific course offerings are usually driven by the training needs of the community and employability of program completers.

Specific vocational instruction is delivered in one of four settings. Area Vocational Centers provide content area vocational instruction in a separate facility with students attending their regular home high schools for academic instruction. Vocational High Schools provide both academic and vocational content area instruction in the same facility. Comprehensive High Schools are traditional high school settings that offer five or more vocational content area programs. General High Schools are again traditional high school settings; however, they offer four or fewer vocational programs. The majority of vocational instruction in the United States is delivered in a Comprehensive High School Setting.

One of the additional requirements in the 1990 Carl Perkins Amendments is for vocational education to reorganize instruction within a TECH-PREP format. TECH-PREP programming acknowledges that if vocational training is to keep pace with the rapid changes in technology, then the amount of training and type of curriculum content must change. Consequently vocational educators are developing programs that will provide

- ☐ two years of high school training plus two years postsecondary training (2 + 2), or
- ☐ four years of high school training plus two years of postsecondary training (4 + 2), or
- ☐ four years of high school programming plus two yearstechnical school plus two years at college (4 + 2 + 2).

In addition to these instructional time increases, the curriculum will include information/communication skills, applied academics, and traditional technical skills in an integrated format. TECH-PREP attempts to bridge the gap between academic and vocational programming.

ROLES OF PROFESSIONALS AND FAMILIES

In this chapter we advocate collaboration among professionals, parents, and students in order to promote effective transition from high school to employment (Elksnin & Elksnin, 1990; Gajar, Goodman, & McAfee, 1993). Individuals representing different disciplines and agencies are instrumental in assuring that students with learning disabilities make a smooth postsecondary transition (Feichtner, 1989; Sitlington, 1986).

Vocational Educators

Vocational educators provide specific vocational training and assist in locating vocational training sites for those individuals who desire postsecondary training. Vocational educators also may collect vocational assessment data and develop vocational Individualized Education Plan and Individualized Transition Plan objectives.

Special Educators

Special educators collect and analyze assessment data, provide consultation regarding program modification, provide supplementary instruction as needed, educate the community about the capabilities of individuals with learning disabilities, and coordinate transition planning.

Vocational Rehabilitation Counselors

Until 1981 individuals with learning disabilities were excluded from vocational rehabilitation eligibility because learning disability was not regarded as a mental or physical disability. Vocational Rehabilitation now considers "individuals who have a disorder in one or more of the psychological processes involved in understanding, perceiving, or expressing language or concepts (spoken or written)" as learning disabled (P.L. 94-142, 34 C.F.R. 300.5 [b] [9]). In order to qualify for services, individuals with learning disabilities must meet these criteria:

1. Their psychological processing disorder is diagnosed by a licensed physician and/or a licensed or certified psychologist who is skilled in the diagnosis and treatment of such disorders; and
2. Their disorder results in a substantial handicap to employment; and
3. There is a reasonable expectation that vocational rehabilitation services may benefit the individual in terms of employability. (Office of Information and Resources for the Handicapped, 1980 [p. 4])

Vocational Rehabilitation is the primary service provider available for individuals with a learning disability as they receive services after public school. A significant gap remains between the number of individuals with learning disabilities served by Vocational Rehabilitation and the potential number of eligible individuals. Vocational Rehabilitation counselors can secure funding for job-related services, such as onsite training, provide vocational evaluation information, facilitate job placement and provide support services, and educate the community to promote integration of persons with learning disabilities in community job settings. The Vocational Rehabilitation Act Amendments of 1984 require that counselors serve secondary-level students who are attempting to make the transition from school to work. Vocational Rehabilitation services include vocational training, academic support services, medical treatment, educational and medical evaluations, and other support services such as transportation, books, tools, and the like (Dowdy, Smith, & Nowell, 1992).

Employers

Employers assist in transition by making job training sites and employment available. Information about job requirements and employer needs is of utmost importance when developing and enhancing learning-disability and vocational programs. Employers' prescriptions of necessary secondary and postsecondary support services are important when developing these services or evaluating existing services.

Parents

Parents contribute to the transition process by helping their adolescent with learning disabilities develop realistic career goals and by helping develop Individualized Education Plan and Individualized Transition Plan goals. It is essential that parents be supportive as the adolescent with learning disabilities explores career and employment options. Parents can foster independence by providing structure and encouragement and by allowing the adolescent with learning disabilities to assume responsibility for home and school tasks.

Students

The adolescent with learning disabilities must assume a high level of responsibility for developing and reaching transition goals. Secondary learning-disability and vocational programs that promote independence and responsibility will assist the student in assuming the role of self-advocate. One approach that can be used to encourage students to become more involved in their Individual Education Plans and Individual Transition Plans is the *Education Planning Strategy* developed by the University of Kansas (Van Reusen, Bos, Schumaker, & Deshler, 1987). *I PLAN* is a motivational strategy students can use as they prepare for or participate in IEP and ITP meetings. *I PLAN* includes these five steps: *I*nventory strengths, weaknesses, goals, and learning choices; *P*rovide inventory information to others at the meeting; *L*isten and respond to others; *A*sk questions during the meeting; and *N*ame your goals.

MAKING THE TRANSITION TO COLLEGE

During the past decade, the number of students with learning disabilities in college has increased tenfold (Learning Disability Update, 1986). Many of these students, however, never complete their college degree programs. It is important that high school learning-disability programs enable students with learning disabilities to acquire the skills they will need in college settings, such as course content, study skills, self-reliance, self-knowledge, and self-advocacy. Secondary teachers and parents must create situations that foster student independence. College transition is a three-stage process: from secondary school to college, from college entrance to college graduation, and from college graduation to employment.

From Secondary School To College

During this stage, students and their parents need information about college options. Information can be obtained through printed materials, workshops, and forums. Students with learning disabilities need a clear understanding of the basic differences between high school and college. Brinkerhoff, Shaw, and McGuire (1993) at the University of Connecticut identified several basic differences, including the amount of time in class (e.g., 6 hours per day for 180 days for high school versus 12 hours per week for 28 weeks for college), study time (more required in college), testing practices (e.g., tests are administered less frequently in college), teacher expectations (e.g., college faculty demand a higher level of independence), and structure (e.g., the high degree of externally imposed structure in high school versus the self-determined structure of college).

Siperstein (1988) also recommended that an Individualized College Plan (ICP) be developed that will enable students to be aware of their strengths and weaknesses, the types of instructional accommodations they may require, the availability of educational and financial resources, and so on. The ICP can be used to develop a plan that will enable students to overcome personal, environmental, and social obstacles to success in college.

When selecting a college for the student with learning disabilities, Strichart and Mangrum (1985) suggest that students and parents closely examine the institution's admission policy. Some colleges will consider results from individual intelligence tests to determine if a student has the aptitude for college. Others will consider subtest scores from alternative administrations (e.g., taped, untimed) of the Scholastic Aptitude Test to evaluate an applicant with learning disabilities. The admissions process may allow for letters of support from content area teachers and on-campus interviews. In addition, the availability of these services should be determined: diagnostic and prescriptive planning, special advisement, remediation of basic skills, tutoring, special courses to acquire critical skills (e.g., study, communication, composition, etc.), auxiliary aids and services such as taped textbooks, and counseling services.

The goal of college selection should be to match the student to the institution. A formal procedure that facilitates this process is the *McGuire-Shaw Postsecondary Guide for Learning*, which considers the characteristics of students, the institution, and available learning-disabilities support programs. Appendix B includes a list of college learning-disabilities guides.

From College Entrance To College Graduation

Success in college for the student with learning disabilities may require a combination of changing the student to match the institution and changing the institution to match the student.

Changing the Student

The college student with learning disabilities may require programs that remediate basic skills and provide academic tutoring. Students may need instruction in study skills and access to learning aids such as taped textbooks and notetakers. The academic and social adjustment of the student may be assisted through individual and group counseling services (Satcher, 1993). Students with learning disabilities may need assistance in selecting courses beyond the help normally provided by a college advisor. An appropriate match between student and course can be achieved by considering the student's learning characteristics along with the course materials, content presentation, methods of evaluation, and classroom standards (Patton & Polloway, 1987). Finally, students need to learn self-advocacy techniques, including sitting in front, asking to tape a lecture, planning assignments in advance, explaining one's learning difficulties to the instructor, asking the instructor for assistance, and going to all classes and being on time.

Changing the Environment

Often a primary role of the college learning-disabilities specialist is to be a liaison with faculty, facilitating modifications such as extended time for tests and assignment completion, provision of lecture notes, use of audiovisual equipment, and adjustment of grading standards, although they often initially meet with resistance. College faculty need to become more sensitive to the needs of students with learning disabilities. Figure 13–1 provides a list of instructional accommodations for college students with learning disabilities that can be provided by college faculty.

Another important function of college learning disabilities services is to identify institutional resources that may be beneficial to students with learning disabilities. These resources may include library services such as books on tape, audio visual aids, and other special equipment; student services such as personal counseling, career/life planning, health services; and learning labs such as writing centers, reading labs, study skills centers, and computer-assisted instruction (see Figure 13–2).

In addition to instructional modifications and accessibility to resources, institutional policy changes may lead to more adaptive environments for the student with learning disabilities. Although not widespread, these policy changes may include modification of admissions requirements, specially designed courses, semester load reductions, and foreign language waivers or substitutions.

Students preparing to make the transition from college to employment will require ongoing career counseling (Satcher, 1993). As graduation draws nearer, the college student with learning disabilities will need to learn job-search and job-maintenance strategies.

CONCLUSION

Individuals involved in transition planning for adolescents with learning disabilities should be aware of the feelings and needs of students and their parents. Parents may recognize the need to allow their child with learning disabilities to become less dependent on them but may have difficulty facilitating independence. The failures and frustrations encountered during the high school years may cause parents to feel apprehensive about their child becoming employed or entering a postsecondary training program. Parents may also anticipate a sense of loss of the familiar educational support system available throughout the elementary and secondary years. For the student with learning disabilities, concerns may relate to lack of postsecondary knowledge and self-advocacy skills and the need to become fully accepting of their learning disability. The learning disability specialist can promote transition for parents and students through these activities (Ness, 1989):

- [ ] Obtaining more information about postsecondary options.
- [ ] Inservicing regular education teachers and guidance teachers to enable them to contribute to the transition process.
- [ ] Assisting the student to understand learning disabilities, to identify personal strengths and weaknesses, and to self-advocate based on this knowledge.

FIGURE 13–1

Instructional Accommodations For College Students With Learning Disabilities

---

TEACHING STRATEGIES

Provide students with advance organizers such as outlines, schedule of due dates for projects, reading assignments, and exams.

Give students an outline prior to lecture.

Use handouts to list important terms, formulas, key points, and so on.

Write and define new terms on the board.

Provide oral summary statement of key points.

Read material written on board or on overhead transparencies.

Permit the student to use a notetaker.

Allow the student to photocopy another student's notes.

Permit the student to tape record the lecture.

Encourage class discussion.

Provide positive and negative examples.

ASSISTING STUDENTS IN THEIR READING AND WRITTEN WORK

Provide students with chapter outlines or study guides.

Permit students to use a dictionary, computer spell check, or proofreader.

Allow students to use readers, scribes, word processors, tape recorders, and typewriters.

Permit students to use a calculator in math or science classes.

Allow students additional time to complete written assignments.

EVALUATION STRATEGIES

Allow students to complete paper and project drafts for critique; permit rewriting.

Give students additional time to complete examinations.

Allow students time to study before administering an examination or quiz.

Be sure examination questions are well-spaced on the page.

Avoid requiring student to transfer responses to an answer sheet.

Allow students to take examination as an oral essay, to tape answers, or to use a transcriber for essay exams.

Allow poor grammar on exams if grammar is not the primary focus.

Permit student to take exam with a proctor in a quiet room without distractions.

Administer short exams frequently rather than one or two lengthy exams.

Divide exam and assess student over multiple sessions.

Provide cues to help students recall information. Consider retesting students.

Be willing to consider a variety of test designs (e.g., essay, multiple choice, matching, true-false).

Consider the use of alternatives to test when evaluating student performance (e.g., demonstrations, taped interviews, slide-tape presentations, photographic essays, and so on).

Allow extra credit assignments.

Be willing to schedule individual conferences during the semester to discuss the student's progress.

FIGURE 13–2

Institutional Resources For College Students With Learning Disabilities

---

PERSONNEL

Special Education Faculty

LD Administrator/Coordinator

LD Specialists

Notetakers

Peer Tutors

Readers

Scribes

SERVICES

Academic Counseling

Access to computers, tapes, taping, videos, etc.

Career Counseling

Diagnostic Services

Personal Counseling

Self-Help Groups

Tutoring

SPECIAL COURSES

Compensatory/Learning Strategies Instruction

Developmental/Remedial Courses

Social/Interpersonal Skills Training

Study Skills Courses

FACULTY AND STAFF TRAINING

Faculty Awareness Activities

Staff Training

- [ ] Assist parents in understanding their child's learning disabilities so they can in turn encourage the child's self-awareness.
- [ ] Providing support groups and workshops for parents that might feature speakers from advocacy organizations such as the Learning DisabilityAssociation of America and the Department of Vocational Rehabilitation Services.
- [ ] Include transition objectives in the student's IEP and begin the transition process by at least the 9th grade through offering the appropriate course work and career development activities.

CHAPTER 14

The Summary Conference

Frank R. Brown, III
Elizabeth H. Aylward

The goal of the interdisciplinary team process, as described in the preceding chapters, is to develop a consensus opinion regarding diagnoses and to formulate a comprehensive treatment plan. An equally essential element of the diagnostic and prescriptive process is to convey findings and recommendations of the interdisciplinary team to the parents (and, when appropriate, to the child) through a summary conference. The individual assigned this responsibility (usually the case manager) has a very difficult and important responsibility; this is the subject of the final chapter.

In theory, and in the best of circumstances, any professional participating in the interdisciplinary team process should be capable of functioning as case manager and could be assigned the responsibility of explaining the diagnoses and therapeutic recommendations to the parents and child. It is imperative, however, that the case manager understand, at least to a reasonably complete degree, all the factors involved in formulating the interdisciplinary diagnoses and therapeutic recommendations. It is not sufficient for the case manager to understand only his or her own discipline's perspective, as the result would reflect this limited perspective and bias. The person conducting the summary conference should have a good breadth of understanding of the child with learning disabilities and his or her family, and should be able to articulate the team's findings and recommendations to the family in a comprehensive, unbiased, and sensitive way. In particularly difficult cases, it may be beneficial to have several team members present at the summary conference in order to support the case manager's presentation.

The case manager may want to begin the conference by asking the parents to reiterate the concerns and goals they had at the time the evaluation was initiated. Concerns of the individual who initiated the referral (if not the parents) should also be discussed. With these concerns and goals in mind, the case manager can conduct a conference that will produce appropriate closure on the parent's agenda and, when necessary, expand this agenda to reflect additional diagnostic concerns and therapeutic recommendations from the team's perspective.

PRESENTATION OF THE DIAGNOSES

Throughout this book we have attempted to clearly distinguish between primary (neurologically based) and secondary (derivative of primary) disabling conditions. It is important that the case manager share this distinction with the parents. By making this distinction, the case manager provides the parents and child with a logical and effective framework for the discussion of diagnoses and therapeutic recommendations.

Diagnoses of Primary Disabling Conditions

In presenting the team's diagnostic data, the case manager will need to define some terms for the parents, especially the term *learning disability*. Throughout this book, *learning disability* has been defined as a discrepancy between cognitive ability and academic achievement, assuming that other conditions have been ruled out (see Chapter 1). It is important that parents understand the difference between intelligence and academic achievement, as many will presume that these concepts are one and the same. The difference between intelligence and academic achievement can sometimes be explained by describing the types of tasks presented on tests of intelligence (which are presumed to reflect underlying cognitive ability) and tests of academic achievement (which reflect the level of mastery of academic skills).

After defining terms, the case manager should review the data from the individual evaluations and highlight those findings that support or refute the diagnosis of a specific learning disability. The case manager can begin by describing any delays in early development that often correlate with subsequent learning disabilities (see Chapter 2). This will help the parents understand the long-standing developmental basis of their child's primary disabling conditions.

Next, the case manager will present data regarding the potential for academic achievement, as defined by the results of the psychologist's formal cognitive assessment. Overall cognitive assessment should be discussed, as well as any significant strengths and weaknesses within the cognitive profile (see Chapters 4 and 5).

When discussing the child's academic achievement, it is important to present both the results of the formal achievement tests and the classroom teachers' present and past perspectives on the child's rate of progress (see Chapter 6). Strengths and weaknesses within the academic achievement profile should also be discussed with the parents.

After the case manager has explained the defining characteristics of learning disabilities and has outlined any significant discrepancies between cognitive ability and academic achievement, the diagnostic conclusion regarding the presence or absence of learning disabilities should be clear to the parents. Definition of relevant individual learning disabilities (dyslexia, dyscalculia, dysgraphia) will further clarify the diagnosis (see Chapter 1). The case manager should help the parents understand how the learning disabilities will interfere with school performance and how the disabilities may prevent the child from learning through traditional approaches.

Following the discussion of learning disabilities, the case manager should introduce any other primary disabling conditions diagnosed by the team (e.g., attention-deficit/hyperactivity disorder [AD/HD], language disabilities, fine and gross motor dyscoordination). As with the discussion of learning disabilities, the case manger will need to clearly define the terms associated with each individual diagnosis. Then data to support or refute each diagnosis should be presented. This data will include test results as well as information obtained through the teacher interview, parent interview, classroom observation, and observation of the child during testing. The case manager should explain how these associated primary conditions will interfere with school performance. For example, parents should be able to easily understand that AD/HD may result in inconsistent application to task, fluctuating academic performance, and failure to follow directions.

Diagnoses of Secondary Disabling Conditions

The case manager should next focus discussion on any secondary disabling conditions that have been diagnosed or are suspected (e.g., poor self-esteem, behavioral problems). Their definitions, diagnostic features, and implications should be discussed. Data relevant to these conditions may include test results but will more typically involve information obtained through interviews and observation.

At this point, it will be helpful for the case manager to review the relevant diagnoses and their definitions and to discuss the relationships among the diagnosed conditions. Parents should understand that the primary disabling conditions are neurologically based, whereas secondary disabling conditions have probably occurred as a result of the primary disabilities.

It is especially important that the case manager clarify the distinction between primary and secondary disabling conditions when discussing AD/HD and attention-seeking behavior (see Chapter 11). It should be emphasized that AD/HD represents a primary disability frequently associated with learning disabilities, which is to a large extent out of the child's control. This is contrasted with attention-seeking behaviors, which are frequently a secondary condition representing the child's underlying frustration in dealing with the primary disabling conditions. These attention-seeking behaviors can, with assistance, be brought under the child's willful control. Although these conditions often overlap and may be very difficult to disentangle, it is important that the parents understand the distinction between them before therapeutic recommendations are presented.

PRESENTATION OF THERAPEUTIC RECOMMENDATIONS

Following explanation of the diagnoses, the parents' first question will probably be "What do we do about these problems?" The case manager should attempt to respond to this question by systematically reviewing the types of treatment and accommodations appropriate for each specific diagnosis. In discussing these recommendations, the case manager will find it helpful to again use a format based on the distinction between primary and secondary disabling conditions.

Therapeutic Recommendations for Primary Disabling Conditions

The case manager should present the team's therapeutic recommendations first by discussing the relatively straightforward procedures used to address the learning disabilities. The issue of special education services should be presented by explaining to parents that their child's learning disabilities prevent him or her from being taught effectively using traditional approaches. Parents should be provided with information regarding the types of special education services that might be available through the school and be introduced to the procedures for obtaining these services. Following this general introduction, the case manager should discuss with the parents some of the specialized terminology they will encounter when they meet with the Individual Educational Plan (IEP) development team at their child's school. Some of this terminology will be used in discussing the amount of time the child spends in special programming (e.g., resource classroom, levels of special education service). Other terms will be used in discussing special education methods to which the child will be exposed (e.g., Direct Instruction, Strategies Intervention Model). It is important that parents be familiar with these terms, as this type of jargon is often used by school personnel during the IEP development conference without adequate explanation. If the interdisciplinary team wishes to recommend any other educational treatment (e.g., tutoring, vocational education) or alternative school placements, these options should also be presented.

Next, the case manager should discuss any special accommodations that the child's teachers (regular or special education) will need to make to circumvent additional primary disabling conditions often associated with learning disabilities. For example, if the child's handwriting is slow and inefficient, the parents need to understand what types of accommodations the child's teachers should be making (see Chapter 10). Similarly, if the child has AD/HD the parents should expect special classroom accommodations to be implemented (see Chapter 11).

The case manager should also discuss the parents' role in the management of primary disabling conditions, especially AD/HD. Specific suggestions for home management of the child (see Chapter 11) should be reviewed with the parents. Strategies for helping the child with homework, organizational difficulties, or other problems associated with the primary disabling conditions should also be presented.

If the interdisciplinary team (with input from the child's physician) has determined that a trial of medication for AD/HD is warranted, the case manager will want to convey this recommendation to the parents. The case manager, depending on his or her familiarity with the medication, may want to provide a full discussion of this topic or instead may want to recommend that the parents speak with the child's physician. In any case, it should always be made clear that the final decision regarding use of medication is to be made by the parents and the child's physician.

Therapeutic Recommendations for Secondary Disabling Conditions

Therapeutic recommendations for the prevention or treatment of secondary disabling conditions should be presented following discussion of the primary disabling conditions. This area of discussion is most important because these secondary disabling conditions, unlike the primary conditions, can almost always be prevented or eliminated, if parents and teachers deal with the child appropriately.

During the evaluation, the interdisciplinary team will have identified inappropriate attention-seeking behaviors that are a cause for concern among parents or teachers. The case manager should explain to
the parents how they can help the child control these behaviors
through a behavior management system (see Chapter 12). It may be
necessary in some cases for the parents and school to coordinate their
efforts in establishing a single behavior management system that covers
inappropriate behaviors both at home and school. Strategies for establishing such a system should be discussed with the parents.

Finally, and perhaps most important, the case manager should discuss strategies for maintaining or improving the child's self-concept.
This area is of vital importance because, when all is said and done, the
child's image of himself or herself and his or her ability to relate to others are probably the greatest determinants of overall success.

Parents need to understand their role in building the child's self-
concept. They should be encouraged to implement some of the specific
strategies discussed in Chapter 12 (e.g., identifying and encouraging
special strengths or talents, encouraging participation in structured
nonacademic group activities). More important, they can accept the
fact that the basis of many of the child's difficulties is neurological and,
therefore, out of the child's control. When parents stop holding the
child accountable for learning difficulties, attention problems, and poor
impulse control, and focus on providing the extra structure and support
needed, the child's self-concept will improve.

Parents also need to understand the school's responsibility for
building the child's self-concept. They may need to work as the child's
advocate to make certain that teachers each year are making the special accommodations necessary to allow the child maximum success.

ANSWERING PARENTS' QUESTIONS

Through a systematic approach of defining terms, presenting data
to support or refute diagnoses, explaining how each disabling condition
will interfere with performance, and presenting therapeutic recommendations to treat or accommodate each condition, the case manager
should be able to convey to the parents a fairly comprehensive understanding of their child's situation. Regardless of the case manager's
skills at conveying this information, parents will no doubt have many
unanswered questions. The most common of these involve the etiology
and prognosis of the disorders.

Discussion of Etiology of Disorders

As discussed in Chapter 1, we view learning disabilities and associated primary disabling conditions as neurologically based. With an un-

derstanding of the neurological basis of learning disabilities, parents are sometimes better able to recognize that the child is not at fault and cannot be held responsible for his or her difficulties. Because neurological damage in children with learning disabilities is subtle and diffuse, the cause of this damage cannot, in most cases, be determined for certain. Parents should be discouraged then from dwelling on "what went wrong," as determination of the precise etiology of the disorders is not usually possible nor requisite in their child's treatment.

Discussion of Prognosis of Disorders

Parents almost always want to ask, "Will my child get better?" The answer to this question can almost always be answered affirmatively, because the child will continue to develop and make academic progress. (The exception to this rule would be the child whose self-concept and attitude toward school have been damaged beyond recovery.)

However, if the question is phrased, "Will my child be normal?" the answer cannot be as reassuring. The neurological damage or dysfunction believed to underlie learning disabilities and concomitant conditions will not disappear. It is known, however, that certain areas of the brain can compensate for damage that has occurred in other areas. In addition, children with learning disabilities (especially those who are bright) will learn strategies to compensate for areas of weakness. Unfortunately, it is not possible to determine the extent to which compensation will occur and it is, therefore, not possible to determine to what extent functions will eventually appear normal. Parents are often told that their children will "outgrow" the primary disabling conditions, especially AD/HD, around the time of puberty. The case manager should caution parents that this expectation is usually unrealistic.

Despite the fact that the neurological damage or dysfunction underlying primary disabling conditions cannot be changed, parents should not be left with the idea that remedial efforts are worthless. Special education teachers can help children with learning disabilities develop strategies for compensating or working around their learning disabilities. Counselors can sometimes help children with AD/HD apply strategies for controlling their impulsivity. Occupational or physical therapists may be able to help the child find easier methods for accomplishing difficult motor tasks. Despite "specialists'" claims to the contrary and parents' desire for a "normal" child, the current level of understanding of learning disabilities and concomitant conditions does not permit a "cure," and parents should not expect special education teachers or therapists to be able to totally remediate the disorders.

Although special education teachers and therapists cannot be expected to completely remediate learning disabilities and concomitant conditions, they do play an important role in determining how the child

learns to accept and handle his or her disabilities. As we have emphasized several times, prevention or remediation of secondary disabling
conditions in children with learning disabilities, especially inappropri-
·ate attention-seeking behaviors and poor self-concept, is vital in determining eventual outcome. Placement in special education classes where
the child is presented with materials appropriate to his or her achievement level will allow the child to experience success he or she would be
unable to achieve in a regular classroom. Accommodations for poor
handwriting, poor organizational skills, or attention problems will
allow the child the opportunity to demonstrate what he or she is capable of doing, preventing unnecessary frustration. By implementing
these strategies as well as special techniques for handling secondary
disabling conditions, parents and teachers will be able to ensure the
best possible outcome for the child with learning disabilities.

PLANNING FOR FOLLOW-UP

Parents should leave the summary conference with the understanding that the interdisciplinary team will monitor implementation of the
therapeutic suggestions, conduct regular evaluations of the child's
progress, and revise the treatment plan as necessary. If possible, the
case manager should outline for the parents any specific tasks they are
expected to accomplish (e.g., meeting with the IEP development team,
contacting tutors, consulting with the child's pediatrician regarding trial
medication for AD/HD, implementing behavior management strategies). The case manager should, of course, provide as much assistance
as necessary to ensure that the parents will be able to accomplish these
tasks. In addition, the case manager should outline the tasks to be completed or monitored by the interdisciplinary team (e.g., preparing the
IEP, helping the teacher develop a behavior management system, coordinating a medication trial with the school nurse).

The case manager should outline for the parents what types of future evaluations should be conducted (e.g., academic achievement testing only, complete psychoeducational reevaluation, additional testing
by allied professionals) and when. Parents should know that the school
will automatically conduct evaluations on a regular basis as long as the
child receives special education. If the interdisciplinary team feels additional testing is necessary (to be conducted either through the school or
privately), arrangements should be made to ensure that this occurs.

Regardless of the case manager's ability to clearly present definitions, data, diagnoses, and recommendations, parents are bound to
have further questions and concerns after they leave the conference.
Problems often arise as parents, teachers, and therapists experiment

with various strategies for dealing with the child's disorders. The case manager should make certain that the parents feel free to contact him or her for further discussion, advice, or assistance.

CONCLUSION

This chapter has addressed the case manager's important role in conveying the results and recommendations of the interdisciplinary team process. We suggested that the case manager present diagnoses and therapeutic recommendations using a format that clearly distinguishes between primary and secondary disabling conditions. In order to help parents fully understand their child's disorders, the case manager must clearly define diagnostic terms, present data obtained through the evaluations that are relevant to each diagnosis, integrate the data to explain how each diagnosis was formulated, and describe how the disorders will interfere with normal functioning. Therapeutic recommendations relevant to each specific diagnosis (of both primary and secondary disabling conditions) are then presented. Common questions regarding the etiology and prognosis of learning disabilities and concomitant conditions are discussed, with special emphasis given to the importance of preventing secondary disabling conditions. The case manager should make certain that parents leave the summary conference with the assurance that the interdisciplinary team will monitor implementation of the therapeutic recommendations, regularly evaluate the child's progress, and revise the treatment plan as necessary. It is hoped that these procedures will make the parent feel that the interdisciplinary team has worked and will continue to work as the child's advocate in obtaining the support and understanding he or she needs for optimal outcome.

Glossary, Appendices, and References

GLOSSARY

Attention-Deficit/Hyperactivity Disorder   Developmentally inappropriate lack of attention and/or poor impulse control with excessive motor activity.

Criterion-Referenced Test   A test designed to determine whether or not the child has mastered specific skills. Unlike scores from norm-referenced tests, scores from criterion-referenced tests do not reflect comparison of the student with peers.

Dyscalculia   Poor achievement in arithmetic, as compared with overall cognitive ability.

Dyseidetic (Dyslexic)   A proposed subtype of reading disability whereby the child has difficulty remembering the visual configurations of letters and words. Dyseidetic dyslexics spell and read words by their sounds and consequently read very slowly, as they must sound out each word as they go.

Dysgraphia   Poor achievement in written language, as compared with overall cognitive ability.

Dyslexia   Difficulty with reading, manifested as a significant discrepancy between reading achievement and expectations based on cognitive potential.

Dysphonetic (Dyslexic)   A proposed subtype of reading disability whereby the child has difficulty relating symbols to sounds and, consequently, difficulty mastering phonetic word analysis. Dysphonetic dyslexics are dependent on their sight-word (visually memorized) vocabulary and make bizarre spelling errors unrelated to the sound of the word.

Dyspraxia   Poor praxis or motor planning.

Educational Quotient (EQ)   A score that reflects the expected level of academic achievement. The EQ is based on a measure of intellectual functioning and takes into account the statistical phenomenon known as regression toward the mean.

Environmental Accommodations   Changes made in the home and school environment to minimize or eliminate the effects of primary handicapping conditions, especially attention-deficit/hyperactivity disorder.

Error of Measurement   An individual's "true score" on a given test is the average of the scores he or she would obtain if the test were given an infinite number of times without any effects from retesting. The error of measurement is the standard deviation of the difference between the true score and the obtained scores. The error of measurement allows the examiner to develop "confidence bands" that indicate a range of scores within which the individual's true score will fall a given percentage of time.

Fine Motor   Movements using hands and fingers for tasks requiring precision.

Gross Motor   Movements requiring the whole body for appropriate execution. Transfer of body weight and postural adjustment is involved.

Hyperactivity   Excessive motor activity, manifested as excessive running or climbing, difficulty sitting still, or excessive movement in sleep.

IEP   Individual Educational Plan. A written outline of instructional and therapeutic strategies that will be used for the remediation of a student in special education.

IFSP   Individual Family Service Plan. A written outline of instructional and therapeutic strategies necessary to meet the preschool-age child's (birth to 3 years) and family's needs. Developed from child and family assessments conducted by a multidisciplinary team and with the family's input.

Interdisciplinary   Format of shared communication, trust, openness, respect, and interdependence between professionals in establishing a diagnosis or developing prescriptive plans.

Learning Disability   Condition whereby an individual's academic achievement level (in any specific academic area) is significantly below the level that would be predicted from the level of intellectual ability.

Minimal Brain Dysfunction (MBD)   Subtle brain dysfunction in which a child exhibits a mixture of some or all of the following: learning disabilities, language disabilities, other inconsistencies among various cognitive functions, attention-deficit/hyperactivity disorder, gross, fine, and oral motor dyscoordinations.

Neurodevelopmental Examination   Examination of the level of development in motor (gross and fine), language (expressive and receptive), visual problem solving, and social adaptive functioning.

Neurodevelopmental History   History of the temporal sequence of development in motor (gross and fine), language (expressive and receptive), visual problem solving, and social adaptive functioning.

Norm-Referenced Test   A test designed to determine how well the child performs on a particular task, in comparison with peers.

Norms   Test scores based on the performance of a representative cross-section of students, usually a national sample.

Perceptual-Motor Integration   The ability to integrate information from sensory channels (e.g., vision, touch, body position) with fine motor skills to achieve the desired outcome.

P.L. 94-142   The Education for All Handicapped Children Act of 1975, which provides for free appropriate education of all handicapped children, including children with learning disabilities, in the least restrictive educational environment.

P.L. 98-524   The Carl D. Perkins Vocational Education Act of 1984, enables students with disabilities and who are disadvantaged to access the full range of vocational programs available to individuals without disability or disadvantage.

P.L. 99-457   Education of the Handicapped Amendments of 1986, which provide new incentives for the development of services to young children with disabilities and their families. Stipulates development of an Individual Family Service Plan (IFSP).

P.L. 101-336   The Americans with Disabilities Act of 1990, further expands and specifies the civil rights (especially in the area of employment) of all individuals with a disability.

P.L. 101-476   The Individuals with Disabilities Act (IDEA) of 1990, which amended P.L. 94-142.

Primary Disabling Conditions   Disabling conditions that have a neurological basis, including learning disabilities, speech-language disabilities, gross and fine motor dyscoordination, and attention-deficit/hyperactivity disorder.

Regression Toward the Mean   A statistical phenomenon whereby students who score higher or lower than the mean on a given test will be expected to score nearer the mean on a subsequent test. Regression toward the mean increases as the correlation between the two tests decreases.

Reliability   The extent to which a test consistently measures what it measures. This includes consistency over time (test-retest reliability), and consistency across forms of the test (alternate form reliability), or consistency within the test items themselves (internal reliability).

Secondary Disabling Conditions   Disabling conditions that do not have a direct neurological basis, but are the result of primary (neurologically based) conditions that have not been properly managed. The most common are poor self-concept and inappropriate attention-seeking behaviors.

Sensory Integration   The ability to perceive discrete stimuli and to combine them into a meaningful whole, generating an appropriate response.

Sensory Integrative Therapy   Treatment involving sensory stimulation (vestibular, proprioceptive, and tactile) with the goal of improving the way a child processes and organizes sensations.

Slow Learner   Term used to describe the child whose learning ability in all areas is delayed in comparison to children of the same chronological age. These children are characterized by low-normal to borderline intelligence, with corresponding slow academic achievement.

Soft Neurological Signs   Neurological findings that are on a developmental continuum; that is, they appear and disappear with development and maturation of the nervous system. Pathology equates with the extent of their presence and the timing of their appearance and disappearance. Mirror movements and synkinesis represent the most commonly encountered.

Standard Score   A type of test score that indicates how far an individual's performance deviates from the mean of the standardization sample (the representative sample from which the standard scores were derived). Standard scores for most tests have a mean of 100 and a standard deviation of 15.

Synkinesis   Overflow or overshooting of muscle movements into surrounding muscle groups when a request is made for movement of an isolated muscle group.

Validity   The extent to which a test actually measures what it purports to measure. A test's validity is determined by how well it samples from the domain of behaviors it was designed to measure (content validity), how well the test correlates with other measures of the same or similar construct (concurrent validity), how well the test predicts the child's future performance (predictive validity), and how helpful the test is in understanding the construct measured (construct validity).

Vestibular System   The sensory system that responds to the position of the head in relation to gravity and accelerated or decelerated movement.

Word-Attack Skills   A child's ability to decode unknown words, based on application of phonic skills (making grapheme-phoneme equivalences) and structural analysis skills (identifying word "parts," including root words, suffixes, and prefixes.

APPENDIX A

Parent Interview Form

Child's Name ——————————————————————————

Interviewee ——————————————————————————

1. Primary concerns: ——————————————————————

2. Source of referral: ——————————————————————

3. Current grade: —————

    school: ——————————————————————————

    teacher: ——————————————————————————

    special education services: ————————————————————

    type of class: ————————————————————————

4. School history:

    preschool?

Grade	School	Services	Repeated?	Problems
K				
1				
2				
3				
4				
5				
6				
7				
8				
9				

5. Current school grades: ————————————————————

6. Teachers' complaints: _____ hyperactive

    _____ distractible

    _____ short attention span

    _____ won't stay in seat

    _____ shy/withdrawn

    _____ sloppy/disorganized

    _____ frustrated easily

    _____ talks out of turn

    _____ fails to complete assignments

                                 _____ destructive

                                 _____ disruptive

7.   Specific weaknesses: _____ reading

                                 _____ arithmetic

                                 _____ spelling

                                 _____ handwriting

                                 _____ speech

                                 _____ fine motor skills

                                 _____ gross motor skills

                                 _____ hearing/vision

8.   Family: _____ father   _____ mother   _____ brothers (ages: ____)

                 _____sisters (ages: _____)   _____ other:

                 parents separated? _____ how long? ____

                 contact with noncustodial parent? _____

9.   Language other than English at home? _____

10. Behavior problems at home?

       _____ fails to listen to and follow instructions

       _____ refuses to obey

       _____ temper tantrums

       _____ lies

       _____ steals

       _____ other

11. Chores required? _____

       type? _____

       problems? _____

12. Homework:

       How much time spent each night? _____

       How much time should be spent? _____

       Supervision required? _____

       Problems? _____

13. Many friends? _____

       Interaction with peers? _____

14. Relationship with siblings? _____

15. Extracurricular activities: _____

       What does the child like to do? _____

       Organized teams/groups? _____

16. Any unusual fears? _____

    Sleeping problems? _____

    Eating problems? _____

    Separation problems? _____

17. Self-concept? _____

18. Previous Testing? _____

19. Family history of learning problems?

    Mother: _____

    Father: _____

    Siblings: _____

    Other family members: _____

20. Medication for attention deficit disorder?

    Started:_____   Stopped:_____

    Current dosage: _____

    Schooldays/evenings/weekends/summers: _____

    Effectiveness: _____

    Problems: _____

    On medication today? _____ Time taken: _____

    Any other medications/health issues that might affect testing? _____

    _____

    _____

21. Other concerns? _____

    _____

    _____

APPENDIX B

Transition Resource List

COLLEGE/POSTSECONDARY TRAINING LD GUIDES

ACLD College List
Learning Disabilities Association
Pittsburgh, PA

College Guide for Students with Learning Disabilities
J. Scalfani and M. J. Lynch
SPEDCO Associates
Farmingville, NY

College Programs for Learning Disabled Students
National Association of College Admissions Counselors
Skokie, IL

A Guide to Colleges for Learning Disabled Students
M. Liscio
Academic Press
Orlando, FL

A Guide to Post-Secondary Educational Opportunities for the Learning Disabled
Time Out to Enjoy
Oak Park, IL

Learning Disabilities, Graduate School, and Careers
Pamela B. Adelman and Carol T. Wren
Learning Opportunities Program
Barat College
Lake Forest, IL

Lovejoy's College Guide for the Learning Disabled
C. T. Straughn
Monarch Press
New York, NY

McGuire-Shaw Postsecondary Selection Guide for Learning Disabled
    College Students
Special Education Center Publications
The University of Connecticut
Storrs, CT

A National Directory of Four Year Colleges, Two Year Colleges and Post High School
    Training Programs for Young People with Learning Disabilities
P. M. Fielding, Editor
Partners in Publishing
Tulsa, OK

Peterson's Guide to Colleges with Programs for Learning Disabled Students
C. T. Mangrum and S. S. Strichart, Editors
Peterson's Guides
Princeton, NJ

ORGANIZATIONS/AGENCIES

Association on Handicapped Student Services Programs in
  Postsecondary Education
P. O. Box 21192
Columbus, OH 43221

College Handicapped and Exceptional Learners Programs and Services
Partners in Publishing
1419 East 1st Street
Tulsa, OK 74127

Council for Learning Disabilities
P. O. Box 40303
Overland Park, KS 66204

Division for Learning Disabilities
Council for Exceptional Children
1920 Association Drive
Reston, VA 22091

HEATH Resource Center
National Clearinghouse on Postsecondary Education for Individuals
  with Disabilities
Publisher of *Information from HEATH*, a newsletter published three times a year.
  (Subscription is free.)
One Dupont Circle
Washington, DC 20036

Learning Disability Association of America (formerly ACLD)
4156 Library Road
Pittsburgh, PA 15234

The National Center for Research on Vocational Education
The Ohio State University
1960 Kenny Road
Columbus, OH 43210

National Clearinghouse of Rehabilitation Training Materials
Oklahoma State University
115 USDA Building
Stillwater, OK 74078

National Information Center for Handicapped Children and Youths
P. O. Box 149
National Resource Center for Materials on Work Evaluation and Work Adjustment
Materials Development Center
University of Wisconsin-Stout
Menomonie, WI 54751

Reference List of Tests

Tests included in this list are not necessarily endorsed by the authors. A number of these tests are discussed in the text and are referenced in the index.

ACTeRS (1988)
MetriTech, Inc.

Analytic Reading Inventory-5th Edition (1995)
M. L. Woods and A. J. Moe
Prentice-Hall
200 Old Tappan Road
Old Tappan, NJ 07675

Basic Achievement Skills Individual Screener (BASIS, 1983)
Psychological Corporation
555 Academic Ct., San Antonio,
  TX 78204-2498

Battelle Developmental Inventory (1984)
DLM Teaching Resources
One DLM Park, P. O. Box 4000, Allen,
  TX 75002

Bayley Scales of Infant Development-II (1993)
Psychological Corporation
555 Academic Ct., San Antonio,
  TX 78204-2498

Behavior Evaluation Scale-2 (BES-2, 1990)
S. B. McCarney and J. E. Leigh
Hawthorne Educational Services
P. O. Box 7540, Columbia, MO 65205

Behavior Problem Checklist-Revised (1987)
H. C. Quay and D. R. Peterson
P. O. Box 248074
University of Miami, Coral Gables,
  FL 32124

Behavior Rating Profile 2nd Edition (1990)
L. L. Brown and D. D. Hammill
PRO-ED
8700 Shoal Creek Blvd., Austin,
  TX 78757-6897

Bender Visual Motor Gestalt Test (1946)
Lauretta Bender
American Orthopsychiatric Association
49 Sheridan Ave., Albany, NY 12210

Benton Visual Retention Test Fifth Ed. (1991)
Abigail Benton Sivan
The Psychological Corporation
555 Academic Ct., San Antonio,
  TX 78204-2498

Boston Naming Test (1983)
E. F. Kaplan, H. Goodglass, and S.
  Weintraub
Lea & Febiger
600 Washington Square, Philadelphia,
  PA 19106

Brigance Comprehensive Inventory of Basic Skills (1983)
Brigance Diagnostic Inventory of Basic Skills (1977)
Brigance Diagnostic Inventory of Early Development-Revised (1991)
Brigance Diagnostic Inventory of Essential Skills (1981)
Brigance Early Preschool Screen (1990)
Brigance K & 1 Screen-Revised (1992)
Brigance Preschool Screen (1985)
Albert H. Brigance
Curriculum Associates, Inc.
5 Esquire Rd., North Billerica,
  MA 01862-0901

Bruininks-Oseretsky Test of Motor Proficiency (1978)
Robert H. Bruininks
American Guidance Service
Publishers Building, Circle Pines,
  MN 55014

California Achievement Tests-5 (1992)
CTB-McGraw-Hill
20 Ryan Ranch Road
Monterey, CA 93940

California Diagnostic Reading Test (1990)
CTB-McGraw Hill
20 Ryan Ranch Road
Monterey, CA 93940

California Verbal Learning Test for Children (CVLT-C; 1994)
D. C. Delis, J. H. Kramer, E. Kaplan, and B. A. Ober
The Psychological Corporation
555 Academic Court, San Antonio, TX 78204-2498

Child Behavior Checklist (1991)
T. M. Achenbach and C. Edelbrock
1 South Prospect Street
Burlington, VT 05401

Child Development Inventory (1994)
Behavior Science Systems, Inc.
P. O. Box 580274, Minneapolis, MN 55458

Children's Apperception Test (1980)
Leopold Bellak and Sonya Sorel Bellak
C. P. S., Inc.
Box 83, Larchmont, NY 10538

Classroom Reading Inventory-7th Edition (1994)
M. J. Silvaroli
Times Mirror Education Publishing Group
2460 Kerper Blvd.
Dubuque, IA 52001

Code for Instructional Structure and Student Academic Response (CISSAR) (1978)
In J. Salvia and J. E. Ysseldyke (Eds.) (1991). *Assessment* (Fifth Edition)
Boston: Houghton Miflin Company

Cognitive Abilities Test (1983)
Robert L. Thorndike and Elizabeth Hagen
Riverside Publishing Co.
8420 Bryn Mawr Ave., Chicago, IL 60631

Cognitive Skills Assessment Battery, Second Ed. (1981)
Teachers College Press
P. O. Box 1540, Hagerstown, MD 21740

Comprehensive Test of Basic Skills-4 (1990)
CTB-McGraw-Hill
Monterey, CA 93940

Curriculum Referenced Tests of Mastery (1984)
Psychological Corporation
555 Academic Ct., San Antonio, TX 78204-2498

Detroit Tests of Learning Aptitude-3 (DTLA-3, 1991)
D. D. Hammill
PRO-ED
8700 Shoal Creek Blvd., Austin, TX 78757-6897

Developmental Indicators for the Assessment of Learning-Revised (DIAL-R) (1983)
Childcraft Education Corporation
20 Kilmer Road, P. O. Box 3081, Edison, NJ 08818-3081

Developmental Test of Visual-Motor Integration, 3rd Rev. (1989)
Keith E. Beery and Norman A. Buktenica
Modern Curriculum Press, Inc.
13900 Prospect Road, Cleveland, OH 44136

Diagnostic Reading Scales-Revised (1981)
G. D. Spache
CTB-McGraw-Hill
Monterey, CA

Durrell Analysis of Reading Difficulty-3 (1980)
D. D. Durrell
Psychological Corporation
555 Academic Ct., San Antonio, TX 78204-2498

Dyadic Interaction Analysis (1969)
J. E. Brophy and T. L. Good
Research Development Center
University of Texas
Austin, TX

Ekwall Reading Inventory-2nd Edition (1986)
E. Ekwall
Allyn-Bacon
7 Wells Avenue, Newton, MA 02159

Enright Diagnostic Inventory of Basic Arithmetic Skills (1983)
B. E. Enright
Curriculum Associates, Inc.
5 Esquire Rd., North Billerica,
   MA 01862-0901

Finger Tapping Test & Grooved Pegboard Test
Psychological Assessment Resources, Inc.
P.O. Box 998, Odessa, FL 33556

Frostig Developmental Test of Visual Perception (1961)
Marianne Frostig and Associates
Consulting Psychologists Press, Inc.
577 College Avenue, P.O. Box 60070,
   Palo Alto, CA 94306

Gates-MacGinitie Reading Tests (1978)
The Riverside Publishing Company
8420 Bryn Mawr Ave, Chicago, IL 60632

Gates-McKillop-Horowitz Reading Diagnostic Tests (1981)
Teachers College Press
1234 Amsterdam Ave., New York,
   NY 10027

Gesell Developmental Schedules: Revised (1980) Manual of Developmental Diagnosis
H. Knobloch, F. Stevens, and A. Malone
Harper & Row
Hagerstown, MD

Gesell School Readiness Test (1980)
Programs for Education, Inc.,
   Department W83
82 Park Avenue, Flemington, NJ 08822

Goldman-Fristoe-Woodcock Auditory Skills Test Battery (1976)
Ronald Goldman, Macalyne Fristoe, and
   Richard W. Woodcock
American Guidance Service
Publisher's Building, Circle Pines,
   MN 55014

Gordon Diagnostic System (1983)
M. Gordon
Gordon Systems
DeWitt, NY

Gray Oral Reading Test-3 (GORT-3) (1992)
Gray Oral Reading Test-Diagnostic (1992)
PRO-ED
8700 Shoal Creek Blvd., Austin,
   TX 78757-6897

Halstead-Reitan Neuropsychological Test Battery: Category Test, Progressive Figures, Color Form Test, Trail Making Test, Sensory-Perceptual Exam
Reitan Neuropsychology Laboratory
1338 East Edison Street, Tucson,
   AZ 85179

House-Tree-Person Technique (1981)
John N. Buck
Western Psychological Services
12031 Wilshire Boulevard, Los Angeles,
   CA 90025

Illinois Test of Psycholinguistic Abilities (1968)
Samuel A. Kirk, James J. McCarthy, and
   Winifred D. Kirk
University of Illinois Press
54 E. Gregory Dr., Box 5081, Station A.,
   Champaign, IL 61820

Iowa Test of Basic Skills (ITBS) (1993)
The Riverside Publishing Company
8420 Bryn Mawr Ave., Chicago, IL 60632

Judgment of Line Orientation, Finger Localization, Tactile Form Perception & Three-Dimensional Block Construction
A. L. Benton, A. B. Sivan, K. DeS.
   Hamsher, N. R. Varney, and O.
   Spreen
Oxford University Press
2001 Evans Road, Cary NC 27513

Kaufman Assessment Battery for Children (1983)
A. S. Kaufman and N. L. Kaufman
American Guidance Service
Publisher's Building, Circle Pines, MN
   55014-1796

Kaufman Test of Educational Achievement (KTEA) (1985)
A. S. Kaufman and N. L. Kaufman
American Guidance Service
Publisher's Building, Circle Pines, MN 55014-1796

KeyMath Diagnostic Arithmetic Test-Revised (KM-R) (1988)
A. J. Connolly
American Guidance Service
Publisher's Building, Circle Pines, MN 55014-1796

Let's Talk Inventory for Children (1987)
C. M. Bray and E. H. Wiig
Psychological Corporation
555 Academic Ct., San Antonio, TX 78204-2498

Luria-Nebraska Neuropsychological Battery: Children's Revision
Western Psychological Services
12031 Wilshire Blvd., Los Angeles, CA 90025-1251

McCarthy Scales of Children's Abilities (1972)
D. McCarthy
The Psychological Corporation
555 Academic Court, San Antonio, TX 78204-2498

Memory for Designs Test (1960)
Frances K. Graham and Barbara S. Kendall
Psychological Test Specialists
Box 9229, Missoula, MT 59807

Metropolitan Achievement Tests (MAT-7, 1992)
G. A. Prescott, I. H. Balow, T. R. Hogan, and R. C. Farr
The Psychological Corporation
555 Academic Ct., San Antonio, TX 78204-2498

Motor-Free Visual Perception Test (1972)
Ronald R. Celarusso and Donald D. Hammill
Academic Therapy Publications
20 Commercial Boulevard, Novato, CA 94947

Multilevel Academic Survey Test (MAST, 1985)
K. W. Howell, S. H. Zucker, and M. K. Moorehead
Psychological Corporation
555 Academic Ct., San Antonio, TX 78204-2498

Otis-Lennon Mental Ability Test (1989)
Arthur S. Otis and Roger T. Lennon
The Psychological Corporation
555 Academic Ct., San Antonio, TX 78204-2498

Peabody Individual Achievement Test-Revised (PIAT-R, 1989)
F. C. Markwardt, Jr.
American Guidance Service
Publisher's Building, Circle Pines, MN 55014-1796

Peabody Picture Vocabulary Test-Revised (1981)
Lloyd M. Dunn and Leota M. Dunn
American Guidance Service
Publisher's Building, Circle Pines, MN 55014-1796

Personality Inventory for Children-Revised (PIC-R, 1984)
R. D. Wirt, D. Lachar, J. K. Klinedinst, and P. D. Seat
Western Psychological Services
12031 Wilshire Blvd., Los Angeles, CA 90025-1251

Personality Inventory for Youth (PIY, 1995)
D. Lachar and C. P. Gruber
Western Psychological Services
12031 Wilshire Blvd., Los Angeles, CA 90025-1251

Preschool Behavior Questionnaire (1974)
Journal of Abnormal Child Psychology, 5, 265-275.

Pupil Rating Scale Revised: Screening for Learning Disabilities (1981)
Grune and Stratton
111 Fifth Avenue, New York, NY 10003

Purdue Pegboard Test
Lafayette Company, Inc.
P. O. Box 5729, Sagamore Parkway North,
  Lafayette, IN 47903

Recognition-Discrimination Test (1982)
P. Satz and J. M. Fletcher
Psychological Assessment Resources
Odessa, FL 33556

**Reitan-Indiana Neuropsychological Test
  (1974)**
R. M. Reitan and L. A. Davison
Clinical Neuropsychology: Current
  Status and Application
Washington, D.C.: V. H. Winston & Sons

**Revised Behavior Problem Checklist
  (RBPC, 1987)**
H. C. Quay and D. R. Peterson
Psychological Assessment Resources
P. O. Box 998
Odessa, FL 33556

**Reynell Developmental Language
  Scales-Revised (1977)**
NFER-Nelson Publishing Co.
Darville House, 2 Oxford Road East
Windson Berkshire SL4 1DF, England

**Rhode Island Profile of Early Learning
  Behavior (1982)**
Jamestown Publishers
P. O. Box 6743, Providence RI 02940

Rorschach Psychodiagnostic Test (1981)
Hermann Rorschach
Hans Huber
Distributed by Grune & Stratton
111 Fifth Ave., New York, NY 10003

School Situation Questionnaire (1987)
R. A. Barkley and C. Edelbrock
In R. J. Prinz (Ed.) *Advances in
  behavioral assessment of children
  and families* (Vol. 3, pp. 157-176)
Greenwich, CT: JAI Press

**Sequenced Inventory of
  Communication Development
  (SICD, 1979)**
University of Washington Press
P. O. Box 85569, Seattle, WA 98105

**Slingerland Pre-Reading Screening
  Procedures-Revised (1980)**
Educators Publishing Service
75 Moulton Street, Cambridge,
  MA 02238-9101

Slosson Intelligence Test-R (1990)
Richard L. Slosson
Slosson Educational Publications, Inc.
P. O. Box 280, East Aurora, NY 14052

Spellmaster Assessment System (1987)
C. R. Greenbaum
PRO-ED
8700 Shoal Creek Blvd., Austin,
  TX 78757-6897

SRA Achievement Series (1978)
R. A. Naslund, L. P. Thrope, and D. W.
  LeFever
CTB McGraw-Hill
20 Ryan Ranch Road
Monterey, CA 93940

Stanford Achievement Tests-7 (1989)
Psychological Corporation
555 Academic Ct., San Antonio,
  TX 78204-2498

**Stanford-Binet Intelligence Scale:
  Fourth Ed. (1986)**
R. L. Thorndike, E. P. Hagen, and J. M.
  Sattler
The Riverside Publishing Co.
8420 Bryn Mawr Ave., Chicago, IL 60631

**Stanford Diagnostic Mathematics Test-4
  (1995)**
L. S. Madden, E. R. Gardner, and C. S.
  Collins
Psychological Corporation
555 Academic Ct., San Antonio,
  TX 78204-2498

**Stanford Diagnostic Reading Test-4
  (1995)**
Psychological Corporation
555 Academic Court, San Antonio,
  TX 78204-2498

Symbol Digit Modalities Test (1982)
A. Smith
Western Psychological Services
12031 Wilshire Blvd., Los Angeles, CA
  90025

System to Plan Early Childhood Services (SPECS, 1991)
American Guidance Service
Publisher's Building, Circle Pines,
  MN 55014-1796

Test of Early Language Development-2 (TELD-2, 1991)
Test of Language Development-Primary:2 (TOLD-P:2, 1988)
PRO-ED
8700 Shoal Creek Blvd., Austin,
  TX 78757-6897

Test of Mathematical Abilities (TOMA, 1991)
V. L. Brown and E. McEntire
PRO-ED
8700 Shoal Creek Blvd., Austin,
  TX 78757-6897

Test of Visual-Perceptual Skills (TVPS, 1988)
M. F. Gardner
Health Publishing Co.
P. O. Box 3805, San Francisco, CA 94119

Thematic Apperception Test (1943)
Henry Alexander Murray
Harvard University Press
79 Garden Street, Cambridge, MA 02138

Token Test for Children
F. DiSimoni
PRO-ED
8700 Shoal Creek Blvd., Austin,
  TX 78757-6897

Utah Test of Language Development, Rev. Ed. (1978)
Communication Research Associates, Inc.
P.O. Box 11012, Salt Lake City, UT 84147

Wechsler Adult Intelligence Scale-Revised (1981)
Wechsler Intelligence Scale for Children-Third Edition (1991)

Wechsler Preschool and Primary Scale of Intelligence-Revised (1989)
Wechsler Individual Achievement Test (1992)
David Wechsler
The Psychological Corporation
555 Academic Ct., San Antonio,
  TX 78204-2498

Wide Range Achievement Test-Revision 3 (WRAT-3, 1993)
Wide Range Inc.
15 Ashley Place, Suite 1A
Wilmington, DE 19804-1314

Wide Range Assessment of Learning and Memory (WRAML, 1990)
D. Sheslow and W. Adams
The Psychological Corporation
555 Academic Court, San Antonio,
  TX 78204-2498

Wisconsin Card Sorting Test Revised (1993)
R. K. Heaton, G. J. Chelune, J. L. Talley,
  G. G. Kay, and G. Curtiss (Manual)
The Psychological Corporation
555 Academic Court, San Antonio,
  TX 78204-2498

Woodcock Reading Mastery Tests-Revised
American Guidance Service
Publisher's Building, Circle Pines,
  MN 55014-1796

Woodcock-Johnson Psychoeducational Battery-Revised (1989)
Riverside Publishing
8420 Bryn Mawr Ave.
Chicago, IL 60631

Woodcock-McGrew-Werder Mini Battery of Achievement (1994)
Riverside Publishing Co.
8420 Bryn Mar Ave.
Chicago, IL 60631

REFERENCES

Abikoff, H., & Gittelman, R. (1984). Does behavior therapy normalize the classroom behavior of hyperactive children? *Archives of General Psychiatry, 41*, 449–454.

Accardo, P. J., Blondis, T. A., & Whitman, B. Y. (1990). Disorders of attention and activity level in a referral population. *Pediatrics, 85*, 426–431.

Achenbach, T. M. (1991a). *Manual for the Child Behavior Checklist and 1991 Child Behavior Profile*. Burlington, VT: University of Vermont Department of Psychiatry.

Achenbach, T. M. (1991b). *Manual for the Teacher's Report Form and 1991 Profile*. Burlington, VT: University of Vermont Department of Psychiatry.

Achenbach, T. M. (1991c). *Manual for the Youth Self-Report and 1991 YSR Profile*. Burlington, VT: University of Vermont Department of Psychiatry.

Amaya-Jackson, L., & Cantwell, D. P. (1991). Controversies in psychopharmacologic management of attention deficit and related disorders. *International Pediatrics, 6*(2), 176–183.

American Academy of Pediatrics, Committee on Children with Disabilities and Committee on Drugs. (1987). Medication for children with an attention deficit disorder. *Pediatrics, 80*(5), 758–759.

American Psychiatric Association (1980). *Diagnostic and statistical manual of mental disorders* (3rd ed.). Washington, DC: Author.

American Psychiatric Association. (1987). *Diagnostic and statistical manual of mental disorders* (3rd ed.-Rev.). Washington, DC: Author.

American Psychiatric Association. (1994). *Diagnostic and statistical manual of mental disorders* (4th ed.). Washington, DC: Author.

Anastasi, A. (1961). *Psychological Testing,* New York: The MacMillan Company.

Andrews, J. R., & Andrews, M. A. (1990). *Family-based treatment in communicative disorders: A systemic approach*. Sandwich, IL: Janelle.

Andrews, M. A., & Andrews, J. R. (1993). Family-centered techniques: Integrating enablement into the IFSP process. *Journal of Childhood Communication Disorders, 15*, 41–46.

Aram, D., Ekelman, B., & Nation, J. (1984). Preschoolers with language disorders: Ten years later. *Journal of Speech and Hearing Research, 27*, 232–244.

Arendt, R., MacLean, W., Jr., & Baumeister, A. (1988). Critique of sensory integration therapy and its application in mental retardation. *American Journal of Mental Retardation, 92*(5), 401–411.

Aylward, E. (1991). *Understanding children's testing*. Austin, TX: Pro-Ed.

Ayres, A. (1972). *Sensory integration and learning disorders*. Los Angeles: Western Psychological Services.

Ayres, A. (1977). Effect of sensory integrative therapy on the coordination of children with choreoathetoid movements. *American Journal of Occupational Therapy, 31*(5), 291–293.

Ayres, A. (1978). Learning disabilities and the vestibular system. *Journal of Learning Disabilities, 11*, 18–29.

Ayres, A. (1980). *Sensory integration and the child*. Los Angeles: Western Psychological Services.

Ayres, A. (1989). *Sensory integration and praxis tests*. Los Angeles: Western Psychological Services.

Ayres, A., & Mailloux, Z. (1981). Influence of sensory integration procedures on language development. *American Journal of Occupational Therapy, 35*(6), 383–390.

Ayres, A., & Mailloux, Z. (1983). Possible pubertal effect on therapeutic gains in an autistic girl. *American Journal of Occupational Therapy, 37*(8), 535–540.

Bailey, D., & Wolery, M. (1989). *Assessing infants and preschoolers with handicaps*. Columbus, OH: Charles E. Merrill.

Barkley, R. A. (1990). Attention deficit hyperactivity disorder: A handbook for diagnosis and treatment. New York: The Guilford Press.

Barkley, R. A. (1994). The assessment of attention in children. In G. R. Lyons (Ed.), *Frames of reference for the assessment of learning disabilities: New views on measurement issues* (pp. 69–102). Baltimore: Paul H. Brookes.

Barkley, R. A., McMurray, M. B., Edelbrock, C. S., & Robbins, K. (1990). Side effects of methylphenidate in children with ADHD: A systemic, placebo-controlled evaluation. *Pediatrics, 86*(2), 184–192.

Barrickman, L., Woyes, R., Kuperman, S., Schumacher, E., & Verda, M. (1991). Treatment of ADHD with fluoxetine: A preliminary trial. *Journal of the American Academy of Child and Adolescent Psychiatry, 30*(5), 762–767.

Bayley, N. (1993). *The Bayley Scales of Infant Development-II*. San Antonio, TX: The Psychological Corporation.

Beery, K. E. (1989). *Developmental Test of Visual-Motor Integration* (3rd Rev.). Cleveland: Modern Curriculum Press.

Bender, L. (1957). Specific reading disability as a maturational lag. *Bulletin of the Orton Society, 7*, 9–18.

Benton, A. L. (1975). Developmental dyslexia: Neurological aspects. In W. J. Friedlander (Ed.), *Advances in neurology* (pp. 1–47). New York: Raven Press.

Benton, A. L., Sivan, A. B., Hamsher, K. deS., Varney, N. R., & Spreen, O. (1994). *Contributions to neuropsychological assessment: A clinical manual*. New York: Oxford University Press.

Berk, R. (1984). *Screening and diagnosis of children with learning disabilities*. Springfield, IL: Charles C. Thomas.

Bernheimer, L. P., Gallimore, R., & Kaufman, S. Z. (1993). Clinical child assessment in a family context: A four-group typology of family experiences with young children with developmental delays. *Journal of Early Intervention, 17*(3), 253–269.

Bernstein, D. K., & Tiegerman, E. (1994). *Language and communication disorders in children* (3rd ed.). Columbus, OH: Charles E. Merrill.

Biederman, J., Baldessarini, R. J., Wright, V., Knee, D., & Harmatz, J. S. (1989a). A double-blind placebo controlled study of desipramine in the treatment of attention deficit disorder: I. Efficacy. *Journal of the American Academy of Child and Adolescent Psychiatry, 28*(5), 777–784.

Biederman, J., Baldessarini, R. J., Wright, V., Knee, D., Harmatz, J. S., & Goldblatt, A. (1989b). A double-blind placebo controlled study of desipramine in the treatment of attention deficit disorder: II. Serum drug levels and cardiovascular findings. *Journal of the American Academy of Child and Adolescent Psychiatry, 28*(6), 903–911.

Black, S. (1993). Portfolio assessment. *The Executive Educator, 15*, 29–31.

Blankenship, C., & Lilly, M. S. (1981). Mainstreaming students with learning and behavior problems: Techniques for the classroom teacher. New York: Holt, Rinehart, and Winston.

Bloom, D.R. (1993). *Psychosocial functioning of achievement-based subtypes of learning disabled children from a multi-method perspective.* Unpublished doctoral dissertation. University of Houston.

Borcherding, B. G., Keysor, C. S., Rapoport, J. L., Elis, J., & Amass, J. (1990). Motor/vocal tics and compulsive behaviors on stimulant drugs. *Psychiatry Research, 33*, 83–94.

Boyce, N. L., & Larson, V. L. (1983). *Adolescents' communication: Development and disorders.* Eau Claire, WI: Thinking Ink Publications.

Bracken, B.R. (1984). *The psychoeducational assessment of preschool children.* Boston: Allyn & Bacon.

Bradley, C. (1937). The behavior of children receiving benzedrine. *American Journal of Psychiatry, 94*, 577–585.

Bradley, L., & Bryant, P. (1983). Categorizing sounds and learning to read: A causal connection. *Nature, 301*, 419–421.

Briggs, M. H. (1993). Team talk: Communication skills for early intervention teams. *Journal of Childhood Communication Disorders, 15*, 33–40.

Brinkerhoff, L. C., Shaw, S. F., & McGuire, J. M. (1993). Promoting access, accommodations, and independence for college students with learning disabilities. *Journal of Learning Disabilities, 25*, 417–429.

Brown, A. L., & Campione, J. (1986). Psychological theory and the study of learning disabilities. *American Psychologist, 41*, 1059–1068.

Brown, F. R., III, & Elksnin, N. (1994). *An introduction to developmental disabilities: A neurodevelopmental perspective.* San Diego: Singular.

Brown, R. T., & Sexson, S. B. (1989). Effects of methylphenidate on cardiovascular responses in attention deficit hyperactivity disordered adolescents. *Journal of Adolescent Health Care, 10*, 179–183.

Buchsbaum, M. S., & Sostek, A. J. (1980). An adaptive rate continuous performance test: Vigilance characteristics and reliability for 400 male students. *Perceptual and Motor Skills, 51*, 707–713.

Buck, J. N. (1981). *The House-Tree-Person Technique, Revised Manual.* Los Angeles: Western Psychological Services.

Budoff, M. (1987). The validity of learning potential assessment. In C. S. Lidz (Ed.), *Dynamic assessment an interactional approach* (pp. 52–81). New York: Guilford Press.

Buschke, H. (1974). Components of verbal learning in children: Analysis by selective reminding. *Journal of Experimental Child Psychology, 18*, 488–496.

Camp, B., Blom, G., Herbert, F., & Van Doornenck, W. (1977). "Think aloud": A program for developing self-control in young aggressive boys. *Journal of Abnormal Child Psychology, 5*, 157–169.

Campbell, D., & Stanley, J. (1963). *Experimental and quasi-experimental designs for research*. Chicago: Rand McNally.

Campbell, S. B., Szumowski, E. K., Ewing, L. J., Gluck, D. S., & Breaux, A. M. (1982). A multidimensional assessment of parent-identified behavior problem toddlers. *Journal of Abnormal Child Psychology, 10*(4), 569–592.

Campione, J. (1989). Assisted assessment: A taxonomy of approaches and an outline of strengths and weaknesses. *Journal of Learning Disabilities, 22*, 151–165.

Carlson, J. S., & Weidl, K. H. (1979). Toward a differential testing approach: Testing the limits employing the Raven's matrices. *Intelligence, 3*, 323–344.

Carnine, D. (1979). Direct instruction: A successful system for educationally high-risk children. *Journal of Curriculum Studies, 11*, 29–45.

Carte, E., Morrison, D., Sublett, J., Uemura, A., & Setrakian, W. (1984). Sensory integration therapy: A trial of a specific neurodevelopmental therapy for the remediation of learning disabilities. *Journal of Developmental and Behavioral Pediatrics, 5*(4), 189–194.

Casat, C. D., Pleasants, D. Z., Schroeder, D. H., & Parler, D. W. (1989). Bupropion in children with attention deficit disorder. *Psychopharmacology Bulletin, 25*(2), 198–201.

Cermak, S. (1985). Developmental dyspraxia. In E. A. Roy (Ed.), *Neuropsychological studies of apraxia and related disorders* (pp. 225–248). New York: Elsevier.

Chelune, G. J., & Baer, R. A. (1986). Developmental norms for the Wisconsin Card Sorting Test. *Journal of Clinical and Experimental Neuropsychology, 8*, 219–228.

Chelune, G. J., & Thompson, L. L. (1987). Evaluation of the general sensitivity of the Wisconsin Card Sorting Test among younger and older children. *Developmental Neuropsychology, 3*, 81–89.

Clark, F., Mailloux, Z., & Parham, D. (1989). *Sensory integration and children with learning disabilities* (2nd ed.). St. Louis: C. V. Mosby.

Cone, T. E., & Wilson, L.. (1981). Quantifying a severe discrepancy: A critical analysis. *Learning Disabilities Quarterly, 4*(4), 359–371.

Conley, R. W. (1973). *The economics of mental retardation*. Baltimore: The Johns Hopkins University Press.

Connolly, A. J. (1988). *Key Math Revised: A diagnostic inventory of essential mathematics*. Circle Pines, MN: American Guidance Services.

Critchley, M. (1970). *The dyslexic child*. Springfield, IL: Charles Thomas.

Cummins, R. A. (1991). Sensory integration and learning disabilities: Ayres' factor analyses reappraised. *Journal of Learning Disabilities, 24*(3), 160–168.

Damico, J., & Oller, J. W., Jr. (1980). Pragmatic versus morphological/syntactic criteria for language referrals. *Language, Speech, and Hearing Services in Schools, 11*, 85–94.

Delaney, E., & Hopkins, T. (1987). *The Stanford-Binet intelligence scale: Fourth edition. Examiner's handbook*. Chicago: Riverside.

Delis, D. C., Kramer, J. H., Kaplan, E., & Ober, B. A. (1994). *California Verbal Learning Test-Children's Version-Manual.* San Antonio: Psychological Corporation.

Denkla, M. B. (1972). Color naming defects in dyslexic boys. *Cortex, 8,* 164–176.

Denkla, M. B., & Rudel, R. (1976). Rapid "automatized" naming (R.A.N.): Dyslexia differentiated from other learning disabilities. *Neuropsychologia, 14,* 471-479.

Deno, E., & Fuchs, L. (1987). Developing a curriculum-based measurement systems for data-based special education problem solving. *Focus on Exceptional Children, 19*(6), 1–16.

Densem, J., Nuthall, G., & Bushnell, J. (1989). Effectiveness of a sensory integrative therapy program for children with perceptual-motor deficits. *Journal of Learning Disabilities, 22*(4), 221–229.

Diamond, K. E., & Squires, J. (1993). The role of parental report in the screening and assessment of young children. *Journal of Early Intervention, 17*(2), 107–115.

Dinnebeil, L. A., & Rule, S. (1994). Congruence between parents' and professionals' judgments about the development of young children with disabilities: A review of the literature. *Topics in Early Childhood Special Education, 14*(1), 1–25.

DiSimoni, F. G. (1978). *The Token Test for Children.* Boston: Teaching Resources.

Doll, E. J. (1990). Review of the Kaufman Test of Educational Achievement. *The tenth mental measurement yearbook.* Lincoln, NB: University of Nebraska press.

Dowdy, C. A., Smith, T. E. C., & Nowell, C. H. (1992). Learning disabilities and vocational rehabilitation. *Journal of Learning Disabilities, 25,* 442–447.

Dunn, W., Brown, C., & McGuigan, A. (1994). The ecology of human performance: A framework for considering the impact of context. *American Journal of Occupational Therapy, 48*(7), 595–607.

Dunn, W., & Campbell, P. (1991). Designing pediatric service provision. In W. Dunn (Ed.), *Pediatric occupational therapy: Facilitating effective service provision* (pp. 139–159). Thorofare, NJ: Charles B. Slack.

Dunn, L. M., & Dunn, L. M. (1981). *Peabody Picture Vocabulary Test-Revised Manual for Forms L & M.* Circle Pines, MN: American Guidance Service.

Ehren, B. J. (1994). New directions for meeting the academic needs of adolescents with language learning disabilities. In G. P. Wallach, & K. G. Butler (Eds.), *Language learning disabilities in school-age children and adolescents.* New York: Macmillan.

Elksnin, L. K., & Elksnin, N. (1990). Using collaborative consultation with parents to promote effective vocational programming. *Career Development for Exceptional Individuals, 13,* 135–169.

Elksnin, L. K., & Elksnin, N. (1995a). Strategies for transition to employment settings. In D. Deshler, E. S. Ellis, & K. Lentz (Eds.), *Teaching adolescents with learning disabilities* (2nd ed., pp. 525–578). Denver, CO: Love Publishing.

Elksnin, L. K., & Elksnin, N. (1995b). *Assessment and instruction of social skills.* San Diego: Singular.

Evans, R. W., Clay, T. H., & Gualtieri, C. T. (1987). Carbamazepine in pediatric psychiatry. *Journal of the American Academy of Child and Adolescent Psychiatry, 26*(1), 2–8.

Exner, J. E., & Weiner, I. B. (1994). *The Rorschach: A Comprehensive System, Volume 3: Assessment of children and Adolescents,* New York: Wiley.

Fawcett, A. J., & Nicolson, R. I. (1994). Naming speed in children with dyslexia. *Journal of Learning Disabilities, 27,* 641–646.

Feichtner, S. H. (1989). *School-to-work transition for at-risk youth* (Information Series No. 339). Columbus: The Ohio State University, ERIC Clearinghouse on Adult, Career, and Vocational Education, Center on Education and Training for Employment.

Felton, R. H. (1992). Early identification of children at risk for reading disabilities. *Topics in Early Childhood Special Education, 12*(2), 212–229.

Fennell, E. B. (1994). Issues in child neuropsychological assessment. In R. D. Vanderploeg (Ed.), *Clinician's guide to neuropsychological assessment* (pp. 165–184). Hillsdale, NJ: Lawrence Erlbaum.

Fennell, E. B., & Bauer, R. M. (1989). Models of inference in evaluating brain-behavior relationships in children. In C. R. Reynolds & E. Fletcher-Janzen (Eds.), *Handbook of clinical child neuropsychology* (pp. 167–177). New York: Plenum Press.

Feurerstein, R. (1979). *The dynamic assessment of retarded performers: The learning potential assessment device; theory, instruments, and techniques.* Baltimore: University Park Press.

Finlayson, M. A. J., & Reitan, R. M. (1976). Handedness in relation to measures of motor and tactile-perceptual function in normal children. *Perceptual and Motor Skills, 43,* 475–481.

Fletcher, J. M. (1985). Memory for verbal and nonverbal stimuli in learning disability subgroups: Analysis by selective reminding. *Journal of Experimental Child Psychology, 40,* 224–259.

Fletcher, J. M. (1988). Brain-injured children. In L. G. Terdal & E. J. Mash (Eds.), *Behavioral assessment of childhood disorders* (pp. 451–489). New York: Guilford.

Fletcher, J. M., Francis, D. J. Rourke, B. P., Shaywitz, S. E., & Shaywitz, B. A. (1992). Validity of discrepancy-based definition of reading disabilities. *Journal of Learning Disabilities, 25,* 555–561.

Fletcher, J. M., Levin, H. S., & Satz, P. (1989). Neuropsychological and intellectual assessment of children. In H. Kaplan & B. J. Sadock (Eds.), *Comprehensive textbook of psychiatry* (5th ed., pp. 513–525), Baltimore: Basic Books.

Fletcher, J. M., Shaywitz, S. E., Shankweiler, D. P., Katz, L., Liberman, I. Y., Stuebing, K. K., Francis, D. J., Fowler, A. E., & Shaywitz, B. A. (1994). Cognitive profiles of reading disability: Comparisons of discrepancy and low achievement definitions. *Journal of Educational Psychology, 86,* 6–23.

Fletcher, J. M., & Taylor, H. G. (1984). Neuropsychological approaches to children: Towards a developmental neuropsychology, *Journal of Clinical and Experimental Neuropsychology, 6,* 39–56.

Fletcher, J. M., Taylor, H. G., Levin, H. S., & Satz, P. (in press). Neuropsychological and intellectual assessment of children. In H. Kaplan & B. Sadock (Eds.), *Comprehensive textbook of psychiatry* (6th ed.). Baltimore: Basic Books.

Funk, J. B., Chessare, J. B., Weaver, M. T., & Exley, A. R. (1993). Attention deficit hyperactivity disorder, creativity, and the effects of methylphenidate. *Pediatrics, 91,* 816–819.

Gaddes, W. H., & Crockett, D. J. (1975). The Spreen-Benton aphasia tests: Normative data as a measure of normal language development. *Brain and Language, 2,* 257–280.

Gajar, A., Goodman, L., & McAfee, J. (1993). *Secondary schools and beyond: Transition of individuals with mild disabilities.* New York: Macmillan.

Gallagher, T. M. (1991). Pre-assessment: A procedure for accommodating language use variability. In T. M. Gallagher & C. M. Prutting (Eds.), *Pragmatic assessment and intervention issues in language.* San Diego: Singular.

Gardner, M. F. (1988). *Test of visual-perceptual skills: Manual.* San Francisco: Health.

Gardner, R. A., & Broman, M. (1979). The Purdue Pegboard: Normative data on 1334 school children. *Journal of Clinical Child Psychology, 8,* 156–162.

Garfinkel, B. D., Wender, P. H., Sloman, L., & O'Neill, I. (1983). Tricyclic antidepressant and methylphenidate treatment of attention deficit disorder in children. *Journal of the American Academy of Child and Adolescent Psychiatry, 22*(4), 343–348.

Gersten, R. (1985). Direct instruction with special education students: A review of evaluation research. *Journal of Special Education, 19,* 41–58.

Gittelman-Klein, R., Klein, D. F., Abikoff, H., Katz, S., Gloisten, A. C., & Kates, W. (1976). Relative efficacy of methylphenidate and behavior modification in hyperkinetic children: An interim report. *Journal of Abnormal Child Psychology, 4*(4), 361–378.

Golden, G. J. (1986). *Manual for the Luria-Nebraska Neuropsychological Test Battery: Children's revision.* Los Angeles: Western Psychological Services.

Golden, G. J. (1989). The Nebraska Neuropsychological Children's Battery. In C. R. Reynolds & E. Fletcher-Janzen (Eds.), *Handbook of clinical child neuropsychology* (pp. 193–204). New York: Plenum Press.

Golden, G. S. (1988). The relationship between stimulant medication and tics. *Pediatric Annals, 17*(6), 405–408.

Golden, G. S. (1992). Commentary: The myth of attention deficit hyperactivity disorder. *Journal of Child Neurology, 7,* 446–448.

Gordon, M. (1983). *The Gordon diagnostic system.* DeWitt, NY: Gordon Systems.

Greenspan, S. I., & Greenspan, N. T. (1991). *The clinical interview of the child, second edition.* New York: American Psychiatric Press.

Gresham, F. M. (1990). Best practices in social skills training. In A. Thomas & J. Grimes (Eds.), *Best practices in school psychology-II* (pp. 695–709). Washington, DC: National Association of School Psychologists.

Guerin, G. R., & Maier, A. S. (1983). *Informal assessment in education.* Palo Alto, CA: Mayfield.

Halperin, J. M., Gittleman, R., & Klein, D. F. (1984). Reading disabled hyperactive children: A distinct subgroup of attention deficit disorder with hyperactivity? *Journal of Abnormal Child Psychology, 12,* 1–14.

Halperin, J., Zeitchik, E., Healy, J. M., Weinstein, L., & Ludman, W. L. (1989). The development of linguistic and mnestic abilities in normal children. *Journal of Clinical and Experimental Neuropsychology, 11,* 518–528.

Handen, B. L., Feldman, H., Gosling, A., Breaux, A. M., & McAuliffe, S. (1991). Adverse side effects of methylphenidate among mentally retarded children with attention deficit hyperactivity disorder. *Journal of the American Academy of Child and Adolescent Psychiatry, 30*(2), 241–245.

Hanft, B., & Von Rembow, D. L. (1992). The individualized family service plan process. In M. Bender & C. A. Baglin (Eds.), *Infants and toddlers: A resource guide for practitioners.* San Diego: Singular.

Hannay, H. J., Levin, H. S., & Grossman, R. G. (1979). Impaired recognition memory after head injury. Cortex, 15, 269–283.

Harbin, G. L., Gallagher, J. J., & Terry, D. V. (1991). Defining the eligible population: Policy issues and challenges. *Journal of Early Intervention, 15*(1), 13–20.

Haring, K. A., Lovett, D. L., Haney, K. F., Algozzine, B., Smith, D. B., & Clarke, J. (1992). Labeling preschoolers as learning disabled: A cautionary position. *Topics in Early Childhood Special Education, 12*(2), 151–173.

Harter, S. (1985). *Manual for the Perceived Competence Scale for Children.* Unpublished manuscript, University of Denver.

Hecht, B. F. (1986). Problems in language development. In B. K. Keogh (Ed.), *Advances in special education: Developmental problems in infancy and the preschool years.* Greenwich, CT: JAI Press.

Hechtman, L., Weiss, G., & Perlman, T. (1984). Young adult outcome of hyperactive children who received long term stimulant treatment. *Journal of the American Academy of Child and Adolescent Psychiatry, 23*(3), 261–269.

Heshusius, L. (1991). Curriculum-based assessment and direct instruction: Critical reflections on fundamental assumptions. *Exceptional children, 57,* 315–328.

Hinshelwood, J. (1917). *Congenital word-blindness.* London: Lewis.

Holmes-Bernstein, J. H., & Waber, D. P. (1990). Developmental neuropsychological assessment: The systemic approach. In A. A. Boulton, G. B. Baker, & M. Hiscock (Eds.), *Neuromethods, Vol. 17: Neuropsychology* (311–371). Clifton, NJ: Humana.

Horn, W. F., Ialongo, N. S., Pascoe, J. M., Greenberg, G., Packard, T., Lopez, M., Wagner, A., & Puttler, L. (1991). Additive effects of psychostimulants, parent training, and self control therapy with ADHD children. *Journal of the American Academy of Child and Adolescent Psychiatry, 30*(2), 233–240.

Horn, W. F., & Packard, T. (1986). Early identification of learning problems: A meta-analysis. *Journal of Educational Psychology, 77,* 557–607.

Horowitz, L., Oosterveld, W., & Adrichem, R. (1993). Effectiveness of sensory integration therapy on smooth pursuits and organization time in children. *Padiatr-Grenzgeb, 31*(5), 331–344.

Howell, K., & Moorehead, M. K. (1987). *Curriculum-based evaluation for special and remedial education.* Columbus, OH: Charles E. Merrill.

Humphries, T., Snider, L., & McDougall, B. (1993). Clinical evaluation of the effectiveness of sensory integrative and perceptual motor therapy in improving sensory integrative function in children with learning disabilities. *Occupational Therapy Journal of Research, 13*(3), 163–182.

Humphries, T., Wright, M., Snider, L., & McDougall, B. (1992). A comparison of the effectiveness of sensory integrative therapy and perceptual-motor training in treating children with learning disabilities. *Journal of Developmental Behavioral Pediatrics, 13*(1), 31–40.

Hunt, R. D., Minderra, R. B., & Cohen, D. J. (1985). Clonidine benefits children with attention deficit disorder and hyperactivity: Report of a double blind placebo-crossover therapeutic trial. *Journal of the American Academy of Child and Adolescent Psychiatry, 24*(5), 617–629.

Hurford, D. P., Johnston, M., Nepote, P., Hampton, S., Moore, S., Neal, J., Mueller, A., McGeorge, K., Huff, L., Awad, A., Tatro, C., Juliano, C., & Huffman, D. (1994). Early identification and remediation of phonological-processing deficits in first-grade children at risk for reading disabilities, *Journal of Learning Disabilities, 27,* 647–659.

Idol, L., Paolucci-Whitcomb, P., & Nevin, A. (1986). *Collaborative consultation.* Rockville, MD: Aspen.

Interagency Committee in Learning Disabilities. (1987). *Learning Disabilities. A Report to Congress.*

Jastak, S., & Wilkinson, G. (1984). *The Wide Range Achievement Test-Revised: Administration manual.* Wilmington, DE: Jastak Associates.

Jenkins, J., Fewell, R., & Harris, S. (1983). Comparison of sensory integrative therapy and motor programming. *American Journal of Mental Deficiency, 88*(2), 221–224.

Jensen, P. S., Xenakis, S. N., Shervette, R. E., Bain, M. W., & David, H. (1989). Diagnosis and treatment of attention deficit disorder in two general hospital clinics. *Hospital and Community Psychiatry, 40*(7), 708–712.

Johnson, C. (1981). *The diagnosis of learning disabilities.* Boulder, CO: Pruett.

Kaplan, B., Polatajko, H., Wilson, B., & Faris, P. (1993). Reexamination of sensory integration treatment: A combination of two efficacy studies. *Journal of Learning Disabilities, 26*(5), 342–347.

Kaplan, E. F., Goodglass, H., & Weintraub, S. (1983). *The Boston Naming Test* (Second Edition). Philadelphia: Lea & Febiger.

Karlsen, B., Madden., R., & Gardner, E. F. (1984). *Stanford Diagnostic Reading Test.* San Antonio: Psychological Corporation.

Kaufman, A. (1976a). Verbal-Performance IQ discrepancies on the WISC-R. *Journal of Consulting and Clinical Psychology, 44,* 739–744.

Kaufman, A. (1976b). A new approach to the interpretation of test scatter on the WISC-R. *Journal of Learning Disabilities, 9,* 160–168.

Kaufman, A. (1979). *Intelligent testing with the WISC-R.* New York: Wiley.

Kaufman, A. (1983). Some questions and answers about the Kaufman Assessment Battery for Children (K-ABC). *Journal of Psychoeducational Assessment, 4,* 205–218.

Kaufman, A. S. (1994). *Intelligent testing with the WISC-III.* New York: Wiley.

Kaufman, A., & Doppelt, J. (1976). Analysis of WISC-R standardization data in terms of the stratification variables. *Child Development, 47,* 165–171.

Kaufman, A. S, & Kaufman, N. L. (1983). *Kaufman Assessment Battery for Children: Administration and Scoring Manual.* Circle Pines, MN: American Guidance Service.

Kaufman, A. S., & Kaufman, N. L. (1985). *Kaufman Test of Educational Achievement Comprehensive Form Manual.* Circle Pines, MN: American Guidance Service.

Kaufman, A. S., & Kaufman, N. L. (1993). *Manual: Kaufman Adolescent and Adult Intelligence Test.* Circle Pines, MN: American Guidance Service.

Kelly, P. C., Cohen, M. L., Walker, W. D., Caskey, D. L., & Atkinson, A. W. (1989). Self esteem in children medically managed for attention deficit disorder. *Pediatrics, 83*(2), 211–217.

Kemph, J. P., DeVane, C. L., Levin, G. M., Jarecke, R., & Miller, R. L. (1993). Treatment of aggressive children with clonidine: Results of an open pilot study. *Journal of the American Academy of Child and Adolescent Psychiatry, 32*(3), 577–581.

Kendall, P., & Finch, A. (1979). Developing nonimpulsive behavior in children: Cognitive-behavioral strategies for self-control. In P. Kendall & S. Hollon (Eds.), *Cognitive-behavioral interventions: Theory, research, and procedures.* New York: Plenum Press.

Keogh, B. K., Major-Kingsley, S., Omori-Gordon, H., & Reid, H. P. (1982). *A marker system for the field of learning disabilities. Syracuse,* NY: Syracuse University Press.

Kinsbourne, M. (1975). The ontogeny of cerebral dominance. *Annals of the New York Academy of Sciences, 263,* 244–250.

Kirk, S. A. (1963). Behavioral diagnosis and remediation of learning disabilities. *Conference on Exploration into the Problems of the Perceptually Handicapped Child.* Evanston, IL: Fund for Perceptually Handicapped Children.

Klove, H. (1963). Clinical neuropsychology. In F.M. Forster (Ed.), *The medical clinics of North America.* New York: Saunders.

Knickerbocker, B. (1980). *A holistic approach to the treatment of learning disorders.* Thorofare, NJ: Charles B. Slack.

Lachar, D., & Gruber, C.P. (1995). *Personality Inventory for Youth (PIY) manual.* Los Angeles: Western Psychological Services.

Larrivee, B. (1989). Effective strategies for academically handicapped students in the regular classroom. In R. E. Slavin, N. L. Karweit, & N. A. Madden (Eds.), *Effective programs for students at risk* (pp. 291–319). Boston: Allyn & Bacon.

Larry P. v. Riles, 343 F. Supp. 1306 N.D.Cal. 1972 (preliminary injunction), affirmed, 502 F.2d963 (9th Cir. 1974), opinion issued No. C-71-2270 RFP (N.D.Cal. October 16, 1979).

Law, M., Polatajko, H., Schaffer, R., Miller, J., & Macnab, J. (1991). The impact of heterogeneity in a clinical trial: Motor outcomes after sensory integration therapy. *Occupational Therapy Journal of Research, 11,* 177–189.

Lazarus, B. D., McKenna, M. C., & Lynch, D. (1989–1990). Peabody Individual Achievement Test-Revised (PIAT-R). *Diagnostique, 15,* 135–148.

Leigh, J. (1986). NJCLD position paper: Learning disabilities and the preschool-child. *Learning Disability Quarterly, 9,* 158–163.

Levin, H. S., Mendelson, D., Lilly, M., & Fletcher, J. M. (1994). Tower of London performance in relation to magnetic resonance imaging following closed head injury in children. *Neuropsychology, 8,* 171–179.

Levine, M., Brooks, R., & Shonkoff, J. (1980). *A pediatric approach to learning disorders.* New York: Wiley.

Levine, M. D., & Melmed, R. D. (1982). The unhappy wanderers: Children with attention deficits. *Pediatric Clinics of North America, 29,* 105–120.

Levy, F. (1991). The dopamine theory of ADHD. *Australian and New Zealand Journal of Psychiatry, 25,* 277–283.

Liberman, I. Y. (1973). Segmentation of the spoken word. *Bulletin of the Orton Society, 23,* 65–77.

Lidz, C. S. (1987). *Dynamic assessment: An interactional approach to evaluation of learning potential.* New York: Guilford Press.

Linder, T. W. (1993). *Transdisciplinary play-based assessment* (Rev. ed.). Baltimore: Paul H. Brookes.

Lindgren, S. D., & Benton, A. L. (1980). Developmental pattern of visuospatial judgment. *Journal of Pediatric Psychology, 5,* 217–225.

Lipkin, P. H., Goldstein, I. J., & Adesman, A. R. (1994). Tics and dyskinesias associated with stimulant treatment in attention deficit hyperactivity disorder. *Archives of Pediatrics and Adolescent Medicine, 148,* 859–861.

Lockwood, S. L. (1994). Early speech and language indicators for later learning problems: Recognizing a language organization disorder. *Infants and Young Children, 7,* 43–52.

Lowenthal, B. (1993). The family interview: A technique of early childhood assessment. *Infant Toddler Intervention: The Transdisciplinary Journal, 3,* 101–108.

Lund, N. J., & Duchan, J. F. (1993). *Assessing children's language in naturalistic contexts* (3rd ed.). Englewood Cliffs, NJ: Prentice-Hall.

Lynch, E. W., & Hanson, M. J. (Eds.). (1992). *Developing cross-cultural competence: A guide for working with young children and their families.* Baltimore: Paul H. Brookes.

Mann, V. A. (1985). Why some children encounter reading problems: The contribution of difficulties with language processing and phonological segmentation to early reading disability. In J. K. Torgeson & B. Y. L. Wong (Eds.), *Psychological and educational perspectives on learning disabilities* (pp. 133– 160). Orlando, FL: Academic Press.

Markwardt, F. C. (1989). *Peabody Individual Achievement Test-Revised.* Circle Pines, MN: American Guidance Service.

Marsh, G., Gearhart, C., & Gearhart, B. (1978). *The learning-disabled student: Program alternative in the secondary school.* St. Louis, MO: C.V. Mosby.

Mattis, S. (1992). Neuropsychological assessment of school-aged children, In I. Rapin & S. J. Segalowitz (Vol. Eds.) *Handbook of neuropsychology, Vol. 6: Child neuropsychology* (pp. 395–415). Amsterdam: Elsevier.

McCarthy, D. (1972). *McCarthy Scales of Children's Abilities.* San Antonio: Psychological Corporation.

McCarthy, J. (1989a). Through my kaleidoscope-1989. Elements from the past with promise for the future. *Learning Disabilities Focus, 4*(2), 67–72.

McCarthy, J. (1989b). Specific learning disabilities in preschool children. In L. B. Silver (Ed.), *The assessment of learning disabilities: Preschool through adulthood.* Boston: College- Hill Press.

McKeever, W., & VanDeventer, A. (1975). Dyslexic adolescents: Evidence of impaired visual and auditory language processing associated with normal lateralization and visual responsivity. *Cortex, 11*, 361–378.

McKinney, J. D., Montague, M., & Hocutt, A. (1993). Educational assessment of students with attention deficit disorder. *Exceptional Children, 60*(2), 125–131.

McLeod, J. (1979). Educational underachievement: Toward a defensible psychometric definition. *Journal of Learning Disabilities, 12*, 322–330.

Milberg, W. P., Hebben, N., & Kaplan, E. (1986). The Boston process approach to neuropsychological assessment. In I. Grant & K. M. Adams (Eds.), *Neuropsychological assessment of neuropsychiatric disorders* (pp. 65–86). New York: Oxford University Press.

Molyneaux, D., & Lane, V. W. (1990). *Successful interactive skills for speech-language pathologists.* Rockville, MD: Aspen.

Morrison, D., & Sublett, J. (1986). The effects of sensory integration therapy on nystagmus duration, equilibrium reactions and visual-motor integration in reading retarded children. *Child Care Health Development, 12*(2), 99–110.

National Joint Committee for Learning Disabilities. (1981). *Learning disabilities: Issues on definition.* Unpublished position paper. (Available from Drake Duane, NJCLD Chairperson, c/o The Orton Dyslexia Society, 8415 Bellona Lane, Towson, MD 21204).

Nelson, N. W. (1993). *Childhood language disorders in context: Infancy through adolescence.* New York: Macmillan.

Ness, J. E. (1989). The high jump: Transition issues of learning disabled students and their parents. *Academic Therapy, 25*, 33–40.

Norris, J., & Hoffman, P. (1993). *Whole language intervention for school-age children.* San Diego, CA: Singular.

Office of Information and Resources for the Handicapped. (1980, January/
     February). RSA task force tackels problems of learning disabled.
     Programs for the Handicapped (pp. 1, 4, & 9), (USPS 461–450).
Otis, A. S., & Lennon, R. T. (1989). *Otis-Lennon School Ability Test, Sixth
     Edition*. San Antonio, TX: The Psychological Corporation.
Ottenbacher, K. (1982). Sensory integration therapy: Affect or effect.
     American Journal of Occupational Therapy, 36(9), 571–578.
P.A.S.E. v. Hannon, 506 F. Supp. 831, N.D.Ill. (1980).
Passler, M. A., Isaac, W., & Hynd, G. W. (1985). Neuropsychological devel-
     opment of behavior attributed to frontal lobe functioning in children.
     Developmental Neuropsychology, 1, 349–370.
Patton, J. R., & Polloway, E. A. (1987). Analyzing college courses. *Academic
     Therapy, 22*, 273–280.
Patton, M., & Westby, C. (1992). Ethnography and research: A qualitative
     view. *Topics in Language Disorders, 12*, 1–14.
Paul, R. (1991). Profiles of toddlers with slow expressive language develop-
     ment. *Topics in Language Disorders, 11*, 1–13.
Paul, R. (1993). Patterns of development in late talkers: Preschool years.
     Journal of Childhood Communication Disorders, 15, 7–14.
Paul, R., Sprangle-Looney, S., & Dahm, P. S. (1991). Communication and
     socialization skills at ages 2 and 3 in "late talking" young children.
     Journal of Speech and Hearing Research, 34, 858–865.
Pediatric News. (1994). Beware of ritalin abuse, *28*(6).
Peloquin, L. J., & Klorman, R. (1986). Effects of methylphenidate on normal
     children's mood, event related potentials, and performance in memory
     scanning and vigilance. *Journal of Abnormal Psychology, 95*(1), 88–98.
Pennington, B. F. (1991). *Diagnosing learning disorders: A neuropsychologi-
     cal framework*. New York: Guilford Press.
Pennington, B. F. (1995). Genetics of learning disabilities. *Journal of Child
     Neurology, 10*, 69–77.
Pliszka, S. R. (1987). Tricyclic antidepressants in the treatment of children
     with attention deficit disorder. *Journal of the American Academy of
     Child and Adolescent Psychiatry, 26*(2), 127–132.
Polatajko, H., Kaplan, B., & Wilson, B. (1992). Sensory integration treat-
     ment for children with learning disabilities: Its status 20 years later.
     Occupational Therapy Journal of Research, 12(6), 323–341.
Polatajko, H., Law, M., Miller, J., & Schaffer, R. (1991). The effect of a sen-
     sory integration program on academic achievement, motor perfor-
     mance, and self-esteem in children identified as learning disabled:
     Results of a clinical trial. *Occupational Therapy Journal of Research,
     11*(3), 155–176.
Pressley, M., & Associates (1990). *Cognitive stategy instruction that really
     improves children's academic performance*. Cambridge, MA: Brookline
     Books.
Public Law 93-112. (1973). The Rehabilitation Act.
Public Law 94-142. (1975). Education for All Handicapped Children Act, S.6,
     94th Congress [Sec. 613 (a) (4)]. Report No. 94-168.

Public Law 98-524. (1984). Carl D. Perkins Vocational Education Act.

Public Law 99-457. (1986, 1991). Education for the Handicapped Amendments.

Public Law 101-336. (1990). The Americans with Disabilities Act.

Public Law 101-476. (1990). The Individuals with Disabilities Act (IDEA).

Rao, K. S., Menon, P. K., Hilman, B. C., Sebastian, C. S., & Bairnsfather, L. (1988). Duration of the suppressive effect of tricyclic antidepressants on histamine-induced wheal and flare reactions in human skin. *Journal of Allergy and Clinical Immunology, 82,* 752–757.

Rapoport, J. L., Buchsbaum, M. S., Zahn, T. P., Weingartner, H., Ludlow, C., & Mikkelsen, E. J. (1978). Dextroamphetamine: Cognitive and behavioral effects in normal prepubertal boys. *Science, 199,* 560–562.

Rapoport, J. L., Zametkin, A., Donnelly, M., & Ismond, D. (1985). New drug trials in attention deficit disorder. *Psychopharmacology Bulletin, 21,* 232–236.

Reed, V. A. (1994). *An introduction to children with language disorders* (2nd ed.). New York: Macmillan.

Reeve, R. C. (Ed.). (1989–1990). Monograph: Assessment for the 1990s— Critical reviews of recent instruments. *Diagnostique, 15,* 1–4.

Reid, D. K., & Stone, C. A. (1991). Why is cognitive instruction effective? Underlying learning mechanisms. *Remedial and Special Education, 12*(3), 8–19.

Reitan, R. M., & Davison, L. A. (1974). *Clinical neuropsychology: Current status and applications.* Washington, DC: V. H. Winston & Sons.

Revelj, E. (1987). Improving learning of minimally handicapped preschoolers using sensorimotor integration therapy. *Practicum II Report,* Nova University.

Reynolds, C. R. (1984–1985). Critical measurement issues in learning disabilities. *Journal of Special Education, 18*(4), 451–476.

Reynolds, C. R. (1985). Measuring the aptitude-achievement discrepancy in learning disability diagnosis. *Remedial and Special Education, 6,* 37–55.

Reynolds, C. R., & Kamphus, R. W. (1992). *BASC: Behavior Assessment System for Children Manual.* Circle Pines, MN: American Guidance Service.

Richard, G., & Hanner, M. A. (1985). *Language Processing Test.* Moline, IL: LinguiSystems.

Roberts, G. E. (1994). *Interpretative Handbook for the Roberts Apperception Test for Children.* Los Angeles: Western Psychological Services.

Roberts, J. E., & Crais, E. R. (1989). Assessing communication skills. In D. B. Bailey, Jr., & M. Wolery (Eds.), *Assessing infants and preschoolers with handicaps.* Columbus, OH: Charles E. Merrill.

Rosner, J., & Simon, D. P. (1971). The auditory analysis test: An initial report. *Journal of Learning Disabilities, 4,* 40–48.

Rourke, B. P. (1989). *Nonverbal learning disabilities: The syndrome and the model.* New York: Guilford Press.

Rourke, B. P. (1993). Arithmetic disabilities, specific and otherwise: A neuropsychological perspective. *Journal of Learning Disabilities, 26,* 214–226.

Rourke, B. P., Fisk, J. L., & Strang, J. D. (1986). *Neuropsychological assessment of children: A treatment- oriented approach.* New York: Guilford Press.

Rourke, B. P., & Gates, R. D. (1980). *Underlining Test: Prelimary norms.* University of Windsor, Department of Psychology, Windsor, Ontario.

Rosner, J., & Simon, D. P. (1971). The auditory analysis test: An initial report. *Journal of Learning Disabilities, 4,* 40– 48.

Safer, D., & Allen, R. (1976). *Hyperactive children: Diagnosis and management.* Baltimore: University Park Press.

Safer, D. J., & Krager, J. M. (1988). A survey of medication treatment for hyperactive/inattentive students. *Journal of the American Medical Association, 260,* 2256–2258.

Salvia, J., & Hughes, C. (1990). *Curriculum-based assessment: Testing what is taught.* New York: Macmillan.

Satcher, J. (1993). College-bound students with learning disabilities: Role of the school counselor. *The School Counselor, 40,* 343–347.

Satir, V. (1988). *The new peoplemaking.* Mountain View, CA: Science and Behavior Books.

Satterfield, J. H., Satterfield, B. T., & Cantwell, D. P. (1981). Three year multimodality treatment study of 100 hyperactive boys. *Journal of Pediatrics, 98,* 650–655.

Satterfield, J. H., Satterfield, B. T., & Schell, A. M. (1987). Therapeutic interventions to prevent delinquency in hyperactive boys. *Journal of the American Academy of Child and Adolescent Psychiatry, 26*(1), 56–64.

Sattler, J. M. (1992). *Assessment of Children: WISC-III and WPPSI-R supplement.* San Diego: J. M. Sattler.

Satz, P., & Fletcher, J. M. (1982). *Manual for the Florida Kindergarten Screening Battery.* Odessa, FL: Psychological Assessment Resources.

Scarborough, H. (1990). Very early language deficits in dyslexic children. *Child Development, 61*(6), 1728–1743.

Scarborough, H. S., & Dobrich, W. (1990). Development of children with early language delay. *Journal of Speech and Hearing Research, 33,* 70–83.

Schumaker, J. B., Deshler D. D., Alley, G. R., & Warner, M. M. (1983). Toward the development of an intervention model for learning disabled adolescents: The University of Kansas Institute. *Exceptional Education Quarterly, 4,* 45–74.

Scott, C. M. (1994). A discourse continuum for school-age students. In G. P. Wallach & K. G. Butler (Eds.), *Language learning disabilities in school-age children and adolescents.* New York: Macmillan.

Sebrechts, M. M., Shaywitz, S. E., Shaywitz, B. A., Jatlow, P., Anderson, G. M., & Cohen, D. J. (1986). Components of attention, methylphenidate dosage, and blood levels in children with attention deficit disorder. *Pediatrics, 77,* 222–227.

(Section {2}a.4(b)(3)). U.S. Congress, *Public Law 94-142, Education for All Handicapped Children Act of 1975.*

Sexton, D., Thompson, B., Perez, J., & Rheams, T. (1990). Maternal versus professional estimates of developmental status for young children with handicaps: An ecological approach. *Topics in Early Childhood Special Education, 10*(3), 80–95.

Shaywitz, S. E., & Shaywitz, B. A. (1988). Attention deficit disorder: Current perspectives. In J. F. Kavanagh & T. J. Truss (Eds.), *Learning disabilities: Proceedings of the national conference* (pp. 369–523). Parkton, MD: York Press.

Sheslow, D., & Adams, W. (1990). *Wide Range Assessment of Memory and Learning: Administration manual.* Wilmington, DE: Jastak Associates.

Siegel, L. S. (1992). Dyslexics vs. poor readers: Is there a difference? *Journal of Learning Disabilities, 25,* 618–629.

Silberzahn, M. (1975). Sensory integrative function in a child guidance clinic population. *American Journal of Occupational Therapy, 29*(1), 28–34.

Simeonsson, R. J. (1986). *Psychological and developmental assessment of special children.* Boston: Allyn & Bacon.

Siperstein, G. N. (1988). Students with learning disabilities in college: The need for a programmatic approach to critical transitions. *Journal of Learning Disabilities, 21,* 431–436.

Sitlington, P. L. (1986). *Transition, special needs, and vocational education.* Columbus, OH: The National Center for Research in Vocational Education, The Ohio State University.

Sitlington, P. L., & Frank, A. R. (1990). Are adolescents with learning disabilities successfully crossing the bridge into adult life? *Learning Disability Quarterly, 13,* 97–111.

Sivan, A. B. (1992). *Benton Visual Retention Test* (Fifth ed.). San Antonio: Psychological Corporation.

Sixth Annual Report to Congress on the Implementation of Public Law 94-142: The Education of All Handicapped Children Act (1984). Office of Special Education, U.S. Department of Education.

Slosson, R. L., Nicholson, C. L. & Hibpshman, T. (1991). *Slosson Intelligence Test-Revised Manual.* Austin, TX: Pro-Ed.

Smith, A. (1982). *Symbol Digit Modalities Test.* Los Angeles: Western Psychological Services.

Snyder, L. (1980). Have we prepared the language disorder child for school? *Topics in Language Disorders, 1,* 29–46.

Sprague, R. L., & Sleator, E. K. (1977). Methylphenidate in hyperkinetic children: Differences in dose effects on learning and social behavior. *Science, 198,* 1274–1276.

Spreen, O., & Benton, A. L. (1969, 1977). *Neurosensory Center comprehensive examination for aphasia.* Victoria, B.C.: University of Victoria, Neuropsychology Laboratory.

Spreen, O., & Strauss, E. (1990). *A compendium of neuropsychological test.* New York: Oxford University Press.

Stake, R., & Wardop, J. (1971). Gain score errors in performance contracting. *Research in the Teaching of English, 5,* 226–229.

Stanovich, K. E. (1988). Explaining the differences between the dyslexic and the garden-variety poor reader: The phonological core variable difference model. *Journal of Learning Disabilities, 21,* 590-604,

Steingard, R., Biederman, J., Spencer, T., Wilers, T., & Gonzalez, A. (1993). Comparison of clonidine response in the treatment of attention deficit hyperactivity disorder with and without co-morbid tic disorders. *Journal of the American Academy of Child and Adolescent Psychiatry, 32*(2), 350–353.

Strichart, S. S., & Mangrum, C. T., II (1985). Selecting a college for the LD student. *Academic Therapy, 20,* 475–479.

Sugai, G. (1985). Recording classroom events: Maintaining a critical incidents log. *Teaching Exceptional Children,* (1986, Winter), 98–102.

Szatmari, P., Offord, D., & Boyle, M. H. (1989). Ontario Child Health Study: Prevalence of attention deficit disorder with hyperactivity. *Journal of Child Psychology, 30,* 219–230.

Taylor, H. G. (1988). Learning disabilities. In E. J. Mash & L. G. Terdal (Eds.), *Behavioral assessment of childhood disorders* (2nd ed.), (pp 402–450). New York: Guilford Press.

Taylor, H. G., & Fletcher, J. M. (1990). Neuropsychological assessment of children. In G. Goldstein & M. Hersen (Eds.), *Handbook of psychological assessment* (pp. 228–255). New York: Praeger.

Tew, L. (1984). *Language therapy and sensory integration therapy in maximizing language gains in developmentally delayed preschool children. Report of results, May, 1983 through April, 1984.* Wabash Center, Inc., Lafayette, IN.

Thal, D., Tobias, S., & Morrison, D. (1991). Language and gesture in late talkers: A one-year follow-up. *Journal of Speech and Hearing Research, 34,* 604–612.

The Medical Letter. (1990). Sudden death in children treated with a tricyclic antidepressant, 32, 53.

Thiele, J. E., & Hamilton, J. L. (1991). Implementing the early childhood formula: Programs under P.L. 99-457. *Journal of Early Intervention, 15*(1), 5–12.

Thorndike, R. (1963). The concept of over and underachievement. New York: Columbia University Press.

Thorndike, R., Hagen, E., & Sattler, J. (1986). *Stanford-Binet intelligence scale (4th ed.): Technical manual.* Chicago: Riverside.

Torgeson, J. K. (1980). Conceptual and educational implications of the use of efficient task strategies by learning disabled children. *Journal of Learning Disabilities, 13,* 19–26.

Torgeson, J. K., & Goldman, T. (1977). Verbal rehearsal and short-term memory in reading disabled children. *Child Development, 48,* 56–60.

Tramontana, M. G., & Hooper, S. R. (1988). *Assessment issues in child neuropsychology* (pp. 3–38). New York: Plenum Press.

Trapani, C. (1990). *Transition goals for adolescents with learning disabilities.* Boston: Little, Brown and Company.

U.S. Congress, *Public Law 93-112, The Rehabilitation Act of 1973.*

U.S. Office of Education. (1977). Assistance to states for education for handicapped children: Procedures for evaluating specific learning disabilities. *Federal Register, 42*(250), 62082–62085.

Van Benschoten, R. (1975). A sensory-integration program for blind campers. American *Journal of Occupational Therapy, 29*(10), 615–617.

Van Reusen, A. K., Bos, C. S., Schumaker, J. B., & Deschler, D. D. (1987). *The education planning strategy.* Lawrence, KS: EXCELLenterprises.

Vellutino, F. R. (1979). *Dyslexia: Theory and research.* Cambridge, MA: MIT Press.

Wagner, M. (1989, March). *The transition experiences of youth with disabilities: A report from the national longitudinal transition study.* Paper presented at the meeting of the Division for Research, Council for Exceptional Children, San Francisco, CA.

Wagner, R. K., & Torgeson, J. K. (1987). The nature of phonological processing and its causal role in the acquisition of reading skills. *Psychological Bulletin, 101,* 192–212.

Wallis, C. (1994). An epidemic of attention deficit disorder. Time, 144(3), 42–50.

Wechsler, D. (1989). *Manual for the Wechsler Preschool and Primary Scale of Intelligence-Revised.* San Antonio: Psychological Corp.

Wechsler, D. (1991). *Wechsler Intelligence Scale for Children-Third Edition Manual.* San Antonio, TX: The Psychological Corporation.

Weiss, B., & Laties, V. G. (1962). Enhancement of human performance by caffeine and the amphetamines. *Pharmacology Review, 14,* 1–33.

Welsh, M. C., & Pennington, B. G. (1988). Assessing frontal lobe functioning in children: Views from developmental psychology. *Developmental Psychology, 4,* 199–230.

Wender, P.H. (1971). *Minimal brain dysfunction in children.* New York: Wiley.

Wender, P. H. (1987). *The hyperactive child, adolescent and adult: Attention deficit disorder through the lifespan.* New York: Oxford University Press.

Werry, J., Scaletti, R., & Mills, F. (1990). Sensory integration and teacher-judged learning problems: A controlled intervention trial. *Journal of Pediatric Child Health, 26*(1), 31–35.

Werry, J. S., Aman, M. G., & Diamond, E. (1980). Imipramine and methylphenidate in hyperactive children. *Journal of Child Psychology and Psychiatry, 21,* 27–35.

Westby, C. E. (1994). The effects of culture on genre, structure, and style of oral and written texts. In G. P. Wallach & K. G. Butler (Eds.), *Language learning disabilities in school-age children and adolescents.* New York: Macmillan.

Wetherby, A. M., & Prizant, B. (1993). *Communication and symbolic behavior scales.* Chicago, IL: Riverside.

Wiig, E., & Semel, E. (1984). *Language assessment and intervention for the learning disabled,* (2nd ed.). Columbus, OH: Charles E. Merrill.

Wilens, T. E., Biederman, J., Geist, D. E., Steingard, R., & Spencer, T. (1993). Nortriptyline in the treatment of ADHD: A chart review of 58 cases. *Journal of the American Academy of Child and Adolescent Psychiatry, 32*(2), 343–349.

Wilson, B. C. (1986). An approach to the neuropsychological assessment of the preschool child with developmental deficits In S. Filskov & T. J. Boll (Eds.), *Handbook of clinical neuropsychology* (Vol. 2) (pp. 121–171). New York: Wiley.

Wilson, B. C. (1992). The neuropsychological assessment of the preschool child: A branching model. In I. Rapin & S. J. Segalowitz (Vol. eds.), *Handbook of neuropsychology, Vol. 6: Child Neuropsychology* (pp. 377–394). Amsterdam: Elsevier.

Wilson, B., Kaplan, B., Fellowes, S., & Gruchy, C. (1992). The efficacy of sensory integration treatment compared to tutoring. *Physical and Occupational Therapy in Pediatrics, 12*(1), 1–36.

Wirt, R. D., Lachar, D. Klinedinst, J. K., & Seat. P. D. (1984). *Multidimensional description of child personality: A manual for the Personality Inventory for Children.* Rev. by David Lachar. Los Angeles: Western Psychological Services.

Witelson, S. (1977). Neural and cognitive correlates of developmental dyslexia: Age and sex differences. In C. Shagaes, S. Gershon, & A. Friedhoff (Eds.), *Psychopathology and brain dysfunction.* New York: Raven Press.

Wolf, M., Bally, B., & Morris, R. (1986). Automaticity, retrieval processes, and reading: A longitudinal study in average and impaired readers. *Child Development, 57,* 988–1000.

Wolraich, M. L., Lindgren, S., Stromquist, A., Millch, R., Davis, C., & Watson, D. (1990). Stimulant medication use by primary care physicians in the treatment of attention deficit hyperactivity disorder. *Pediatrics, 86,* 95–101.

Woodcock, R. W., & Mather, N. (1989). *Woodcock-Johnson Test of Achievement.* Allen, TX: DLM Teaching Resources.

Zelko, F. A. (1991). Comparison of parent completed behavior rating scales: Differentiating boys with ADD from psychiatric and normal controls. *Journal of Developmental and Behavioral Pediatrics, 12,* 31–37.

Zentall, S. S. (1993). Research on the educational implications of attention deficit hyperactivity disorder. *Exceptional Children, 60*(2), 143–153.

Index

O

P

Tests *(continued)*
   occupational therapy use, 166
   selection for cognitive-
     achievement comparison,
     180–181
Tutorial model, 256

V

Visual perceptual/fine motor skills
  development, 43
   assessment, 46–48, 54–56
Visual-spatial
  processing/constructional skills
  assessment, 77–78
Vocational education,
  258–259

Vocational rehabilitation,
  260–261

W

Wechsler Intelligence Scale for
  Children-Third Edition, 95–101,
  181, 182
   for older children, 101
   for preschool-age children, 101
   subtest scatter, 110–112, 114–117
Woodcock Johnson
  Psychoeducational Battery-
  Revised, 126–127
Work-study model, 257
Written language disability, 5
   treatment accommodations, 225